THE WILD EDGE

Philip Kopper

THE WILD EDGE

*Life and Lore of the Great
Atlantic Beaches*

Illustrated by Anne E. Lacy

Times
BOOKS

Published by TIMES BOOKS, a division
of Quadrangle/The New York Times Book Co., Inc.
Three Park Avenue, New York, N. Y. 10016

Published simultaneously in Canada by
Fitzhenry & Whiteside, Ltd., Toronto

Library of Congress Cataloging in Publication Data
Kopper, Philip.
  The wild edge.

  Includes index.
    1. Seashore biology—Atlantic coast (United States)
2. Beaches—Atlantic coast (United States) 3. Atlantic
coast (United States)—Description and travel.
I. Title.
QH92.2.K66   500.914′6   78-20684
ISBN 0-8129-0818-X

Manufactured in the United States of America

for
Mary née Carll
naturally

Contents

PART II: THE PHYSICAL BEACH

PART III: THE ARTS OF BEACHING

THE WILD EDGE

Sea oats along the Outer Banks.

Introduction

Catching the Beach Bug— The Whys of This Book: An Explanation

I was born on an island, though one so drastically altered that it hardly counts. Suffice it that the delivery occurred no farther west of a certain tidal river than a fiddler crab could creep before running into a York Avenue bus. But if Mimi did her lying in on Manhattan, she says I was conceived on another island and my earliest memories—no, not *that* early—involve summers beside salt water. The gentle Great South Bay made waves barely high enough to breach a sand castle wall. Its placidity may explain why my infancy was alive with horseshoe crabs: unforgettable creatures when you're barely twice their size. They slid out of the swash on invisible feet to perform some deliberate business mute as old men's chess. Then they slid back into the sea again, their round prows pressed so close to the sand it was a wonder they didn't wriggle under it, like a boy beneath a sealskin rug. They were peaceful enough right-side up. But capsized, waving their pincered legs and arching their backs with spear-sharp tails stabbing the sand, they seemed dangerous, threatening, utterly alien creatures. We stoned them to death—or pebbled them, or tried to—in our fright, pride and xenophobia.

On special days the family went out toward Montauk, the eastern end of the land. Mimi took a snapshot near a dune out there of a human pyramid—well, more like a cairn of kin. Dad crouches in the sand, my brother kneels on his back, I perch on his, and our sister leans on the grinning lot of us. My parents must have prized that exposed and wild beach because gas was rationed and it was miles from home; there was a war on. Sometimes a khaki halftrack showed up—the Army's hybrid of a pickup truck and a Caterpillar. Its helmeted crew would point an enormous machine gun at the horizon and wait. That's where the Axis lay, I understood; the world spun around Hitler and Tojo just as a birthday party revolved around the kid who had the worst tantrum. The patriotic gunmen stared out to sea for interminable periods, or longer than an after-lunch rest under a beach umbrella lasted, then disappeared behind the dune again. I ran up the sand hill to see them go, but the beach grass had hidden spikes and hurt my feet. It seemed hateful stuff, so pretty in the wind and so painful.

The surf out there could be huge, or taller than me. But there were stout ropes strung from the beach to floating buoys a little way offshore. I'd grab a rope with both hands (unable to grasp around it with one) and inch my way out. The waves lapped my ankles, my knees in turn, my crotch, and belly. Then one got me wet all over and I went squealing back to the dry hot sand to start again and get a little farther out. Melinda was my first love, the first I didn't understand. (Her father was the doctor who delivered me so you can guess the age we got together; we were both in diapers. It was an affair of convenience, our mothers'.) Melinda hated surf. When it rose any higher than a clam shell, she'd stamp her feet and scream bloody murder. I couldn't fathom how she'd stay away from the semifrightening waves that held such frothy excitement. After all, everything good could have barbs inside. The world was full of barking dogs, cross streets, two-wheel bikes, cozy bedtime and then The Dark, artichokes. My point is that every familiar thing in childhood can turn to terror—even elevators with bright brass gates (that jammed) or a doting cook (who went crazy when she drank once a year). And every fright could hold a laugh or a present, like Halloween or a Grimms' fairy tale.

The world was a place that a four- or five-year-old forayed into, then came home from, washed his hands for supper and had a story. The beach was part of that outside world; a place to play in the water and get nipped by a crab. In childhood one takes what comes. Gold stars in front-room windows were normal; didn't everyone have a neighbor die in the Pacific? One moved to Dayton, Ohio for the War Effort's sake as a matter of course. (Ever been to Dayton? That's where the cook brandished a butcher knife. An inherently primitive place.) In childhood one learns that "saving the best for last" is risky in summer because ice cream melts. We did save gum wrappers and made huge balls of tinfoil. We had bonfires by the water and picnics and sang "America, the Beautiful" when the A-bomb lit up an unseen sky, in innocent childhood. So many things seemed of the same magnitude from a viewpoint three feet high: spiked grass, merry-go-rounds, the horseshoe crab, white margarine, Christmas, fear of drowning, rice pudding with raisins, grandma's cancer, Walt Disney's *Bambi,* Victory Gardens, war, reading, parents' divorce, cotton candy and the beach itself.

Peace came for a few years, its bright promise overshadowed (for me) by the immediate siege of adolescence with its dedication to pressing priorities. White bucks outshone piano lessons; the new Gregory Peck epic at the Garden Theater surpassed a solar eclipse any Saturday afternoon. I was away from the beach for most of those years. I fled the familiar across the great plains' seas of grass to summer jobs on ranches in the Rocky Mountain West. The beach surfaced again, in college, as a place for terribly serious winter weekends in cold summer houses where herds of us would congregate like untimely turtles, then sneak off in pairs to talk about Camus and woo.

Life in several cities working in various corners of the fourth estate brought me back to beaches, older and a stranger, looking for joy or solace, not existentialism. I was briefly a born-again New Yorker who returned like the prodigal son to what people said was the center of the universe. But it couldn't be the hub—everything spun too fast and randomly for that. The reaches of Long Island offered freedom from artificial deadlines, cool clean air and a little quiet in the night. A Columbus Avenue grocer sprinkling salt on his sidewalk (to save customers from slipping in a puddle of stab-wound blood) suggested that the margins of civilization might be nicer. By design I headed west again and got as far west as Baltimore before my trusty Chevrolet coupe slipped its rusty radiator like an ill-fitting denture. But a newspaper there offered the perfect job and I hired on before learning that a cub reporter's first duty tour was the solo, all-night, every night "lobster trick." The morning rewrite man who relieved me at 7 A.M.—he was a perennial old pro with all the tattered trimmings—offered counsel in psychological survival techniques. Rx: nickel blackjack, bourbon and the Gayety Burlesque's Saturday Morning Show.

The reward for surviving both "Lobster" and its prescription was a long weekend; I asked my mentor for new advice on where to go for a change in scene. "Booze, gambling and girls?" he queried, pouring half his carry-out coffee in the wastebasket. "Life," I answered. "I'm gray as a mushroom from not seeing the sun and haven't touched a body of water larger than a highball since July." Tomorrow was Labor Day. "Ocean City," he said, filling his paper cup with rye from the bottle in his bottom drawer. He hadn't been there since he was married the day before embarking on a free trip to the beaches of gracious North Carolina, sunny California and Guadalcanal. But in his day Ocean City was where young bloods went, he said, tearing obits from the teletype.

I slept, packed the car and arrived at sundown. The place was not as he described. It had aged and grown respectable with a vengeance. No alcohol could be had in the entire county on a Sunday; even most Communion services offered grape juice. The only gaming was Thursday Night Bingo in the firehouse. And each single female parading along the boardwalk sported as many plastic curlers in her hair as she had years on this earth—between nine and fifteen, depending on head size. I was glumly choosing between an auction sale of "oriental" rugs (woven in the east of Belgium) and a prayer meeting as the evening's entertainment when some college kids staged the parody of a riot. It was an odd relief. I went to work covering the inanities of young rowdies tossing empty beer cans at a burly, brutal police chief who replied with something close to martial law. He locked up twenty slightly soused jejune delinquents, they spent the night in two two-man cells and I got my first by-line. Ocean City had a beach, but during the recess in a kangaroo magistrate's court the next noon I didn't see it for all the beach towels, folding chairs, lotioned flesh and litter.

That experience taught me to save extra days-off for planned vacations: in Mexico, Puerto Rico, the Caribbean, Martha's Vineyard, Nantucket, the Maine coast, Cornwall—places like that. They had two things in common: seashore and distance. Why not? It seemed that anywhere closer to the eastern megalopolis had only beery collegians, bullish cops and blue laws. These distant places had (variously) friendly strangers, odd customs, rum, tides, scuba diving, shells for the picking, clams for the digging, waves for the surfing, sailboats, stunning scenery, whales, bikinis or less, fresh seafood, nesting birds in season, dunes to nap on, palm trees to read beneath, stretches of hard sand to run along, cliffs to climb, breakers to romp in and countless peninsulas to round, each one guarding another private cove that ended with another promising point. They had beaches.

In time I found some closer to home—by then the nation's capital, where I first chased fire trucks, wrote obits and covered suburban sewer plans. I crashed the White House press room at 2 A.M. when President Kennedy swapped an obsolete Russian spy for Ike's U-2 pilot, interviewed Commander in Chief Emeritus Harry Truman on a railroad platform, and covered the Third Annual Labor Day Riot in Ocean City, which was sillier than the first. Jaded by stuff of such transient importance, I swaggered across the newsroom to the Sunday Department as a budding critic in search of real theater and significant cinema. After seeing too many movies before too-many-martini lunches, I quit the paper to free-lance and found myself seeking out more beaches. The wages of free-lancing are odd: articles about the sociopolitical lion of the instant, and traffic flow through the perfect car-repair shop, and a psychiatric team that performed transsexual therapy. After assignments like these I'd simply wander to any natural place that nurtured fundamental things, where I could watch the tides rise and listen to ghost crabs. There is nothing faddish about gulls flocking to a low-water bar as avidly as cognoscenti jamming a Kennedy Center gala benefit. There is no contrived moral question in a crab's molt, nor anything trendy in the wind's change before a squall. National atrocities could occur in the name of narrowly partisan principle; hems could rise, fall or surrender entirely to pants; Nixon could enter disgrace and Capote re-emerge from alcoholic ashes. But back at the beach it was retreat and renewal in endless succession. There was always either overwhelming peace or natural fury—violence without malice. Back at the beach it was predation as usual and reproductive life. Thoreau wrote, "I love nature, partly because she is not a man but a retreat from him. None of his institutions control or pervade her; there a different kind of right prevails. . . . He is constraint; she is freedom for me. He makes me wish for another world; she makes me content with this."

I even came to love Ocean City, as a twelve-year-old running back named Christopher loves pro football; i.e., from a distance. One July

Fourth the Chamber of Commerce proudly announced the number of people packing the beach there. It was either 100,000 souls or 1,-000,000; the difference between 10^5 and 10^6 can be a typographical error. I love Ocean City because another beach not much farther from my desk has no neon-bright boardwalk by night, no people cluttering every horizon by day and no high-rise structures at any time except a lighthouse. If Ocean City's pathologically popular playland weren't where it was, some of the hordes would appear on my empty beach and change it into a very different place. Not that I'm an anthrophobe. It's just that among organisms in vast numbers, I prefer nesting terns or even menhaden to man, who swarms so erratically.

Learning something new on every trip came naturally—not as a compulsory challenge but as the inevitable. At first the beach was more bewildering than a room with mirror walls—a place of myriad specifics and infinite interactions. Trying to distinguish them, I turned to books; the field guides first, of course. Perhaps they'd at least identify all the birds, beasts, shells, shrubs, trees, animal tracks, marine mammals, edible plants, fishes, crabs, coelenterates, minerals and more. Soon my purportedly portable nature library grew too large to tote, even in an L. L. Bean bag. Each book was more encyclopedic than the last, which became more curse than blessing. Every memoir reported a species or behavior pattern I'd never seen, but failed to mention what I encountered that morning. An impressive anthology like the Sierra Club's *Mind in the Waters* offers enormous lore about the titanic and intelligent whales. But narrative literature neglects the multitudes of whiffets (by definition "small or insignificant" animals).

Something as important as the beach, I decided, a place so complex, dynamic and perpetual, deserved a better press and this book was conceived. I set out to write the single volume I would have liked to pack along in the beginning of my beachings. It would be an anthology, of sorts; a compendium of the several natural sciences encountered along the edge of the land where the Atlantic Ocean makes the shore. These sciences per se are not natural, of course, but man-made. They are the categorized results of man's awkwardly systematic rummagings to explain to himself what the starfish and osprey take for granted. They are the unravelings of the practical, physical mysteries that surround us. Look around. Every object, organism, sprig or stone raises a question. How does the tide move? When does a lobster mate? Where do jellyfish go in winter? What does beach grass need to grow where nothing else can survive? What makes sand build into seemingly stable dunes?

Consciously looking around became a compulsive task. Instead of packing a library to the beach, I'd take an empty pack and return with it full of shells, rocks, bleached branches, bones, seaweeds, unidentifiable litter and an occasional corpse. (Often a live specimen would go astray on the drive home and end up hiding under the bucket seat while the Mustang spent a few summer days parked on a city street. More than one common crab and whorled whelk gave up a fulsome ghost to haunt my car for weeks.) A reporter by training and writer by trade, I'd explored several scientific realms before, one at a time. This job was different. So many scientific disciplines apply to the beach: botany, ornithology, ichthyology, geology, animal behavior, tide mechanics, invertebrate biology, barrier island dynamics, human physiology, and more. It would take a lifetime to explore each cul-de-sac of every disciplinary subdivision.

In desperation I got a big Jeep to cover more shifting ground. It extended my range. Like any vehicle it served as an effective bird blind. It offered shelter when I was too lazy to pitch a tent, even provided a place to read and write at a makeshift desk. It took me the lengths of islands and to the outermost ends of peninsulas. But a Cherokee Chief is not a guru and my enlightenment remained a dappled thing, like the surface of the sea when the moon starts breaking through a hurricane sky. In libraries and on the beaches I finally realized why all the books fail to contain all answers. Because no book can articulate every question about each thing we see, let alone what we can't see: objects hidden by time or distance—the oceanic birth of a skate from its batlike egg case or the once-a-year matchmaking shivaree of terns on remote islands.

By design then, this book is not intended to tell everything about anything, i.e., the sex life of the oyster (though some intimate details are bared). To tell all would require the patience of Job for every reader and leave me no space to say anything about sea rocket's succulence or the gemstones in sand. My chosen task is to examine the obvious, the commonplace, the apparent and often-encountered: such things as birds, grasses, crabs, clams, flots- and jetsam, algae, empty shells, fetid fish, hazards to human health, marine delicacies and prime movers of the beach itself. The goal became to describe the visible tips of disciplinary icebergs and outline the different scientific glaciers that spawned them. T. S. Eliot warned "I will show you fear in a handful of dust." I hope to tell how to find life in a hatful of sand. Dylan Thomas remembered among his Christmas presents in Wales "Books that told me everything about the wasp except why." This book will describe the things most commonly encountered along a natural beach; readers will have to guess many whys for themselves and come up with more answers than mine.

As finally born, this book is a hybrid. It owes something to the great clans of field guides and something to didactic scientific monographs. While it attempts to discuss some important biological matters, it ignores obfuscatory terminology. What's sauce for scientific method can be souse for simple clarity and the nonspecialist's understanding. While I have tried to be as accurate as possible, I've not split every hair of biology's luxuriant pelage nor outlined every bone of scientific contention. I chose to use common popular names for beasts and vegetables while also indicating the latest in Latin. Call a spurge a spurge, but *Euphorbia polygonifolia* as well in case someone wants to pursue the scientific literature. Likewise, I'll use whatever convention of measurement suits the subject—inches for lengths of animals for example—rather than bow to the sacred cow *(Bos indicus)* of the metric system.

The layman is often seduced into believing that painstaking science has an answer to every question. That notion—which more laymen infer than most scientists imply—is false. The natural world, even that corner of it found along the littoral, is too complex for total human comprehension. One can grasp many pieces of the puzzle, learn their shapes and patterns, even put some of them together. But the whole picture is too huge to articulate completely. Don't worry about it. However elusive total knowledge may be, it isn't a prerequisite for comprehensive appreciation. Let it be enough, somehow, to get glimpses and continue wondering. Only a know-it-all knows it all. Study what you can; look, then let the intuition leap and in passing, perhaps, nod courteously to the Beach Goddess, whoever she might be.

This volume describes a ribbon of a region running from the pug nose of Maine to the sandy underbelly of the Outer Banks—1,200 miles as some shorebirds fly but nearly 20,000 if one walked every mile of the convoluted littoral. It does not explore every cove and bay along the coast. It will, I hope, open doors to many rooms in the *oikos,* the Grecian house we leased to build the scientific and humane theater called ecology. Part horizontal field guide, part anthology of the natural sciences, it surveys the many constituent parts of the beach which have been broken down for the convenience of scientists and beach strollers alike.

Take it as a given: Scientific inquiry has always been a ponderous cart behind the horse of simple human curiosity. At its worst, Science can become a more blinding opiate than the most parochial dogma. At its best it is an avenue for exploring places and things that antedated our interest and will survive our passing. One compelling attraction of the beach is the undeniable certainty that it will be there long after us. (Insects are a good deal less vulnerable to radiation than mammals; if the "highest" animal of them all succeeds in finally using his most heinous toys of war, the bugs will probably survive even if we don't.) Physically the beach will remain, as dynamic as ever, long after *Homo sapiens,* with its cerebral subspecies of poets and physicists, has become extinct. But for as long as we can, people will continue visiting this partially hospitable place. It draws us for as many reasons as there are human beings. When I get fed to the teeth with petty politics, grand opera or argumentative scientists, I visit a stretch of coast to encounter the ineffable. When Wilbur and Orville Wright wanted to fly, they went to the Outer Banks. William Blake, in all his internal and external wanderings, sought

> To see a World in a Grain of Sand,
> And a Heaven in a Wild Flower,
> Hold Infinity in the palm of your hand
> and Eternity in an hour.

To each his own along the shore.

My real reason to go beaching is recreation—or re-creation. But I've learned why beach grass hurts in early summer and gotten a peek at its miraculous regenerative ways. I've gained a fond respect for the horseshoe crab, which has the engaging habits of eating with its shoulders and swimming upside-down after dark. (I haven't wantonly killed one in years, except to eat.)

And if science couldn't reveal all, neither would nature. Each time I walked another stretch of beach to the farthest point seen from the starting place, I found new frustration—or so it seemed. I secretly kept hoping that beyond the next point of sand or rocky head the littoral would offer up all the answers, that windrows of knowledge would be washed ashore to explain what the books didn't. Instead there'd be just another cove alive with seaweed and raucous birds—or utterly empty, provoking another question. And there would be another dim point in the distance. So I'd go away again, back to the city, the libraries, the laboratories, the museums, the typewriter, knowing one thing for certain: While I'm gone and when I return the beach will be there still shifting, changing, mystifying, reassuring, continuing.

Driftwords:

The Longest Meal

The tide rises along a narrow empty island's shore; the sun slides down behind the continent. This place—for the miles I can see in any direction —is mine alone. It was a willet's when I arrived, but the bird fled, flashing its chevrons and complaining prettily.

Pour a shot over the last ice and break out peanuts. Quick, tidy up before the light goes completely and find that shell book among the tackle and oilskins. Do it now; it's easy enough to pitch the tent after dark on a clear, calm night like this. Light the safari lamp and study a bird guide, learn field marks for tomorrow; the sandpipers all looked alike again today. (No more peanuts. Buy peanuts next time you see a store.) Set up the stove, heat the soup, choose the entrée—canned hash or the fish that didn't bite? A good old Carolina boy said fishing will be bad for days after this onshore wind. "It makes the water mulky." *Mulky.* We spoke at noon and I haven't seen a brace of people to talk to since. The word lingers.

(Will you please pitch the tent and roll out the bag so it's ready when you are? All right.) When that chore's done, the soup's ready. Then take a walk to clear the palate; go see what the tide dragged in . . . nothing to write home about yet. Whet the knife, chop an onion, sauté in butter with four twists of fresh pepper, start the hash. (Buy no more hash! Tiresome hash.) While it's browning, sort the day's crop of shells and sprigs: *Quercus virginiana* (live oak from a hummock near the marsh) and *Atrina serrata* (a pen shell from the swash.) R. Tucker Abbott's field guide shows how to tell the pen shells apart by internal muscle scars. He says the critter's edible, like a scallop. Or was. Mine's dead, an empty shell, but one valve's intact. A lucky find. Alive it grew narrow-end down, anchored by byssus threads like a mussel. The external scales helped hold it and provided attachments for barnacles, oysters and worms. *Seashells of North America* reports:

> The soft parts of these clams are unique in possessing a finger-like pallial organ and gutter-like waste canal. These organs remove pieces of broken shell, rejected food, and other debris. . . . Within the mantle cavity of this

bivalve a small crab, *Pinnotheres* receives protection and feeds upon surplus food particles.

Elsewhere I've read that *Pinnotheres ostreum* in particular inhabits oysters commensally too, doing them no harm. Those pea crabs, no bigger than lima beans, are said to be delicious.

Abbott does not say pen shells are rare; they are southern animals with thin, fragile shells. I've found only fragments before. (Save it in a jar filled with water as a cushion.) "The brittleness of the shell is due in part to the very large size of the prismatic crystals, which can be easily seen with the aid of a hand lens." (Where the devil has the lens gone? That can wait. The hash is crusty.) (Would you like a glass of once-chilled chablis *ce soir?* With hash, don't be gauche. *Absolument non,* crack a beer and bring Thoreau to dinner.)

In *Cape Cod,* Thoreau tells of a place a thousand miles back and a dozen decades ago. He walked its length more than once, lodging with local folks and lighthouse keepers, an interesting way to travel. (Today all the lighthouses have signs warning the public to stay away—even several standing from his time.) One of the first things he sees is the new wreck of the British brig *St. John* on Grampus Rock off Cohasset. Shipwrecks were common in the 1840s; scores of immigrants drowned. (Put on your editor's cap and punctuate the leagues-long sentences of his transcendental sermon.)

Why care for these dead bodies? They really have no friends but the worms or fishes. Their owners were coming to the New World, as Columbus and the Pilgrims did. They were within a mile of its shores. But before they could reach it they emigrated to a newer world than ever Columbus dreamed of. Yet one of whose existence we believe that there is far more universal and convincing evidence—though it has not yet been discovered by science—than Columbus had of this: not merely mariners' tales and some paltry drift-wood and seaweed, but a continual drift and instinct to all our shores. I saw their empty hulks [their bodies, he means] that came to land. But they themselves, meanwhile, were cast upon some shore yet further west, toward which we are all tending, and which we shall reach at last. It may be through storm and darkness, as they did. No doubt we have reason to thank God that they have not been "shipwrecked into life again." The mariner who makes the safest port in Heaven, perchance, seems to his friends on earth to be shipwrecked, for they deem Boston Harbor the better place. . . .

Clean-up is fast and easy. Wash the pot, pan, cup and plate in the swash. Flatten empty cans to pack them out again. Close up the car.

Brush the teeth. Do the little one can to help a rising tide. Check the stars again while coffee water boils. Open a can of fruit. (Save half for breakfast, damn it. Stop nagging.)

There's dew enough now to wipe the salt off the windows. Walk the berm with the six-volt torch pinning ghost crabs that flee, then cower in the beam. (Never heard of anyone eating a ghost crab, anywhere.) Oh hell, nearly midnight; you have a date with a fish at dawn. And so to bed. Crawl in. Zip up. Lights out. Pray for a shifting wind and the wit to fool a flounder. (Good night. Nice party. Thanks. Good company. I hate eating alone.)

Outer dunes: beach grass, sea rocket and sand.

Prologue

What's Going On Here?

Since there are no certain boundaries, start in the middle. The mid-Atlantic beach is a blurred entity. To the north lies glacier-made New England with its hard rock coast. Below the Outer Banks, climate, sand composition and animal populations become significantly different. But the notion of a mid-Atlantic beach is conceptually useful; the place has its characteristics. The ocean doesn't strike firm land here as it openly pounds the west coasts of Europe and America. This coast is mostly made of barrier islands, no matter how much man has done to camouflage that fact. Starting parallel to Long Island, sand barriers are the rule. Though often linked to the mainland by low-tide bars, natural isthmuses or artificial causeways, islands constitute the New Jersey Coast, the Delmarva (for Delaware/Maryland/Virginia) Peninsula above Chesapeake Bay and the Outer Banks below it. Between, behind and among these islands—protected from the ocean's raw force—lie inlets, bays, sounds and lagoons lined by uncounted miles of marsh, a realm of astonishing ecological importance to human and marine life.

Concentrate on the beach itself. Between surf and terra firma lurks a bewilderingly complex place, one we take for granted. The seashore is like sex: easy to enjoy without knowing much about how it works. And mysterious as it is, sex might be the simpler to understand—just two major elements: anatomy and emotion. The beach involves many more particulars: rocks, plants, animals, weather, water all tangled together like a surf row of seaweed, spider crabs and tidal lint in the wide-meshed fishnet of natural science. Energy and change are the only constants in this ribbon of a region where old, sloping land meets the kinetic ocean. This shoreline is the result of movable objects meeting a resistible force. (The ocean is presently winning as its level rises inches a century, though the next ice age will take it all back, if you care to stick around.)

Traveling from deep inland, one crosses the Eastern Shore with its pulpwood stands and vast flat fertilized fields that grow three crops a year. At the northeast corner of that land, where Delaware Bay enters the Atlantic, is Cape Henlopen and a state park where I saw two-toed tracks in the sand early one morning several springs ago. (Deer are common enough on almost any mid-Atlantic beach with a trace of wildness left; they forage in nearby woods and marsh but usually stay hidden from human day-trippers.) Then a small white-tail scampered around a dune and headed into the surf. Though a slight sea was running, the animal swam toward where Cape May lay hidden a dozen miles away beneath the low sky. Yes, deer swim to reach islands or elsewhere. An easier way to go northeast is by the ferry that plies between Lewes, Delaware and Cape May, which shelters one of Roger Tory Peterson's favorite birding spots. Many land birds reluctantly cross water they can't see across, so the south end of a landmass like New Jersey is a migratory bottleneck.

Turning south from Cape Henlopen, wild and settled stretches are interspersed. The coast road runs straight down the barrier islands between a plain of bracken on the left and the meandering bays. The sea is hidden behind a line of man-made dunes; the snow fences that collected them grain by grain stand buried to stubs in the sand. There are World War II watchtowers, widely spaced parking lots with plastic aqua waterclosets like vertical coffins. Towns lie off the main drag: clapboard cottages for young families and clusters of new identical second-homes with identically steep roof lines and price tags. At man-made Indian River Inlet, where fishermen cast from the rock breakwaters that guard the channel, the road arches across a bridge tall enough to let the charter boats pass with their outriggers erect in the sockets.

Then, on this island of shifting sand, the condominiums of Ocean City rise ahead: towers, pyramids and monoliths, some now standing barely 50 feet from the high-tide line, some of their footings washed by storm tides. The beach is "eroding" here and bulldozers pile up the sand in a steep, uneven line of dunes, a wishful wall against the inevitable storms. But a prominent geologist says "Ocean City doesn't have enough little Dutch boys." He wonders when a condo, its footings awash in an abnormally high tide, "will fall seaward like a Douglas fir."

Cross streets number into the hundreds, all of them dusted with a little sand. This is a city of amusements: roller coasters, arcades, pizza parlors, rent-a-bikes, auction houses, stout turn-of-the-century hotels facing the beach across a boardwalk strong enough to carry trucks. The most feral thing might be the purple moose head on the wall of its namesake saloon or the monsters in the Morbid Manor Fun House at the foot of the fishing pier. Visitors can rent all sorts of accommodations, from a porch swing (in a pinch) to a scarlet suite in a high-rise built by a celebrated felon. In a bar at sundown a pretty PR gal and a handsome accountant said they loved the town. They came all the way from Seattle and Philadelphia respectively "just to have an affair" which was going swimmingly. For people who like people in numbers, who seek the anonymity or opportunity of crowds, this must be the place.

Just beyond the Ocean City Inlet lies Assateague National Seashore, a 35-mile island that was saved from development—and just as well. In the last few years the north end of Assateague has moved west more than its original width. All the planned house lots are under the Atlantic now, though the island seems intact; it simply migrated. Erosion along the entire chain of East Coast islands naturally proceeds at a few feet a year. "There'll always be a beach," says another geologist. "It just won't stay where it was and may not be where someone wants it."

A beach is a sometime thing. It constantly shifts and moves as countless grains of sand answer the ceaseless winds and waves. The motion of the sea is fascinating, mesmerizing—like firelight certainly, or a TV tube perhaps. But that motion makes this a most difficult place for humans to settle and "improve" because it has no respect for stability or arbitrary property lines. Wild inhabitants of the coast and surf zones are wiser. None tries to beat a wave on its own mobile turf. They have adapted their ways to the place and roll with each oceanic punch.

Several miles down-island lies a stretch of old macadam, a remnant of road from the once-intended summer town. Only a few rods of pavement remain, crumbling at the edges and cracked clear through. Behind it a tall dune rises, covered with American beach grass on its seaward side. The dune, in turn, protects plants that secure its landward side. Below it grows an impenetrable thicket: alder, holly, bayberry,

loblolly pine. None grows taller than the dunes because spray blowing
off the sea keeps these trees pruned back. A chunk of dune side has slid
away to reveal layers of dark sand, garnet and magnetite. These minerals
become concentrated in layers when fierce wind blows away the lighter
grains of quartz that were mountains geological ages ago and which
make up most of the beach today.

Along the water are the constant birds: laughing, herring and ring-
billed gulls; busy sandpipers and their vocal kind all pecking their
livings from the wet sand. There are the remains of many marine animals: crabs, clams, snails. Like any beach where wild species outnumber
Homo sapiens, this place is both alive and cluttered with the remains of
things now dead. Ocean water is a cold soup of tiny nutrients. Microorganisms live in the open sea and in the tiny channels of water among
the sand grains wherever the beach is wet. So in one respect the living
is easy for small creatures that patronize the generous tidal caterer.
Because the ocean is an endless source of small meals, many slightly
larger animals learned to put up with the oceanic headaches of constant
pounding. They'd grow complacently fat if they didn't spend their lives
evading the larger animals that learned to feed on them. Each animal
lives and dies, eats and is eaten. Each generation's success is measured
by a single criterion: Did it create another generation? As Samuel Butler
said, "A hen is only an egg's way of making another egg." As Harvard
sociobiologist Edward O. Wilson updates the notion "the organism is
only DNA's way of making more DNA."

One can walk to the south end of Assateague or drive the long way
around: down Route 13 to T's Corner gas-station-grocery-and-bus-
stop. Turn left past forlorn signs to the candle factory and X-rated
drive-in, past the roller rink, Satellite Motel and miles-long cyclone
fence protecting the distant dish antennas of NASA's Wallops Island
tracking station. Then the road curves right to cross miles of marsh to
reach the low island of Chincoteague.

It's a curious place where traditional livelihoods survive the crowded
tourist seasons. Clapboard motels take in paying guests a clam shell's
toss from packinghouses. Offshore dredgers and seiners dwarf the
sport-fishing boats along the bulkhead. Local folks brag about their
"salt oysters" which have far more flavor than the Chesapeake Bay or
Long Island Sound bivalves that just taste slithery.

Stands selling decoys, painted shells and clam sandwiches line the
road northeast of town. Where they thin out, the marsh begins again,
patrolled by "cranky birds" (herons) afoot and a-wing. Beyond the toll

gate, a bridge, low, noisy and rickety, seems to emphasize the breadth of the tidal gut. Crossing that bridge stresses the fact that an island lies at the other end. Predictably the powers that be are replacing the old truss span with a soaring thing on concrete piers to ease access to the south end of Assateague Island National Seashore and the Wildlife Refuge that surrounds it. It's a pity; well-connected islands lose their special feeling.

A park ranger reports that a harbor porpoise came ashore last week. The books say this animal ranges only from Greenland to New Jersey, which is two states north, and watchers delight at the chance to see a local rarity. The ranger can tell the dried scat of fox from raccoon because the fox's contains undigested feathers while the coon's has broken shells. The Fish and Wildlife people, who have the bureaucratic upper hand here, have declared war on foxes, which eat birds; soon there may be fewer small mammal signs to distinguish. This war is a shame; I've seen one red fox here, a saucy prince who trotted past my car one night as if he owned the right-of-way. The Park Service would declare peace and let nature arbitrate between animal and Aves, prey and predators who seem to know the inherent dangers of overkill. But the "managed habitat" here is managed for the benefit of proliferating waterfowl. There were no brants twenty years ago; this poor member of the goose family is abundant now, perhaps because of the sanctuary's "management techniques," perhaps because modern reaping machines on the huge Eastern Shore farms nearby leave far more gleanings. In addition there are 250 other bird species here; it's another migratory bottleneck and wintering ground as well.

Botany time. Marsh alder grows down to the high-tide line in the marsh. So does salt meadow grass *(Spartina patens)* which farmers used to mow for hay that cost them only the price of labor. Where the salt hay stops, its cordgrass cousin begins. *Spartina alterniflora* is hinged near the ground and falls in a high wind to create mats like mattresses of reeds. The fiddler crabs live below it, their million burrows ventilating the mud at low tide, irrigating it when the water rises. There's phragmites too, hollow reeds of the sort the ancients carved into the first pens. Saltwort *(Salicornia)*, which adds zest to salads, thrives in the tide flats, its spikes shiny from expelled salt. Snails creep up and down the flat grasses eating algae and keeping above the reach of the water whence their ancestors came. Seemingly sterile salt pans—flat areas of empty mud—are actually alive with different colored algae that migrate up and down as conditions change by the hour.

Sometime in June the marshes will be kept nearly people-free by mosquitoes. Why not annihilate them? Because their larva is prime food for the shell- and fin-fish that spend their youth in shallow marsh waters. Without the eggs of these bloodsucking pests three-fourths of the fish we eat would go hungry before growing large enough to go to sea. Raymond B. Manning, a Smithsonian Institution crustacea curator, offers this datum: Recent catches of marsh-dependent seafood amount to 535 pounds per acre of estuary: This is nearly twice what a well-managed and heavily capitalized Maryland farm can grow in livestock. Comparative agronomists say that acre for acre, a marsh is the most productive land on earth except for a well-fertilized pineapple field. And it does its fecund work alone—cleaned and fertilized alike by diurnal tides—if it is left alone.

Closer to the beach there's poison ivy, a plentiful source of berries for at least sixty species of birds. Sea lavender and seaside goldenrod grow on the dunes. "Terns used to nest here," the ranger says walking the beach near Tom's Cove, where some vehicles are allowed now. But their odd mating rite, which includes paired flights across the rookery and gifts of ritual food, must be seen elsewhere. Their rites have the same surprising purpose as the heron's ungainly spring dance: for one individual to discover another's gender from its role. These birds must *act* male or female since both sexes look alike, even to their own kind.

Another drive south, another spring day, another guide. Retired waterman George West, Jr. of Cheriton, Virginia steers his inboard-outboard out of the small fishing port of Oyster below Assateague off Virginia's Eastern Shore. West has plied these waters, oysterman and boy, as his father and grandfather did and he's old enough to be a grandfather himself by now. But these bays are treacherous. Underwater shoals wander about like sad bores at a cocktail party. Creeks open and close before they're printed on any chart. We're headed for the dozen barrier islands that make up the new 35,000-acre Virginia Coast Preserve. These islands were recently bought by the Nature Conservancy which will see that they're not tampered with in perpetuity: Metomkin, Cedar, Cobb, Wreck and the rest. People are welcome to visit by day so long as they don't disturb the wildlife or pick the plants. The Conservancy will leave the islands to their own devices as they shrink, grow, rotate and migrate, supporting gently balanced and well-studied ecosystems all the while.

Going outside onto the edge of the Atlantic, the boat is surrounded by a herd of feeding porpoises. Minutes later West says, "I owned a thousand acres right about here." The islands once lay farther east; the course he steers crosses where his family lived before the hurricane of '33. "All got in safe except my grandfather and old Mr. Cobb. We didn't know anything about hurricanes then—called them northeasters. Nobody could conceive a tide could come that high. . . . Any man says he can build something the ocean won't tear up is overlooking a whole lot. He's a damn fool pure and simple. And that covers it all."

Much of the coast once looked like these islands now: low, with broad beaches that slope gently to a short dune and, behind that, grassy plains, salt marshes and fresh ones where rainwater lies in a convex "lens" on top of the heavier saltwater table. There are a few wrecked ships and the bones of stranded whales and stuff that drifted all the way from Spain to these beaches. In the spring there are rookeries and later, no doubt, more man-eating bugs than grains of sand when the summer wind is wrong. These islands appear modest: so unimposing—and unimposed on.

Smith Island, the southernmost, lies even with Cape Charles, the tip of the Eastern Shore. I rounded that point one hot afternoon, in order to have the luxury of a beach walk that didn't backtrack over the same ground. I'd walked south down the bay side and climbed an imposing fence that announced "No Trespassing: U. S. Government Property," an offensive statement since the government is not properly the owner of anything, just a trustee. I'd seen thunderheads crossing the Chesapeake. When they reached the narrow land again—it's barely a sliver there while the bay mouth is 20 miles wide—their forward edge began rolling up like sterile cotton into its blue paper. It was an extraordinary sight, standing almost directly beside an invisible column of air that rose straight up forcing the moving cloud to twist itself up seemingly tighter and tighter like a magazine rolled into a bat. The leading edge stayed bright and fluffy in the sun as it rolled, and the roll itself stayed right overhead. But the rest of the cloud, spreading back across the bay, went from a gentle gray to sooty black.

There was no thunder or lightning, suddenly just rain. It blew horizontally in gill-sized drops, and the sun went out as if snuffed by the wall of wind that bent every tree and carried spring leaves away. I'd just passed an old artillery bunker from a nearly forgotten war and stumbled back to it as the rain turned to hailstones big as mothballs. Drenched and stung, I hid in the dark, dank, man-made cavern with a dripping ceiling and rusty rails running across the oddly even floor. The storm passed, leaving the land veiled with rising mists and sparkling sunlight.

Now the peninsula road becomes the Chesapeake Bay Bridge-Tunnel leading to Norfolk and the summer metropolis of Virginia Beach. Motel towers offer all the comforts of home, plus views of Navy ships heading in. The sky is alive with jet fighters on training flights. The beach below the concrete breakwater/promenade is covered with young. A bald jogger puffs by. Four slim blond, coiffed, men sway in counterpoint like herons. A young couple in street shoes pushes a stroller along the hard wet sand. Two girls in electric bikinis flip a Frisbee. Hundreds of others lie face down, basking with their bra tops untied, all pointing in the same direction as if conforming to a solartrophic law.

In a nearby office complex, incongruously, Dennis Holland fields phone calls about a pair of peregrine falcons, fastest birds on earth. The species is scarce now, but this pair is nesting on a bank building in downtown Norfolk and getting fat on pigeons as they used to do before DDT reduced the clan to endangered status. Holland is boss of the Back Bay Wildlife Refuge. The road there winds around small farms, reaches the water at Sandbridge, and turns south again between the new summer homes on stilts high enough to look over the barrier dunes—if another house isn't in the way.

Romie Waterfield, who is nearing retirement and has worked at Back Bay nearly half his life, explains, "My forefather was shipwrecked on the dune." The English sailor's great-great-grandson, born near the refuge, remembers eating swan at a time when a man could shoot whatever he chose if he couldn't get a goose. Now Waterfield tends the birds: "hell diver" (the pied grebe which sinks to hide underwater when frightened); snowy egret ("when he jumps up, look on his yellow dancing slippers"); "puddle ducks" that feed on the surface; "dabbling ducks" that forage below it; "ditty birds" including everything from song sparrows to mocking birds, and 18,000 whistling swans that winter here. "There are those that think ducks was created for hunters to shoot. It couldn't be farther from the truth." Waterfield points out there is a species with every length of neck to feed on every kind of aquatic plant in the marsh. While eating, "he's tearing roots up, knocking seed off and covering it up. What he's doing is cultivating better than a man can. Other than that you wouldn't have nearly as good a crop of aquatics as you have"—to feed the birds. He knows every bird in the place and every plant.

Inside the narrow stretch of barrier dunes runs a line of hardwood trees that usually only grow much farther inland. Some visionaries have proposed a road because the presence of the trees seems to suggest that the land is apparently more stable here. Waterfield wishes the policy-makers had better outdoor sense. The inland trees grow only in the narrow lee of the dunes which force the salt-filled sea winds up and over in an atmospheric wave. More stable soil has nothing to do with it; rooted in sand, these trees grow in a fresh-air tunnel behind the wall of sand, protected from the salt spray.

He dislikes the Refuge beach today with its buggies driven by "people who don't want to know you" and occasional bare sunbathers whom he reports to the police. "I remember when the birds nested on this side of the dune," he says, steering a battered pickup along the beach. He hasn't seen them in years and wants to blame the traffic. He knows this beach "used to have lots of birds and few cars. Now it has lots of cars and few birds." He drives near a doomed gannet, its feathers clotted with bilge oil, sitting immobile just above the swash. It looks like a judge, its straight sharp beak pointed down, the frost blue eyes unblink-ing. "There's nothing to be done," Waterfield says. He has found his first killdeer nest of the year. The robin-sized bird rushed him first, all puffed up like a cartoon turkey, then fled, feigning a broken wing. The nest holds four speckled eggs.

Two hours south over back roads cross another causeway, beyond Kill Devil Hills where the Wright Brothers made history and Roanoke Island where Virginia Dare was born, the Cape Hatteras National Sea-shore begins. Eddies of the Gulf Stream sometimes launch flying fish near shore and roll God-knows-what along the bottom from the tropics. There are bottlenose dolphin "in numbers," grampuses, pilot whales, sea turtles, a few otters, even fewer and shyer cottonmouth water moc-casins, all sorts of crabs, bivalves and innumerable fish.

"You should have been here yesterday" was the early morning word south of Nags Head. The bluefish had been running; corpses of bait fish, each with a piece of flesh missing, clutter the beach in dead proof. Light rain began an hour after dawn, and most of the surfcasters went in for breakfast. Only one young man stayed, with his child, Shannon, while the mother slept. Then, very quickly, the shallow surf was alive with shiny fish, eight or ten inches long, swimming in tight-packed schools to the top of the wash. Then sloping fins sliced among them: the tails of big blues at an orgy. They'd take one bite from a silverside and go for another. They took Shannon's father's lure on almost every cast. He'd reel in, cut the hook loose and run down the beach to cast into the swarm again. Other fishermen returned quickly until they ranged the beach ten yards apart, sharing the spoils. They must have been watching from the porches like gulls.

The bait fish came in such tight schools that I could wade among them in the numbing water and slap a few ashore. The fishermen couldn't say whether they were shoaling to spawn. "I don't know much about this," said Shannon's dad. "I just like to catch the big blues."

From a fishing pier where the kill seemed greatest, it appeared that when one bluefish fought the hook another swam below, veering in counterpoint. Judging from caps and coveralls, many major corporations were represented: Exxon, Caterpillar Diesel, even your Orkin Man. Four buddies from Norfolk carted off eighty blues load by load in a little red wagon. Beach vehicles are popular here because when the blues are running fishermen can cast until the school passes, then drive a few miles ahead and fish again. So the 58 miles of broken beach are rutted like a racetrack between the wet sand and the dunes.

Marcia Lannon, "the Littlest Ranger" at about 5 feet flat and 90 pounds, works out of the old Coast Guard Station by the Hatteras Lighthouse which was build 1,000 yards from the surf and is now 100 yards away. In spring, along the dunes, sea oats and beach grass are hard to tell apart, she admits, sharing her fount of random comparative botany. Later the sea oats grow tall stalks with tattered flags of seed pods, which people like to carry home but mustn't lest they undermine the fragile dunes. The leaves of both curl in hot weather to conserve moisture. The two most numerous terns are easy to tell apart, once Lannon has compared them. The Royal has an orange bill, the Caspian a red one.

Local folks' accents sound strange; more like Liverpool than Carolina and probably most like Elizabethan England, according to theory. At the lower end of Hatteras, ferries shuttle west to Ocracoke and back, followed by swarms of laughing gulls begging for food. On a stormy day, waves wash over the notorious Diamond Shoals from every direction, meet head on and fly straight into the air—high as a house.

This last island is utterly dry (alcoholically) and inkeepers turn away solos in case a larger party arrives on the last boat. But the water is warm from the Gulf Stream and delightful swimming. It's springtime still; the beach is empty except for an occasional commuting camper and the constant shore birds pairing.

Alta VanLandingham and her husband may be the island's most cosmopolitan couple. He was a military man and she kept busy overseas collecting shells, which she now sells from a shop by the side of the road. She has pet spider crabs and sea horses, which feed from her hand in aquariums. Collecting live shells, she works at low tide. In warm weather she prefers the early morning ebbs because fewer visitors are there to interrupt and ask what she's doing. It's simple; she's digging the beach, her way.

Heading north finally, I know that Prufrock was wrong:

> I shall wear white flannel trousers and walk upon the beach.
> I have heard the mermaids singing, each to each.
> I do not think that they will sing to me.

Mermaids are found only on camper doormats and mirrors behind condominium bars. There are better, living things to see and hear: choirs of gulls, ghost and hermit crabs, migrating clams in migrating sand, fastidious grass, and the ocean's endless energy.

Part I

The Zoological Beach

The shore—from surf across swash zone, foreshore, berm, barrier dune and swale to marsh and bay—supports what's arguably the most varied visible fauna of any habitat in the temperate world. This is the place marine turtles and ancient arachnids seek to lay their eggs in summer sand. Birds abound here at every time of year: spring and autumn migrants, winter residents and summertime brooders. Predatory fishes hunt within reach of well-cast bait while dangerous rays lurk in shallow water and stinging jellies drift aimlessly. An occasional whale strands itself; hundreds of different crustaceans go about their business sideways. Carnivorous mammals leave the maritime forest to scout the littoral for food, rodents ply the grasses, snakes slither down to the swash from time to time and mollusks by the millions inch about on both sides of the land. This place is alive; its denizens are easily seen by anyone who comes here and cares to watch.

Family portrait: Crustaceans.*

Chapter One

The Crabs
—True, Blue and Otherwise

At the outset of this first catalogue of common beach creatures, a few words on terminology are mandatory. Take it as a given: Among the familiar animals in general (and crabs in particular) misnomers and confusing repetitions are the first rule. Confusing duplications are the second. The Atlantic blue crab is mostly green. Horseshoe crabs aren't crabs at all, zoologically speaking, but members of another general category of critters. Further, the barely edible horseshoe crab goes by the alias "king crab" along some stretches of the Atlantic coast while in the Pacific Northwest the same words signify a long-legged delicacy. Thus "king crab" may refer to an East Coast cousin of spiders and scorpions or to a proper decapod from the wrong address. Clearly,

*Crustacea cooperate and compete. The hermit crab inhabits a moon snail's shell crowned with barnacles. A young lobster lurks by its rock shelter and a lady crab flees to feed.

common nomenclature can be confusing. But the scientific idiom has shortcomings, too, superficially at least, because few folks speak Latin with any ease. (Ask your friendly neighborhood fishmonger "How's your *Callinectes sapidus* today?" and he's likely to take it amiss.) The scientific names are unfamiliar and unredeemingly polysyllabic—though frequently mellifluous when untangled properly. More important, they have the advantage of being particularly specific while also indicating some basic relationships between organisims.

Before anyone's enthusiasm curdles in the face of the Latinate, consider the background. The terminological ball game played by biologists today was kicked off by an eighteenth-century Swede whose own name most often appears in its Latin form: Linnaeus. Carl Linné (1707–1778) was so slow as a boy that his father nearly apprenticed him to a shoemaker, according to one account. A more laudatory biographer says the curate's son was so fond of flowers that he was dubbed "the little botanist" at the age of eight. In either event he became famous in his own time as a trailblazing botanist, and incidentally an explorer as well, though he trained as a physician. In the days when modern science was in its confused and adventurous infancy, a medical diploma provided entree not only to patients' bedsides but to every corner of the scientific world as well. The ambitious man of science was surrounded by field after field of uncharted territory; the natural world was so haphazardly known that a kind of anarchy reigned. Linnaeus brought some order to it.

Having successfully practiced medicine and taught at the university in Uppsala, he switched professorial chairs and published landmark works on the classification of plants and methods of classification. Of paramount importance, he was "the first to enunciate the principles for defining genera and species and to adhere to a uniform use of the binomial system for naming plants and animals." He called his system "a concise methodical and ingenious synopsis whereby a mineral, a plant or an animal could be referred to a definite place within the system and associated with a name." The legendary eleventh edition of the Encyclopaedia Britannica opines, "He made many mistakes [in actual classification]; but the honor due to him for having first enumerated the principles for defining genera and species, and his uniform use of specific names, is enduring." In recognition for his scientific preeminence he was admitted to the nobility and given the honorific "von." Curiously, he offered one revolutionary hypothesis which caused little hoopla. In the tenth edition of his *Systema Naturae,* published in 1758, he placed man among the other primates. When Charles Darwin expanded similar ideas in *The Origin of Species* 101 years later, he scandalized the world.

Linnaeus' system depended on Latin, then the accepted international language which survives to this day as a kind of scientific Esperanto for biologists of every tongue. Like any good cataloging system from the phone book to Dewey Decimal, it is essentially open-ended and infinitely expandable. As new groups of flora and fauna were studied during Linnaeus' lifetime and after, his system found room for them. They might not be always accommodated with alacrity, but the method worked; a species could be put in its place and retrieved at will if further research showed it had been misplaced originally. The barnacle, for example, because of superficial appearances was long assumed to be a kind of mollusk and was so classified. But after its life cycle and anatomy were examined more closely it was reclassified as an arthropod, one of the jointed-legged animals like crabs and insects.

This points out one of the traps of attempting absolute scientific accuracy: Many biological truths have a certain transience. One reputable taxonomist says "every authoritative text is obsolete by the time it gets to the printer" because ongoing research constantly reveals newer information and prompts revisions. Over the years there has been a great deal of pulling, stretching and downright unpleasantness among taxonomists. A generation ago the International Commission on Zoological Nomenclature, which keeps tabs on things, was moved to issue a Declaration "On the need for avoiding intemperate language in discussions on zoological nomenclature." But then Linnaeus himself, the father of taxonomy, died after a fit of apoplexy.

Nonetheless, the system he invented evolved into a complex matrix within whose cubbies taxonomists continue to work and wrangle. It depends on an "Obligatory Hierarchy of Ranks" in a declension from the general to the specific (literally) which runs as follows:

Kingdom
  Phylum
    Class
      Order
        Family
          Genus
            Species

But that's just the bare bones of it. As the life sciences became increasingly sophisticated, these categories proved insufficient to accommodate all the distinctions and commonalities that were perceived. Hence a variety of interlinear classifications came into being so that today the full classification of an organism can stipulate its membership in each of the following groups and more: kingdom, subkingdom, phylum, subphylum, superclass, class, infraclass, cohort, superorder, order, suborder, superfamily, family, subfamily, tribe, genus, species and subspecies. Think of it all as an unspeakably big family tree: The closer you find two leaves on a twig, the closer their kinship; branches of the same limb are related in ways that other branches are not, but everything originally came from the same stem. Yet, like a family geneaology commissioned by a social climber, any branch of it may be of dubious legitimacy. One expert can prove a connection to his satisfaction and his client's delight; another may call some favorite ancestral prince a bastard and the issue remains in doubt.

Climbing down out of this hyper-ramified baobab (i.e., from the specific to the general) one can trace a lineage of sorts for a crab which turns up in Cape Cod lobster pots. I've heard it called both the rock crab and the Jonah crab, but the Latin name specifies: *Cancer borealis.* With one other species in coastal Atlantic waters it represents the family Cancridae, which in turn fits into the infraorder Brachyura or true crabs, a group that also includes blue crabs, spider crabs, calico crabs, ghost crabs, etc. They all constitute one of five groups in the suborder of decapods (Decapoda). These ten-footed creatures share the distinction of belonging to the class Crustacea. In turn this class belongs to the phylum Arthropoda which comprises all animals with jointed legs and segmented external skeletons.

It bears mentioning that Linnean categories are not of equal size; the tree is not evenly pruned, to continue the botanical metaphor. Class Crustacea for example, contains 30,000 species while another category of the same rank contains more than a million insects. By the same token many species have numerous cousins of the same genus while some species are the only surviving members of the genus and family and may be considered biologically isolated as far back as the order level.

After finding something's phylum there's nothing left but its biological kingdom, a choice for larger life-forms between animal and vegetable, though many smaller organisms manage to keep a foot in each field.

There are—ready or not—five kingdoms, three of which succor a variety of microscopic organisms such as the viruses, bacteria, some algae, molds and fungi (which occupy an entire taxonomic realm of their own). Most larger members of the world's biota belong to either the kingdom Metaphyta (plants from the true algae on up) or the kingdom Metazoa (higher animals), which has been rent into two subkingdoms. One is devoted to sponges. The other, the subkingdom Metazoa (just to obscure things), contained 27 phyla* at last count, all but one of which belong to invertebrates. (The remaining phylum, Chordata, includes the subphylum Vertebrata, class Mammalia, order Primatae, suborder Anthropoidea—as opposed to the Prosimii like lemurs and such —family Hominidae, genus *Homo,* species *sapiens. Homo sapiens,* modern man, is the only extant member of the hominids.)

Thus, the living world by scientific tradition is divided first into kingdoms and then into phyla. One of those 26 invertebrate phyla is phylum Arthropoda. It contains 3 subphyla. The first is for sea spiders and the second with classes for horseshoe crabs on the one hand plus mites, spiders, ticks, and pseudoscorpions on the other. The third subphylum, Mandiibulata (whose members have similar mouth parts), includes the class Insecta and the class Crustacea. Kenneth L. Gosner writes with authority that "Crustaceans are so diverse an assemblage that, beyond defining them as arthropods with mandibles and two pairs of antennae, a useful yet concise statement of their collective traits is impractical." Suffice it that they all stem from the same branch of the phylogenetic tree; in generally Linnean and Darwinian terms they share a common ancestor and thus are taxonomic cousins. Alas, "the classification of higher Crustacea has had a tortured history." They are now distributed among 8 subclasses which comprise everything from the wood louse and fairy shrimp to the barnacle and lobster.

More to the point, the crustacea class includes 4 superorders, one of which includes the order Decapoda or ten-legged animals that are now considered arthropods. Within this order are 5 infraorders including Brachyura, the true crabs, and we are back (terminologically speaking) where we started. Obviously it is easier to speak of true crabs than brachyurans. But if one jumps the binomial fence into the field of common names one finds a number of commonly visible creatures which are called crabs even though they aren't, e.g. horseshoe crabs. On another hand some noncrabs have much in common with the Brachyura since they are fellow crustaceans, notably the lobster and barnacle. For

*Phyla is the plural of phylum, as taxa is the plural of taxon, the term designating any formal category.

the sake of the reader's convenience (and the writer's sanity), this chapter will deal with animals that share two obvious unscientific traits. Crabs in name or in fact, they have shells which they molt (unlike the mollusks,) and they live along the Atlantic littoral. People plying those beaches are likely to see these creatures, dead or alive.

Consider their outstanding common characteristic first. A crab, like every arthropod, has an exoskeleton. This exterior structure serves the same purpose as our internal skeleton: It's a solid framework for flexible muscles. It also serves as the animal's primary defense. The crab's shell is composed of chitin, a polysaccharide that in and of itself is soft and flexible. Calcium salts and/or the formation of links between protein molecules harden the shell into effective armor. But unlike other kinds of body covering, i.e. human skin, the crab's exterior is composed of rigid plates that don't grow progressively apace with the inner animal. Rather, growth occurs in seemingly abrupt stages that are triggered by hormones.

When a crab grows too large for its shell it bursts at the seams, crawls out and proceeds to grow a new, larger shell with plenty of room inside for muscle and organ growth. The process of the actual molt is called ecdysis, a Greek word H. L. Mencken borrowed to coin the term ecdysiast for the exotic dancers of Baltimore. While the crab's molt is a most dramatic event—far more so than a stripper's peel—the animal is actually in a constant state of preparing for or recovering from ecdysis, just as an adolescent boy is constantly growing out of and into his clothes. "Immediately before and after the casting of the old exoskeleton, water is taken into the animal to expand the soft new cuticle," according to A. P. M. Lockwood, lecturer in biological oceanography at the University of Southampton. "The consequent increase in size is sometimes loosely referred to as 'growth' but strictly the process is only one of expansion. True growth, the incorporation of new tissue, occurs during the later stages of the cycle."

Before an existing shell is shed, an inner skin covering the muscles begins absorbing calcium from the existing outer shell. Softened as a result, the outer shell splits and the animal faces the arduous business of getting out of it. This is a far worse struggle than a balding veteran wrenching his way out of the twenty-year-old uniform he managed to squeeze into for the Memorial Day Parade. In lobsters a claw or leg may be lost in the convulsive process of shedding a too-small shell. Figuratively speaking, if the animal can't get out of a sleeve, it sheds that part of the suit with the musculature still inside. The beast will then grow a new appendage which will be clearly smaller than its opposite number until it catches up in size and appearance two or three molts later. Its overall growth will be slowed, but it can survive the loss of a limb.

Exposure to sea water hardens the new exoskeleton, typically in a matter of days. When it has hardened to become a functional shell, excess water is expelled from the muscle tissue, which shrinks, leaving room for actual growth inside. But molting is a perilous process at best. First there are the mechanical problems of getting out. Then there is a period of defenselessness when the soft-bodied, often immobile animal is easy prey for any carnivore. In addition there is the biochemically tricky business of extreme changes in tissue- and cell-fluid composition as water is absorbed and expelled.

Some arthropods may double their body weight with the premolt absorption of water. Many expand one-quarter in size with each molt. Typically the decapods split open at the rear of the carapace, or upper body segment. This means a lobster opens around his belt line, backs out of the front part of the shell and shucks the rest like sweatpants, more or less. Shrimps eat their cast-off shells, apparently as a handy source of the calcium they need to harden their new shells. After molting, the process of true growth resumes—until things tighten up again. Components of the old shell begin to be reabsorbed, the shell softens, and the cycle begins again. The true crabs, exemplified by the European *Cancer pagurus,* go through the following cycle, according to Dr. Lockwood's timidly titled *Aspects of the Physiology of Crustacea.* This is a fair model for all marine arthropods:

Stage One: The animal molts and can't eat. Often it can't even walk. The new exoskeleton is initially so soft that the crab's limbs won't support its weight; and it gains weight alarmingly fast as muscle tissues absorb water in large quantities. Water content of the whole animal reaches a high of 86 percent. *Stage Two:* The new shell calcifies and a new layer of shell is secreted. Water content declines. *Stage Three:* Feeding resumes and major tissue growth occurs. This stage lasts for more than two-thirds of the cycle. Metabolic reserves accumulate as tissue growth concludes. Water content falls to 60 percent. *Stage Four:* Calcium from the existing exoskeleton is absorbed as outer layers of the subsequent shell begin to develop. Calcium reabsorption continues and the shell cracks, admitting water which the muscles begin to absorb. *Stage Five:* The animal, instinctively alerted to find the safest possible place to hide, struggles out of the old shell and absorbs water rapidly, preparing to create a new exoskeleton.

And so it goes, all over again.

The preeminent prerequisite for biological success is reproduction (should anyone wonder why zoologists are so interested in procreative methodology, e.g. sex). Crustaceans lay eggs. Most protect them one way or another. Typically the female carries them until they ripen, which accounts for the "berried" lobster or "spongy" crab carrying a mass of roe beneath her. The larva develops through a series of remarkably dissimilar body shapes with several molts. These changes can be more distinct than Dr. Jekyll's metamorphosis into Mr. Hyde. Gosner puts it this way: "Morphological differences between larva and adult and between successive larval stages may be so great that one would not guess them to be consecutive manifestations of the same ontogeny." In other words, a baby crab don't look like pa.

TRUE CRABS

Atlantic Blue Crab *(Callinectes sapidus)*

A popular prototype, the common and justly famous Atlantic blue crab is green on top and whitish below. The female's claws are tipped with red while the male's have bright azure highlights. Gender (and in the female, maturity) can also be told by the shape of a structure on the bottom shell called "apron" by diners or "abdomen" by biologists. The male's resembles the stem of a champagne glass, its foot aligned with the back edge of the shell. In the virginal female or "she-crab" the apron is an isosceles triangle. The sexually mature (and almost invariably pregnant) "sook" wears a semicircular apron with a small triangular point during the last stage of her life.

"No other crab has been fished so intensively and thus observed so much," writes William W. Warner in his elegantly entertaining natural history of the animal and its human pursuers, *Beautiful Swimmers.* Its generic name translates into Warner's title while *sapidus* means tasty or savory; it is as delightful at the table as it is nimble in the water. Its swimming ability results from the flattened oarlike shape of its fifth pair of legs which enable it to dart reasonable distances as fast as a fish or to leisurely cross the Chesapeake Bay at will. The fourth, third and second pairs are walking legs. The first pair is armed with sharp, quick claws that bite painfully. The broad body has sharply pointed sides that may be useful defensively since it usually moves sideways.

This outstandingly belligerent and sharp-sighted animal willingly attacks people—or so it seems. They'll go for a tired sailor's toe dangling from the back of an anchored boat, I can assure you, with an alacrity that seems purely malicious. Reputed to be largely creatures of estuaries, they regularly seek the ocean, as when the spent female goes offshore to die after shedding her last eggs and when the larval and intermediary "megalops" stages, drift far out at sea. (Some summers these mites become beach pests, unpopularly called "sea fleas" that cling to swimmers and leave rashes of bites.) By far the largest live specimens I've encountered were caught by a boy in a pond that drained barely 50 yards into the Atlantic across Martha's Vineyard's south beach. They were nothing special, he said, the fruit of twenty minutes' wading with a crab net and bucket in hand. Both were wider across the back than my binoculars, which measure 7 1/2 inches.

Economically important, blue crabs are marketed in two stages. The "hardshell" or "steamer" is the more common. The more expensive "softshell" is the same beast in a state of exoskeletel undress right after ecdysis. Before molting, the soon-to-be vulnerable crab hides in shallow bay waters among eelgrass. When commercial crabbers catch a "peeler" with its characteristically pliable shell, they set it aside in a floating pen until it sheds. The pens must be checked frequently because crabs in captivity cannibalize each other, though there's no evidence that this occurs in the wild. Aggressive and sly, crabs actively hunt minnows and small crustacea. Burrowing in sand or mud, they lie in wait buried up to their stalked, compound eyes which have almost a 360-degree range.

Blue crabs usually mate in fall at the time of a female's final molt. Following an active courtship dance, the male carries his chosen mate through the water, cradling her beneath him for a matter of days until she casts her shell. Warner writes:

> Protection is afforded the female by the male's urge to find good cover and, when the female's moult begins, his habit of standing guard over her by making a cage with his walking legs. He does this very patiently, since the moult may consume two or three hours. When at last the female lies exhausted and glistening in her new skin, he allows her some moments to rest and swallow the water that is necessary to fill out her weakened stomach and muscle tissues. This done, the male gently helps the female turn herself about—she may well have gotten impossibly oriented in the final throes of ecdysis—until she is on her back face-to-face beneath him. It is a most affecting scene. You cannot possibly mistake these actions for anything other than lovemaking. . . . When the female blue crab is ready, she opens her newly shaped abdomen to expose two genital pores. Into these the male inserts his pleopods or two small appendages underneath

the tip of his elongated abdominal apron. When all is in place, the female so extends her abdomen that it folds around and over the male's back, thus effectively preventing any risk of coitus interruptus. Truly, blue crabs are locked in love's embrace. They remain so, blissfully, for from five to twelve hours. Daylight or night, it makes no matter.

The female may brood two batches of eggs—2,000,000 at a crack—before her swan song. After shedding her eggs in spring, it's deep water curtains for her; she cannot molt again. Perhaps two from each batch may reach maturity after going through as many changes in metamorphic rank as a Mason. An individual that starts life measuring one one-hundredth of an inch goes through seven, sometimes eight larval stages. Each zoeal form has a functioning tail, huge eyes and varying numbers of appendages. Then comes the intermediate "megalops" stage which normally lasts less than two weeks. But if water conditions aren't right, the potential crab may remain in this premature limbo for three months before becoming a recognizable crab the size of a pinhead. By November, when it buries itself in mud for the winter, the crab will measure an inch or two. Having once molted every three to five days, it now goes for periods of more than a month. In all, a blue crab may molt more than twenty times in addition to its larval changes. Mating typically occurs at the end of an individual's second summer.

Calico Crab *(Ovalipes ocellatus)*

A close cousin of the blue crab, the "lady" or "calico" crab has a rounder body which is speckled with pink or lavender dots. A member of the same family (Portunidae) this crab is also euryhaline; it survives wide variations in water salinity. But it frequents ocean shallows more often than its relative, and consequently is found more often on the Atlantic beach.

The lady ranges as far north as the Gulf of Maine and, despite her name, is as pugnacious as the blue. This trait gets the animal into frequently fatal trouble. A Portunid would rather fight than flee under almost any circumstances. Attacked by a lobster, it will take a boxer's stance and snap back, first losing one claw to its larger antagonist, then the other, and finally its life.

Green Crab *(Carcinus maenas)*

Some individuals of the species are very well named—they're very green indeed, though others may be orange or brick red. Regardless of color, *Carcinus maenas* looks a lot like other members of the Portunid family, the blue and calico crabs, with quick claws and nimble, gracefully pointed walking legs. However it lacks the broadly flattened rear pair adapted for swimming.

Common along the littoral from New Jersey to Maine, green crabs are easily found at low tide hiding under rocks and among beds of seaweed.

Jonah Crab *(Cancer irroratus)* and Rock Crab *(C. borealis)*

Although the Cancer crabs share the northern part of the blue crab's range, they are not likely to be confused with the Portunids because of their rounder shape and more passive behavior. Caught in a trap, they won't try to bite their captor, but cower instead. In the wild, this craven manner helps the rotund animals survive, if their shells happen to be thick enough. Attacked by a lobster, a Cancer crab tucks its appendages tight beneath its body and sits things out rather than putting up its dukes and getting them bitten off one by one.

The two species, which grow to 5 or 6 inches across the carapace, differ in the sculptured edges of their shells. In the rock crab each "tooth" of the shell's edge has several tiny points and notches; its body margin looks like an irregular hacksaw blade. In the Jonah each tooth along the body edge has just one low-angled point.

Steamed *C. irroratus* are delicious—sweeter than blue crabs, though not as meaty and harder to make a meal of. The claws of large individuals are marketed. However, this is an economically insignificant species compared to its Pacific Coast kin.

Spider Crabs (Family Majidae)

Several members of this family frequent the littoral. Their common name derives from the fact that they look like long-legged spiders. Their bodies may grow as big around as tennis balls. *Libinia emarginata* has nine bumps in a row down the middle of its back. *L. dubia* has six bumps in that row. Their bodies are quite round while *Pelia mutica* and the two species of the genus *Hyas* have oval bodies. *Pelia* has a two-pronged nose, *Hyas* has a simple pointed nose.

This may be the most lethargic clan of the entire order, or so I thought before meeting Alta VanLandingham, the celebrated seashell seller of Ocracoke. Her living room is filled with huge aquaria, one of which is the domain of Lady, a spider crab she's raised from infancy. When Mrs. VanLandingham enters the room, Lady scampers delicately over rocks and mollusks to the near corner of the aquarium to greet her mistress and only her mistress, who reaches down into the water. The crab clings

1. Green crab (*Carcinus maenas*); 2. Rock crab (*Cancer irroratus*);
3. Spider crab (*Labinia emarginata*); 4. Lady or calico crab (*Ovalipes ocellatus*); and 5. Blue crab (*Callinectes sapidus*).

to the woman's fingers—hoping to be fed, no doubt—with the eagerness of a spoiled spaniel.

Spider crabs are commonly found on beaches tangled in surf rows of seaweed and lost nets. On land they seem like sluggards, but this may simply be because they're out of their element and dying for water. They recover quickly enough when put back in the wash. Caught in a dredger's net and tossed back overboard, they sink like so many stones since they lack the flattened rear swimming legs.

The spider crab uses camouflage to conceal itself on the sea bottom, whether for offensive or defensive reasons. They take bits of algae, sea lettuce or eelgrass and fasten it to the hooked hairs on the top of the carapace. The algae will grow there until the crab looks like a local rock. Of course after ecdysis they must put on new makeup.

Ghost Crab *(Ocypodea quadrata)*

Sharing the land with us, ghost crabs are among the most easily observed crustaceans. But it still takes some patient doing both because of human ways and the crab's natural caution. The dry upper portion of Atlantic beaches as far north as Delaware is this spry animal's natural habitat, but the first problem is to find a beach sufficiently natural to nurture the critter. Many resorts clean their sands with huge machines that scrape up the surface and sift out anything much larger than a matchstick. These beaches are certainly clean—to the point of sterility; a self-respecting ghost crab can't eke out a living on them. So to see *O. quadrata,* find a moderately wild beach, look for a stretch of sand marked with holes the size of a nickel or larger, then sit still and wait.

Ghost crab (*Ocypodea quadrata*) outside its burrow.

Though some generally reliable texts say ghost crabs are strictly nocturnal, I've seen these whiffets busying about beaches from Delmarva
to the bottom of the Outer Banks at every time of day. Their business
includes carrying sand out of their yard-deep burrows and finding food
both dead and alive. They eat carrion when they find it. They also hunt
beach fleas, mole crabs and almost anything else smaller than themselves. (The body of a full-grown adult may be an inch and a half wide,
but the span of their legs just about triples their apparent size.) About
the color of the sand they inhabit—whether gray, white or tan—they
have smooth squarish bodies and nimble legs that carry them sideways
at such brisk speeds that they're known as "the rabbits of the crustacea." They spend a great deal of energy keeping out of larger creatures'
way by scurrying down their burrows.

Descended from a marine ancestor, they have not become entirely
terrestrial but must return to the shallow swash several times a day to
wet their gills. Like most crustaceans, they have stalked eyes but, oddly,
not very acute vision. Dr. Austin Williams, a crab expert with the
U. S. Fish and Wildlife Service, says they cannot perceive sharp images
—only shadows and moving objects. Flipping the stalked eyes up in the
manner of spasmodic windshield wipers, they peer over sand ridges or
the rims of burrows like doughboys using periscopes to scan the enemy
trenches.

O. quadrata, which is alone in our range, represents a genus containing
a score of species worldwide. Its family also includes the fiddler crabs
found in muddy marshes and backwaters.

CRABS OTHER-THAN-TRUE

Hermit Crab (Superfamily Paguroidea)

Though the hermit crab molts, the shell you see is not its own, but
the recycled remains of a mollusk. In fact it lives in a stolen shell,
walking around the ocean floor (and often burying itself up to the eyes)
like a turtle with a short lease. The true exoskeleton (as opposed to the
borrowed shell) that the hermit crab sheds is composed of softer material than a true crab's. Only the hermit crab's head and claws are heavily
calcified—so it seeks the protection of a borrowed shell for its soft parts.
When it molts and outgrows one borrowed shell, it seeks out another
that fits. A venerable hermit crab that started out in the husk of an acorn
barnacle may live to plod around in the cast-off shell of a moon snail.

This decapod begins life as a free-swimming larva that lives on plank-ton and is barely visible to the naked eye. After several metamorphoses it takes on a curiously asymmetrical appearance. The naked adult looks something like a shrimp-sized lobster gone wrong, with unequal claws that are characteristic of each species and two well-developed pairs of walking legs. But it's rarely seen naked. When attacked in its borrowed shell (by a man or other predator), it hangs in there so tightly with its last two pairs of highly modified legs that usually it can't be removed in one piece.

Two families of hermit crabs inhabit the western Atlantic. The Di-ogenidae are found no farther north than Virginia. Four of the Paguroids may be found on the littoral while another ranges as deep as 3 miles. Some of the shallow-water species can tolerate extreme variations in salinity and may be found in marshes.

I've found hermit crabs scavenging in the dune grass on Assateague, but they do not survive out of water very long, even though they look like the air-breathing species sold in pet shops. (One thoroughly de-lightful and factually accurate child's introduction to natural science is a hermit crab's biography—*Pagoo,* by Holling Clancy Holling.)

Mole Crab *(Emerita talpoida)*

Not a true crab, the gregarious mole crab is the single local member of the family Hippidae. It burrows in shoals of thousands where waves break on sandy beaches from Cape Cod south to Hatteras and beyond. Each wave tumbles the animals and surface sand around; before the next wave breaks, the mole crabs bury themselves back into sand again up to their antennae. They use these delicate appendages to sift food particles from the backwash. As tides and storm surges come and go, this misnomer migrates up and down the summer beach, always staying in the active surf zone. In winter it evidently seeks out deeper water. Since these animals live on plankton and are themselves prey for a host of larger animals from blue crabs to bass and gulls, they are a key link in the food chain.

Mole crabs are very easy to catch on hat or hand. Absolutely harmless —they tickle your palms while burrowing in a handful of wet sand— they're good momentary pets for small children, especially squeamish tots who are normally afraid of animals. Shaped rather like moles or minute armadillos, they behave more like terrified bunnies.

The female of the species grows larger and lives longer than the male. About half an inch long, the little males cling to a husky mate during summer breeding seasons and soon die. The inch-long females often survive a second winter.

Barnacles *(Subclass Cirripedia)*

Louis Agassiz, the great nineteenth-century naturalist who urged his students to "study nature not books," described the barnacle as "a little shrimp-like animal standing on its head in a limestone house and kicking food into its mouth." That may sound absurd, but it fairly states the case. The barnacle is a catholic and successful creature that has adapted in myriad ways. Its subclass comprises 1,000 species around the world. More than a dozen are found in Atlantic coastal waters; five of these are goose barnacles, while the rest belong to two acorn-barnacle families. The latter in particular are the common animals that foul boat hulls and cover tidal rocks with thousands of individuals per square yard.

The typical barnacle eggs mature and hatch within a parent's shell before the larvae, armed with three pairs of legs, swim free. After several molts and a complete metamorphosis, the animal looks somewhat like a bivalve mollusk. In this form it settles head first on a hard surface, a ship's hull, dock piling, rock or the epidermis of anything from a whale to a horseshoe crab to another barnacle. Glands on its antennae excrete a cement which anchors the animal before it undergoes a final metamorphosis into the adult form which has neither eyes nor sensory appendages. The shell, composed of six plates to form a rough cone, was responsible for barnacles being considered mollusks for so long. It is secreted by a highly modified version of this crustacean's carapace. The adult's six pairs of legs have become "cirri" which the animal projects like feathery fans that wave rhythmically in the water to catch plankton and other minute food particles. In a falling tide, the barnacle retracts its cirri and closes the plates of its shell, sometimes with an audible click, to avoid drying out before the tide returns.

Barnacles are typically hermaphroditic. While self-fertilization can occur, the animal usually mates with a neighbor in its closely packed colony by means of a slender sperm tube that reaches into a nearby shell.

A goose barnacle looks rather like its acorn barnacle relatives atop a wormlike extension cord. The nether end attaches to some hard surface while the lightly shelled business end waves at the top of the flexible neck. Along the Atlantic beach these are most often found attached to driftwood or fishnet floats that wash in from deep water after a long time at sea. Both in ancient Greece and Britain, folk myth held that this kind of creature spontaneously spawned various geese. Hence, in parts of Catholic Europe, goose could be eaten on traditionally meatless fast days—because it was sired by an aquatic animal. Pope Innocent IV put a stop to that in medieval Europe. Religious doctrines aside, people in some parts of the world eat the larger species of barnacles.

Horseshoe Crab *(Limulus polyphemus)*

Upwards of 600 million years ago, before the Devonian age of fishes, before even the advent of sharks or insects, an ancestral arachnid inhabited the Precambrian seas. This creature produced the prolific trilobites which dominated marine life for millennia, but they became extinct along with the kindred sea scorpion which presumably used its spike tail as a weapon. In time—according to widely accepted but unproven theory—some of its descendants crept onto the land to evolve into spiders, ticks, mites and terrestrial scorpions. One group which has remained marine and essentially unchanged for some 200 million years is the horseshoe crab. Four species of this once-cosmopolitan class remain, curiously only on the western sides of the great oceans. The only individual that inhabits our waters is *Limulus polyphemus,* a crab in name only, a recognized "living fossil," and a beast that deserves far higher esteem than it usually receives along our shores.

Ponderous when it comes ashore to breed, it is agile in the water. For example, the shape of the shell apparently functions like a hydrofoil: As the animal walks against a current, water passing over its shell presses the creature down against the sand. In addition, it can swim— usually at night and upside-down at that—when the shell shape forces the water flow to keep the animal off the ocean floor. Its five pairs of walking legs and five pairs of book gills move sequentially to provide the locomotion.

However familiar it may be on a sheltered beach where you may step on one with every pace, *Limulus* looks bizarre—something like a rusty antique helmet with a plate to guard the nape of some Tartar's neck and a sharp spike hanging out aft. A two-foot-long horseshoe crab doesn't use its tail aggressively but only as a self-righting device when it's capsized—either accidentally or when the animal settles down after an inverted swim.

The location of its book gills—behind the legs—is unique. So is its eating apparatus. The mouth is located between its paired legs which are equipped with short-spined grinders. Mollusks and worms pulled from sea-bottom burrows with tweezerlike pincers are "chewed" by the animal's "shoulders" and passed into the mouth. Consequently *Limulus* can't eat while standing still. But if it lacks manners by dining on the run—or the crawl—it is a certified blueblood. Like some crustaceans and mollusks, the horseshoe crab's blood has a blue tinge due to the copper it contains instead of iron to carry oxygen. This blood is a valuable commodity for medical research since it will not support the growth of bacteria. One important commercial use of this blood is testing the purity of manufactured drugs. The animal's nervous system, which functions like our own but is much simpler, also provides food for scientific thought. In 1968 Haldan K. Hartline of Harvard won a Nobel Prize for describing how our optic nerves transmit photoelectric impulses. His investigations depended largely on horseshoe crabs as neurological guinea pigs.

The animal's four eyes are rather special, too. One pair is compound, the pair that looks like caricatured "Dragon Lady" eyes at the front corners of the shell. When *Limulus* molts, these eyes are shed with the old shell; the animal grows new compound lenses. Solar engineers recently proved that the special shape of these components—a slightly rounded cone with a blunt end—is the most efficient light-gathering form imaginable. Its second pair of eyes are the two small black dots on either side of the median line near the front edge of the shell. These are sensitive to ultraviolet light and may be the secret to the animal's navigational competence.

Living on the ocean floor and often rummaging around the surf zone like a snowplow with its front edge scraping under the surface of the sand, this whiffet can startle an unsuspecting wader by moving underfoot. But it's not known to strike anything in anger (or hunger) much

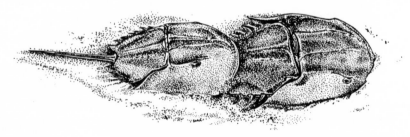

Horseshoe crabs (*Limulus polyphemus*) come ashore to mate.

larger than a marine worm. Alive, horseshoe crabs come ashore only to breed, yet their inanimate shells wash up from one end of the year to the next. Though they appear to be whole animals, these are husks not corpses, that result from molting. Unlike the crustaceans that typically crawl from a shell backwards (more or less), the horseshoe crab splits the forward edge of its outgrown shell and walks straight ahead. Then the shell often seals shut again before ending up on the beach. Find a shell that's still split and you can see the compound eyes still transparent and intact.

Horseshoe crabs start crawling ashore in early summer and a female may return ten times a season. Perhaps she's making up for lost time, having molted 16 times before reaching maturity at the age of 9. She scrapes out a depression in the sand just below the hightide line and lays 1,000 eggs at a crack with her mate in tow, literally, semi-piggyback style. He holds on to her shell so tightly that the boxing-glove-shaped claspers on his first pair of legs may leave dents in her shell. The female, which is larger than the male (and has five identical pairs of pincers), drags her mate across the nest while he deposits sperm. The next wave or tide covers it all with fresh sand. About a tenth of an inch in diameter, the round light-green eggs hatch in a matter of weeks and tailless "trilobite larvae"—so called because they resemble those extinct oddities that once ruled the Precambrian seas—crawl out and head for the water. Needless to say, not all the eggs hatch; many are eaten by birds, fishes and crabs.

Aboriginal Americans are said to have used the animals' tails (or telsons) as spearheads and to have feasted on *Limulus.* In parts of the Far East horseshoe crabs are considered a delicacy today—though one Pacific Ocean species is said to be poisonous to man. English colonists reportedly sneered at them as human food. Having considered the possibility for some time, I steamed a fresh horseshoe crab like a blue crab and sampled it as Fourth of July hors d'oeuvre. The taste resembled lobster—tainted by a rank beach at low tide.

Lobster *(Homarus americanus)*

Lobsters copulate in the "missionary" position, face to face (as near as they can manage). For the female that supine coupling, which occurs soon after her summertime molt, is the onset of an astonishingly dedicated pregnancy. She carries the live sperm for anywhere from a month to a year until underwater conditions trigger ovulation which is independent of her molt/mating calendar. She turns over on her back to stand on the tripod of claws and arched tail. The eggs emerge from small openings at the base of the second pair of walking legs and pass over the seminal receptacle between the last pair of legs which releases the stored sperm. Her swimmerettes (the pairs of small flat appendages along the tail) beat rhythmically to pass the fertilized eggs along the underside of the tail where they are secured by a sticky secretion.

Right-side-up again, she will carry the eggs for as long as another year with her tail curled beneath her to cradle and protect them as they ripen. During this period her active swimmerettes will keep them supplied with a steady stream of cleansing and oxygen-rich water. At first the eggs are black; as they mature, they become golden-brown and microscopically highlighted with the iridescent eyes of the embryos. When the eggs are fully ripe and water conditions dictate, the female walks straight into a current high on her legs while vibrating her tail and swimmerettes to shake loose larvae as they hatch. She starts this one evening at twilight, apparently to give the larvae as much protection of darkness as possible, since the clouds of young attract foraging fishes. She may have as many as 100,000 eggs, which are released in several batches every night for as long as two weeks.

As the larvae leave the eggs they float toward the surface. During their early stages of life, they are planktonic and drift at the mercy of the currents. Eaten by a variety of larger organisms, the lobster larvae themselves eat whatever they encounter, including each other. After the fourth molt, when the nascent lobsters have gained some power of locomotion, they settle toward the bottom where they will live the rest of their lives. With the fifth molt they look and act like lobsters.

The mature lobster hunts by night, haunting the bottom for mollusks, worms, crustaceans and fishes. Evidently it prefers live prey to carrion. By day the lobster seeks shelter in crannies or under rocks, wedging itself backward into an impregnable lair with its claws guarding the entrance. In water with clay bottoms, the animal will even dig burrows to hide in. When threatened in the open it may fight or retreat, its long antennae feeling the way behind it. And it can swim backward with quick spasms of its powerful tail.

Juvenile lobsters molt two or three times a year as they outgrow their shells. Curiously, a molted individual returns to its aggressive ways hours after it has cast its shell—before the new exoskeleton has hardened completely. In fact it may still be somewhat vulnerable, but its manner belies this and the bluff apparently works in the wild. Large lobsters may molt only every two or three years. They live for fifty years or more; lobsters weighing about 45 pounds have been caught and creatures estimated at 50 pounds have been sighted by divers.

The lobster mates for the first time when it is four or five years old, after the female molts. The sex of a lobster can be determined externally. The female's first pair of swimmerettes is feathery and soft; the male's is hard and grooved to carry sperm into her seminal receptacle. An active courtship dance prior to copulation may last half an hour, though the act of mating is over in a minute. Today lobsters are taken legally in large numbers before they've grown large enough to mate. Hence the breeding stock is being removed from seabed to table. Another problem that threatens their future is pollution. Minute amounts of petrochemicals in the water raise havoc with the lobster's navigating ability. (While young ones stay close inshore and don't travel far, large lobsters have been captured 100 miles away from the deep canyons where they were tagged.)

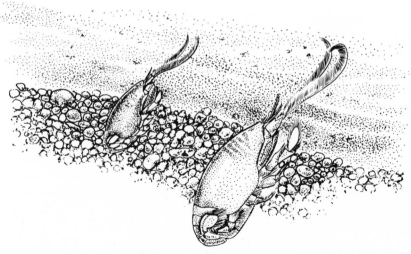

Mole crabs (*Emerita talpoida*).

Driftwords:

How Old?

The "Big Bang" kicked off the universal ball game on the order of 15 billion years B.P. (Before Present), say Nobel Prize-winning physicists Arno Penzias and Robert Wilson. According to the *Scientific American,* which keeps track of things a little closer to home, earth didn't emerge until 4.6 billion years back, and it took another billion years for the first living cells to get organized. Two billion years ago photosynthetic bacteria began pumping oxygen into the atmosphere—a landmark event. Multicellular organisms appeared a billion and a half years later, and things biological began accelerating. Vertebrates arrived 400 million years back, the first mammals half that long ago, and Neanderthal man reared his ugly head about 100,000 years B.P. So what? These staggering figures don't amount to much that's conceptually useful.

Look at it another way. Let the standard unit of time be the traditional biblical lifespan of three score years and ten. L = 70 years. That puts the publication of this book only 28 L into the C.E. (Christian Era). Today we are about 1,400 L away from Neanderthal man. This means that if all my college classmates had appeared on this earth sequentially (instead of virtually en masse), the valedictorian might have been the first man to carry a torch in prehistoric times.

The first mammals appeared 2,857,142 lifetimes ago, and the numbers become incomprehensible again. But stay with it a little longer. Earth began 64 million lifetimes ago. And if the universe began with a bang c. 15,000,000,000 B.P., that was 214,285,714 L ago—just about the number of lifetimes laid end to end as there are Americans today. The number of lifetimes necessary to reach back to the beginning of recorded history could fit on a rush-hour bus. The great whales' ancestors wriggled back into the sea about 900 human lifetimes ago and it's taken us only two to nearly render several species extinct. We did in the passenger pigeon about 1 L ago.

Look at earth's age another way, word by word. The Stradivarius of encyclopaediae, the eleventh edition of the Britannica, contains 32 volumes (including supplements) of about 1,000 pages each. It spans a shelf longer than three feet in my office. If its contents were equally apportioned to cover the history of the world, the first seven volumes would describe a lifeless planet. Leafing through it, the following not-quite-random items would appear on the following pages:

Anerobic bacteria	Volume 8,	page	638
Oxygenated atmosphere	" 19,	"	54
First mollusks	" 28,	"	834
First fishes	" 29,	"	528
Diversified jawed fishes	" 30,	"	292
First amphibians	" 30,	"	570
First reptiles	" 30,	"	917
First mammals	" 31,	"	612
First birds	" 31,	"	939
Last dinosaurs	" 32,	"	549
Neanderthal man	" 32,	"	931
Stonehenge	" 32,	"	998
Birth of Christ	" 32,	"	999
Invention of gunpowder	" 32, last page.		
Atomic Age	The letter *d* in the phrase "The End."		

Scallops flee the starfish.

Chapter Two

The Way(s) of the Mollusk

"He was a bold man that first eat an oyster," wrote Jonathan Swift. It would be a very wise man who simply sums up the beast and all its mollusk kin. Collectively, the edible oyster, reclusive octopus, chiton, tusk shell, periwinkle, et al. constitute a phylum of 100,000 living species and 20,000 known fossilized ones. Since descending from an archetypal ancestor that vanished without a trace before the Cambrian period, the mollusks have had more than 600 million years to improvise. They've used the time so well and found niches in so many habitats that few statements about them can be made categorically without adding catalogues of exceptions. Most are marine and have shells; many aren't and/or don't. They range in size from some Yucatan snails, which can line up fifty strong before making an inch-long train, to a squid that can grab morsels 48 feet away from its mouth with a tentacle.

Their behavior and characteristics are equally diverse. The chambered nautilus, a biological submarine, rises and sinks in the water by adjusting the volume of gases trapped in its shell's compartments. Scallops swim via jet propulsion and have as many as 100 eyes to scan their surroundings. Somewhat sedentary, mussels anchor themselves with bussus threads and replace these mooring lines when they break. The semitropical cone shell has a poisonous lance to stab both prey and suspected predators, including humans. A few mollusks can soar through the air, if not actually fly. Coquina clams can jump in the surf. The lavender janthina snail, which is sometimes beached along the Outer Banks, floats its eggs in a mid-ocean raft made of parentally blown bubbles. The New England neptune lays her eggs in columns as big around as herself and somewhat taller.

In sum, the mollusks are a figurative barrel of worms, monkeys, beer, laughs, nails and anything else that comes kegged. As G. Alan Solem writes in his engaging text, *The Shell Makers:* "No two malacologists agree on how many orders and suborders of bivalves should be recognized, exactly how they are related, and what should be the limits assigned to each." He recommends R. Tucker Abbott's field guide as "a best buy . . . packed with facts" yet the two authorities use different names for the chitons' class. Malacologists agree that mollusks are complex but differ on the degree of that complexity and many other matters.

A Victorian ventured the opinion that "In point of intelligence, mollusks must be relegated to a very low position. They give evidence of possessing no more than the most primary instincts, those of self-preservation and reproduction." But they must have been doing something right to have continued multiplying since a time when not much else was around but algae and each other. And how they thrive without a real brain—depending on those instincts alone—certainly denotes an astonishing kind of competence.

When told the size of the bumper grape crop in postwar Champagne, the chronically thirsty Winston Churchill said: "So much to do and so little time." Much of what's being done in malacology today relates to correcting old errors. The first was made by no less a light than Aristotle, who coined the phylum's name from the Greek word *mollis* meaning "soft." He had the sea hare in mind, not the conch which pries open its bivalve prey with its own shell. But the name stuck. (And Aristotle was no slouch. He made some observations that systematic scientists wouldn't confirm for 2,000 years.) Some confusions derive from the fact that European sophisticates began collecting shells as curiosities several centuries ago; the casual study of shells as exotic objects proceeded independently of serious biological interest in the creatures that made them. Far earlier than that—30,000 years ago—settlers in central France treasured sea shells as jewelry. Virgil, among other Romans, collected shells for diversion; a collection was found in the ruins of Pompeii.

Regardless of when folks started examining shells for whatever reasons, the objects themselves cooperated very little with the growth of either malacology (the science of mollusks) or conchology (informally the study of shells per se). "Most mollusks are very secretive creatures, often less than 1 inch in size [only one species in 20 exceeds 3 inches] and frequently nocturnal in their activity," Solem writes. "They do not bite like mosquitos, buzz like flies, or scamper through walls like mice. Rarely do mollusks call human attention to themselves."

They must have better things to do. They were here before us; the gastropods alone adapted to more habitats than mammals, the presumably "highest" of which willy-nilly alters habitats to suit himself. Some mollusks don't seem to care. In the 100 years or so since we began polluting the oceans with oil-laden ships, the common periwinkle has quietly marched all the way south from Labrador to the Chesapeake Bay. Mollusks pay less attention to us than we to them.

In the last decade, as many papers on their kind were published as had been written before 1890. There are now 100,000 tracts—though not one describing every living species, many of which haven't even been named. Alas, the more science knows, the more must be revised.

About twelve dozen mollusks are common along large portions of the beach from the Bay of Fundy to Ocracoke Inlet. Extend the range to Florida and the number doubles. Describing so many species individually would be tedious; reading about that many is worse. (There's much about the mollusks that doesn't bear repeating.) Instead, it seems more worthwhile to concentrate on frequently encountered members of various taxa whose habits are representative or interesting.

Malacologists generally agree that seven classes of mollusks exist. Two taxa comprise small, rare, deep-water groups. The remainder are the chitons (polyplacophores—though there's some disagreement on this); the snails and slugs (gastropods); tusk shells (scaphopods); clams, oysters, mussels, etc. (bivalves); and finally the squids, octopi and chambered nautilus (cephalopods). Each class is represented in our shallow coastal waters; many end up dead or dying on the beach—though many more can be seen alive along the littoral by a diligent searcher. One learned malacologist, as softspoken as might be expected of a man who's spent a career with snails, offers some valuable caveats about finding these elusive creatures: "Mollusks are very cryptic," says Joseph Rosewater at the Smithsonian. Before searching for specific animals, he calculates "where they ought to be" and when they're likely to be there. Working the rocks and tide pools mostly at night—which presents its own problems—he encounters "things you never see in daylight." Snorkeling or skindiving reveals an entirely new molluskan world.

In general, mollusks possess two zoologically unique structures: the mantle and the radula. The fleshy mantle secretes a sea snail's continually growing shell which emerges somewhat like a stream of newspaper pages off a very slow rotary press. The shell is not molted, as in the crustaceans; instead it grows as its creator grows. Pigment centers on the mantle are responsible for giving the shell color and pattern. A uniformly colored shell is the work of evenly distributed pigment cells in the secreting tissue. Some mantles have pigment cells of several colors which produce a multicolored shell. When a distinct color center remains in one place on the mantle it creates a stripe of color in the shell; when it migrates across the mantle, it makes a slanting band on the shell. If the pigment center starts and stops producing (due to changes in diet or water salinity), dots can result on the shell.

The radula is a ribbonlike tongue bearing sufficiently abrasive teeth to rasp rock or, with the help of excreted acids, to bore through the shells of the hardest molluscan prey. It goes without saying, many mollusks feed on their zoological cousins. (This is no closer to cannibalism than a man eating another mammal like a cow.) Evidently after the first mollusks began thriving on the endless supplies of vegetation and plankton they found in the primeval seas, the next mollusks learned how deliciously easy it was to live off the herbivores. That was the beginning of real diversity among the mollusks. In time the bivalves gave up their radulae as they became addicted to microscopic food strained from the primeval soup. (They gave up their heads too.) The squids modified their radulae and, in addition, developed parrotlike beaks to grasp and kill slippery prey, like fishes. But overall, every mollusk has some if not all of the following structures: a muscular foot for locomotion; a distinct head; a visceral mass containing organs; a radula; a mantle and the protective shell it makes; a mantle cavity which offers a place for excretory and reproductive organs to empty.

As to the mollusk's sex life, it is as varied as the phylum and, in human terms, bizarre. The male squid creates a dense mass of sperm within a chitinous tube. Then he plucks the tube from his body and places it within the female's mantle. Some male snails that lack a penis manufacture two types of sperm cells: the ordinary kind that inseminates and a sort of messenger variety. It piggybacks the other through the water on its conceptive errand which the absent penis would otherwise perform. Mollusks come male, female, hermaphrodite, and all of the above. The individual sexually agile oyster changes its gender— sometimes repeatedly. But enough of generalities.

THE BIVALVES

Taxonomically the bivalves are a mess. It isn't their fault; they never asked to play the game of systematics. Nor is it a matter of scientific caprice—contentiousness perhaps. The puzzle of their genealogical relationships is composed of too many pieces that *almost* fit too many ways, while fitting perfectly in no way at all that is scientifically satisfactory. Bivalves of two genera that appear closely related in terms of dental work (i.e., the interlocking teeth near the shell's "hinge") may have dissimilar organs or vice versa. Two clams may seem closely related by one anatomical or embryological criterion but only distant kin by another. The results are differences of scientific opinion which the bivalves themselves do little to resolve. (What is less communicative than a clam?) However, they are astonishingly clever about knowing their own exact kind, and the devil take the in-laws. Witness the female American oyster that spills her eggs minutes after nearby males cloud the water with sperm; any kind of oyster sperm isn't good enough, she will react only to the seed of her own species.

The confusing and maddening upshot is that three generally authoritative texts use three different taxonomic systems to describe the higher categories of bivalves. Fortunately they agree on the lower taxa and specific names, which points up the beauty, flexibility, and utility of the Linnean system. Taxonomists can wage war on one level while sharing a single arsenal on another. Fighting about principles, they use the same esoteric language—like lawyers. But as it happens, the Latinate nomenclature is almost dispensable here because many of the most conspicuous bivalve families are known by commonly accepted culinary names. So I'll use the happy expedient of kitchen argot and risk the ire of malacologists. But first some more anatomical terms.

Predictably, the garden-variety bivalve has two "valves," i.e., shells. These are hinged by an "elastic ligament" which normally holds them slightly apart. It works against one or two "adductor muscles" which close the shell from the inside. (The only part of a scallop usually eaten by Americans is the single adductor muscle, though the rest of the animal is used in European recipes. In a quahog, bits of its paired adductor muscles are what cling to the shell.) The typical bivalve has a muscular foot, an ordinary set of visceral organs, and a mantle that secretes the shell. In addition the mantle forms two siphons; one brings in water which the other expels after the gills have removed its dissolved oxygen and microscopic food particles. Since a bivalve strains its food from the water, it has no need for a radula, which it lacks along with a head.

Consider the oyster in some detail, one of the more familiar, best studied and familiar bivalves. Fifteen years ago—a lifetime in terms of some scientific knowledge—Fish and Wildlife Service biologist Paul S. Galtsoff wrote *The American Oyster*. Weighing in at 480 pages, this tome is the unabridged *Oxford English Dictionary* so far as oysters are concerned; an apotheosis of detail that's not likely to be surpassed despite its sometimes turgid prose. It covers everything from the structure of gill cilia (which are "indistinguishable from that of the cilia of vertebrates, protozoa, or the tails of spermatozoa") to characteristics of a good oyster habitat. Galtsoff writes:

> In several respects the anatomy of the oyster is simpler than that of other bivalves. . . . Only the posterior adductor muscle is present and there are no specialized organs of sight, although the animal is sensitive to changes of illumination. On the other hand, the edge of the mantle is fringed with highly sensitive tentacles abundantly supplied with nerves leading to the ganglia. As in other bivalves, the nervous system is not centralized . . . a condition which undoubtedly results in a high degree of coordination among the various parts of the organism. In addition to performing their principal functions, several organs of the oyster also participate in other activities. The gills, for instance, are not only the organ for respiration but collect and sort food as well. The mantle is used extensively in control of the flow of water through the body; the coordinated action of the adductor muscle, gills and gonad is necessary for the effective discharge of eggs by the female oyster. In other animals such functions are performed by special organs, but in the evolution of the oysters the high degree of coordination developed among different parts of the body eliminates the special structures, and new and complex functions are successfully performed by synchronizing the work of the existing parts.

Yet there remains great variety in oysters. The family Ostreidae now contains more than a dozen living genera. The genus *Ostrea*—the name translates into "oyster"—once comprised all edible species that were considered dues-paying members of the group. Then some important anatomical and reproductive differences raised their metaphoric heads. The genus *Crassostrea* ("thick oyster") was hypothesized in 1897 and validated in the International Commision on Zoological Nomenclature's own sweet time fifty-eight years later. Why? For one thing, members of the genus *Ostrea* are typically hermaphrodites: Each individual functions simultaneously as both male and female. *Crassostrea* are normally male or female—given the proviso that an individual changes back and forth.

Several species are found along the Atlantic coast. But who's kidding whom? The one that most people care about is *Crassostrea virginica,* the Eastern or American oyster that ranges from Canada to the Gulf of Mexico. Epicures may call their favorites "Chincoteagues" or "Blue Points" but these names only indicate the place where they were harvested. Most oysters eaten in America are *C. virginica.* It is a very fine species and one worthy of Galtsoff's considerable attention.

To begin with, this oyster's sex life involves a degree of togetherness

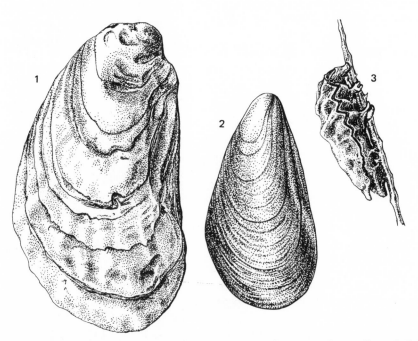

1. American oyster (*Crassostrea virginica*); 2. Blue mussel (*Mytilus edulis*); and 3. Coon or leafy oyster (*Ostrea frons*).

that borders on mass hysteria. An oyster bed is a den of simultaneous iniquity, and for good reason. Lacking external equipment, the males (pro tem) release abundant sperm into the water when they sense the presence of other sperm. When one male ejaculates—normally in response to a rise in water temperature—every male in chemosensory reach follows suit within seconds. Minutes later the females get into the act by releasing enormous batches of eggs. The best Galtsoff could do was estimate in his laboratory that one five-inch female laid 114.8 million eggs without exhausting her supply. While she might produce ova in such quantities two or three times during a six-week summer breeding season, biostatisticians suggest that only a dozen eggs in a batch reach maturity. The rest fail to find a suitable place to spend their adulthood, succumb to various infections, becoming food for other marine animals or simply fall by the aquatic wayside.

One practical reason for the massively simultaneous mating activity by both genders is that the females, however prolific, never developed much of a muzzle velocity. The eggs they exude (with little, coordinated spasm of muscle and shell) don't travel far. Since these eggs sink only inches away from their spawning dam, their best chance for a vital future depends on being released when the surrounding water is saturated with sperm so that catch-as-catch-can fertilization occurs before they touch bottom.

If all oyster eggs were fertilized and survived to breed, according to one theoretical estimate, we'd be buried in a pile of living oysters eight times as large as earth itself within four oyster generations. George L. Clark, solon of the Woods Hole Oceanographic Institution, once wrote "The prodigious fertility of nature is a measure of the destructive action that is received from the environment." But that "destructive action" keeps the environment's other inhabitants alive. A simple rule of thumb holds that the greater the number of potential young a species naturally produces, the more "destructive" is its particular habitat and the more unsure the future of any one ovum. The corollary: Animals with the riskiest reproductive methods spend the greatest effort on them.

So let it be with the oyster, whose largest internal organ at maturity is the versatile gonad. Furthermore, the sexual health of a local oyster population is a fair indicator of environmental purity. Galtsoff writes: "Oysters living in waters highly polluted by various trade wastes have, as a rule, poorly developed gonads." This is ecologically bad business, of course, and something close to culinary catastrophe as well; an oyster with enlarged sex organs is a fat, delicious one.

The reasons oysters change their sex remain unclear. Suffice it that "the sexes are . . . unstable and once a year a certain percentage of oysters change their sex. . . . This change takes place after spawning during the indifferent phase of gonad development." Indifferent indeed. "Spawning may last from a few minutes to nearly one hour, depending on the amount of mature eggs in the ovary. . . . The spawning reaction is always followed by a refractory period of two to several days during which the female is not responsive to stimulation." In other words, after parturition she retires and frequently gives up on maternity by becoming male for the following season.

After fertilization the oyster egg—like all mollusks—develops into a trochophore larva. This stage may last no more than 24 hours. The next stage, or veliger, is an increasingly complex organism that develops eyespots, a protective shell and a velum (hence its name). The velum is composed of two semicircular folds with large cilia along their edges. It enables the organism to swim freely, yet the structure is also retractile and after the shell develops can be quickly withdrawn inside.

When the oyster veliger's foot develops, it possesses a byssus gland, like the organ that mussels use to spin the replaceable mooring threads that anchor them to rocks. As the future oyster grows heavier it sinks, and with its developing foot begins to crawl over hard surfaces until it finds a suitable spot to settle down for life—typically on another oyster shell.

The foot extends beyond the edge of the shell and the animal reclines on its left side (usually), becoming permanently attached in minutes with a cement secreted by the byssus gland. Then the veliger, which measures about one one-hundredth of an inch, hastily changes into a minute oyster. Within a few days it reorganizes its permanent organs. The ones not needed for a sedentary life disintegrate or are absorbed: the eyespots, byssus gland, foot, and velum. The minute animal, called a spat, fundamentally has nothing left to do but grow and multiply. In fact, the animal becomes anatomically and neurologically simpler. Galtsoff explains:

> The high degree of specialization of larval organs may be regarded as an adaptive organization of a free-swimming organism to its environment. . . . The pelagic larva of a bivalve has a double task: to distribute the species and grow into an adult. . . . When the larva attaches to the substrate, the velum and the foot are no longer needed.

I find it intriguing to think how differently adult humans might behave if we could shuck more of the traits required and acquired in infancy. (Unleavened Freudian theory suggests that we pack every one of them throughout life.) If an oyster didn't give up the velum of its youth, it could never settle down to the immobile but otherwise constructive business of being an adult oyster. It can't move or relocate; the only thing it can change thereafter is its gender.

Crassostrea virginica contorts the shape of its rough, usually oblong shell to grow as best it can in the crowded space of a natural oyster bed. The off-center scar of its adductor muscle and the edge of its shell lining are tinged with purple. In the wild, its varied shape can lead to misidentification; growing in a spacious bed, the individuals may be rather thin-shelled and almost circular. The tidiest shapes are found among oysters raised in controlled conditions. At the University of Delaware experimenters predict that "domesticated" oysters can be raised to market size in nine months instead of the three years they need in the wild. Predictably the secret is an artificial habitat with lots of food, no predators and ideal water. A dean of the College of Marine Studies there reports that mariculture can do for oysters and clams in the near future what agriculture did for grain crops at the dawn of recorded history. "We are just now crossing the frontier from hunting and collecting marine species for man's use to properly managing and husbanding them."

Ostrea equestris, called the horse or crested oyster, lives in saltier water than the American oyster. Found from Virginia to Texas, it is a smaller animal than its more famous kin and has a pale muscle scar at the center of its nearly round shell. The coon or leafy oyster *(O. frons),* which is favored by raccoons, ranges south from the Outer Banks.

Pursuing the other bivalves by culinary category, the clams constitute the informal group of the next greatest importance. The name *Mercenaria mercenaria,* chosen for the northern quahog by Linnaeus, comes from the Indians' use of its shell to make wampum beads which were used like money after European traders arrived. Those made from the white portions of the shell were small change compared with those made from the small purple parts near the adductor muscle attachments. *M. mercenaria,* which ranges along the entire East Coast, is more oval than round and grows 4 inches in length. Outside of scientific circles, it's called littleneck clam, cherrystone, round clam or quahog.

The larger southern quahog *(Mercenaria campechiensis)* grows up to 6 inches, lacks the interior purple stains and has more definite concentric growth ridges on the outside of the shell. At extreme low tides I've

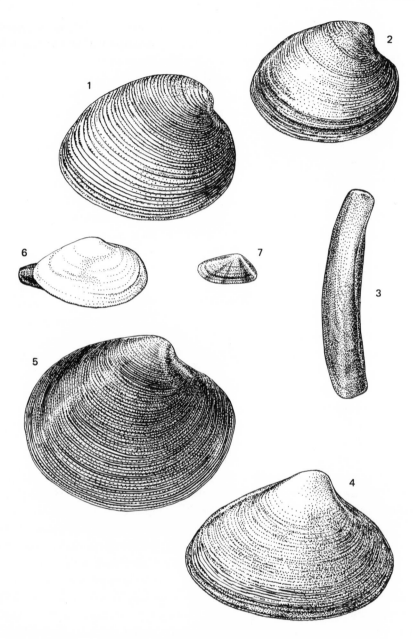

1. Southern quahog (*Mercenaria campechiensis*); 2. Northern quahog (*M. mercenaria*); 3. Razor clam (*Ensis directus*); 4. Surf clam (*Spisula solidissima*); 5. Ocean quahog (*Artica icelandica*); 6. Softshell clam (*Mya arenaria*); and 7. Coquina clam (*Donax variabilis* or *fosser*).

found these sitting on sandbars near the mouth of Chesapeake Bay, high and dry until the tide returns. One explanation is that a spring tide falls so fast that the surface sands dry out before the clam can dig itself in. While it is then somewhat vulnerable to mammal or bird predators, the stoutness of an adult's shell offers real protection from almost anything short of a clam knife. One zoologist says it represents "the highest type of shell development among the bivalves." It is exceptionally hard and strong without being ponderously heavy and it contains ample space inside.

The quahogs belong to the Venus family (Veneridae). Several other clams have clans of their own. The Atlantic surf clam *(Spisula solidissima)* is a larger, shallower, more triangular clam dredged from the continental shelf at depths as low as 100 feet. Its thinner shell is fairly smooth despite the growth rings and cream-colored or brown depending on the color of the sea bottom where it lives. Before this animal is considered edible it must be cleaned of its very sandy viscera: a process that involves separating muscles from internal organs. The flesh is then chopped or shredded to find its way into millions of trademarked clam rolls.

Clams of the family Solenidae are the slender bivalves that many epicures believe to be the tastiest. The largest member of the family is the Atlantic jackknife clam *(Ensis directus)* which grows 6 inches in length. Quick and delicious, it is hard to capture since it burrows straight down with surprising speed. (When digging these be careful how you grab them because their shells seem as sharp as the name implies.) Its shell is covered with a thin dark brown layer, the periostracum. For inexplicable reasons, the jackknife clam looks like a horn-colored antique straight razor. The razor clams are shorter animals closer in size and shape to pocketknives.

Softshell clams *(Mya arenaria)* often surface under various aliases such as steamer (which might also be a crab), littleneck (which might be *Mercenaria*) or, unmistakably, pissclam. This precise if vulgar designation derives from the animal's habit of betraying its presence in a mud flat at low tide by shooting a stream of water into the air as it digs itself deeper in the face of danger. When walking a New England shoal, look ten yards or so ahead for these telltale fountains which come from a sheathed siphon, the animal's uppermost extremity. The thin, fragile shell is white inside and pale or stained outside (sometimes nearly black) depending on the local bottom.

A Massachusetts Shellfish Officer on the town dock in Duxbury

offered some behavioral insights about various clams one quiet day
apropos of the temporary closing of local shellfish beds. A moratorium
had been declared, not because of pollution but to give *Mya arenaria* time
to repopulate. The clam flats had been raked nearly clean and Maine
clams were brought in. But they didn't cotton to Massachusetts waters
and died. Hence the decision was made to simply let the decimated
population reproduce in peace since there was no hope that new stock
would spontaneously migrate in from nearby waters. *Mya* doesn't migrate worth a damn, the clam cop said. Once a pissclam larva settles, it
hardly moves—except up and down a little. Quahogs, on the other
hand, move about a fair amount, while the razor clams are veritable
gypsies. Not long ago they were numerous in a certain mud flat in
Duxbury harbor, said the officer, and "almost overnight spread along a
beach two to three miles away."

Donax clams inhabit the surf zone along open beaches, migrating up
and down the wet sand to stay in the highest reach of spent waves. Tiny
and rather triangular, they come in a rainbow of colors that seems to
grow brighter and fade as multitudes dig themselves in and out of the
sand as the waves come and go. Found south of Virginia, the Florida
coquina *(Donax variabilis)* grows to almost an inch or more in length.
Donax fossor, which ranges from Virginia to New York, is half that size
and not quite as colorful. "Some species jump out of the sand as soon
as they feel the acoustic shock of a breaking wave," according to Abbott, who notes that 1,500 of the tiny creatures may be found on a
square foot of beach. The *American Museum of Natural History Guide to Shells*
reports some experts believe *D. fossor* is just *D. variabilis* stunted by a
poorer environment. "However, this point has not finally been settled;
it has met with vigorous opposition by some malacologists."

Scallops are the least sedentary of the bivalves. The first time I saw
them in the wild, while snorkeling in a brackish Chappaquiddick Island
bay, I was mesmerized by their antics. Equipped with bright iridescent
eyes around the edge of the mantle just inside the shell, they bounce
about in the water like silent castanets clapping their valves. Though
their jerking jumps seem random, they can control direction by changing the shape of the mantle within the shell and forming distinct directional nozzles. A water jet fired straight from the front of the shell forces
the animal backward; two jets pointing obliquely aft from either side
of the hinge propels the animal forward. It can also turn acrobatically
in the water and swim upward from a standing start. When a starfish,
one of the scallop's natural enemies, comes near, the would-be prey gets

agitated and actively tries to escape. Left to their own devices, scallops
sit on the bottom, dining on a puree of microorganisms at their leisure
and peering all around like tourists.

The scallops I first saw were Atlantic bay scallops, *(Argopecten* or
Aequipecten irradians), which with its subspecies, *concentricus,* ranges along
the coast as far south as Florida. They grow to 3 inches and have
many-ribbed shells with undulating edges. The smooth-shelled Atlantic deep-sea scallop *(Placopecten magellanicus)* grows as large as 8 inches and
ranges in deep water from Labrador to the Outer Banks.

The mussels, another family of edible bivalves, are notable for their
anchors. While a juvenile oyster's byssus gland atrophies after its ce-
menting work is done, the mussel's gland remains active throughout
life. It secretes threads which the foot secures to rocks or pilings like a
boat's mooring lines. Set in divergent directions, these threads anchor
the animal in any current as the bivalve twists to present its narrowest
edge against the current. If the threads break in a storm sea the mussel

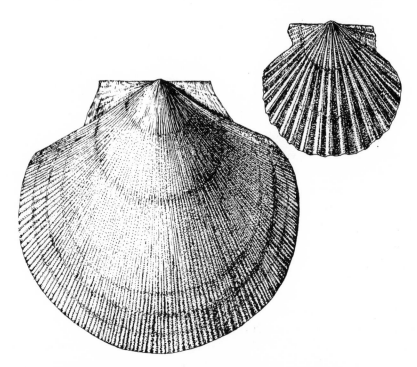

(LEFT) Atlantic sea scallop (*Placopecten megellanicus*).
(RIGHT) Atlantic bay scallop (*Argopecten irradians*).

secretes more to replace them. Cast completely adrift, it can find another place to anchor itself and spin a complete new set of byssal threads.

The common blue mussel *(Mytilus edulis)* ranges in coastal waters from the Arctic to South Carolina. Its shiny exterior, marked by oval growth lines, is a deep blue-black. Individuals may live seven years and grow to three inches in height. The females can lay 12 million eggs a season and 6,000 bushels of adults may grow in an acre of healthy bay, which hints at the enormous amount of microscopic nutrients found in sea water. The ribbed mussel *(Modiolus* or *Guekensia demissa)* frequents brackish water, sometimes in salt marsh mud flats, and has radiating ribs on its exterior.

Jingle shells are a family of common bivalves with a hole near the apex of the lower shell. The byssus extends through this hole to attach the animal to a rock or to another shell. The heaviest concentrations of the Atlantic jingle *(Anomia simplex)* are found in beach houses where people string them together through the byssal holes and hang them up as wind chimes. They tend towards translucent pastel colors, though some shiny black dead shells wash ashore.

THE CHITONS

Most scientists agree that chitons are among the most primitive mollusks still around. Built low to the rocks they are oval-to-oblong and rather flat—like a coolie's hat—with a foot that occupies most of the underside. Uniquely, a chiton's shell is composed of eight overlapping plates. These valves, running in a row down the back, are held in place by the surrounding muscular girdle, the margin of the mantle. The mouth is in front and the anus aft (which isn't always the case among mollusks). Gills run along the chiton's underside, between the girdle and the foot. The animal can lift any part of the girdle to admit oxygen- and food-bearing water. Some species have microscopic eyes and scattered tactile organs in the plates of their shells. These animals must be seen alive or not at all since an individual disintegrates and the valves scatter soon after death.

Three fastidious species inhabit along rocky sections of the Atlantic coast. The mottled red chiton *(Tonicella marmorea)*, which roams as far south as Massachusetts, has a smooth girdle and sharply arched valves. The northern red chiton *(Ischnochiton ruber)*, which ranges south to Connecticut, has wrinkled valves and a girdle that looks granular. Both are about an inch long. The common eastern chiton, little more than half the size of its cousins, is found in protected places between Florida and Massachusetts. Also known as the gray or hairy chiton, *Chaetopleura apiculata* has some hairs on its narrow girdle.

SEA SNAILS & COMPANY

By one count, the phylum's largest and most varied class contains 3,000 fresh water species, 24,000 terrestrial types and 40,000 marine inhabitants. The gastropods include unshelled slugs, shelled snails, everything that looks remotely like them and some things that don't. Their distinguishing characteristic is that when a shell exists the gastropod has only one; it is a univalve. The limy shell is made of calcium carbonate removed from the blood by the process of osmosis and concentrated. Glands in the mantle then excrete this material in layers of crystals. As a gastropod grows, the mantle continues to excrete material and the shell grows apace, unrolling and spiraling larger to accommodate its occupant/creator.

Over the course of evolutionary time gastropods experienced "torsion" so that their gills, waste vents and sexual outlets moved toward the head. In addition the typical shell was skewed to one side; instead of becoming a regular jellyroll affair, it twisted as it grew, like a magazine rolled up on a bit of a bias. The little end of the growing, rolling shell, where the whorls are smallest (since the animal was youngest when it made them), was typically on the right side. The obvious

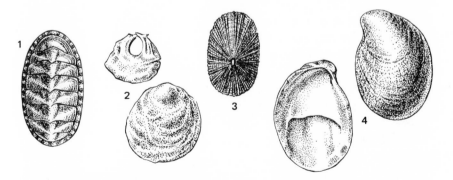

1. Northern red chiton (*Ischochiton ruber*); 2. Jingle shell (*Anomia simplex*); 3. Keyhole limpet (*Diodora cayenensis*); and 4. Common Atlantic slipper (*Crepidula fornicata*).

imbalance this caused would naturally tend to twist the shell to the right. Whatever the sequential reasons—and theories differ—these changes had very practical results: The vertical height of a whole animal was minimized without loss of shell capacity or body size. Room appeared in the front of the shell for the head to hide in when danger threatened. The gills on the right side typically atrophied or changed while gills on the left side grew larger to shoulder the whole respiratory burden. Then, a single stream of water could enter the shell from the front left, areate the gills, make one easy hairpin turn past the anus and sexual vents, then exit from the front right side of the shell. In addition, most species developed a horny operculum, the trapdoor that seals the shell's aperture after the head and foot retreat inside to safety.

Some of these changes found in the higher gastropods are absent in the lower families. Primitive Pacific Ocean abalones have an arc of holes near the edge of the shell through which water and wastes pass. On our coast the adult keyhole limpets each have a single hole near the middle of the shell. It too is an exit hole for water. This aperture is all that remains of an anal slit that is still found among some gastropods that are more symmetrical, hence considered more primitive.

The keyhole limpets are vegetarians that scrape algae from tide-zone rocks and in the process erode the rocks themselves with their rasping radulae. Two rather flat, oval species are reported along Atlantic beaches. Linne's puncturella *(Puncturella noachina)*, a half-inch-long gray-brown shell, ranges from the Arctic as far south as Massachusetts. The Cayenne keyhole limpet *(Diodora cayenensis)*, which lives from New Jersey to Brazil, is dark gray and has bumpy ridges radiating from the apex of its shell.

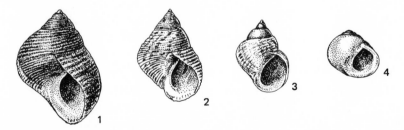

1. Common European periwinkle (*Littorina littorea*); 2. Marsh periwinkle (*L. irrorata*); 3. Northern rough periwinkle (*L. saxatilis*); and 4. Northern yellow periwinkle (*L. obtusata*).

The true limpets represent a certain amount of biological advancement and morphological backsliding. One Atlantic limpet, showing its relative sophistication, has a single set of gills. But, its shell, shaped much like a coolie's hat, represents a case of secondary evolution: The animal's ancestors first developed a coiled shell which then evolved into its flatter, simpler shape as the limpet found its niche along exposed rocky shores. In that turbulent environment a coiled shell could be a fatal impediment; the new shape that evolved uses wave action to the creature's advantage. Waves breaking on it simply press the limpet closer to the rock on which it feeds; its external shape disperses their force.

Limpets rummage around feeding on algae at night, then typically return to the same spot on the rock by day. The sexes are separate and these animals mate from April to September, laying tiny mucus-protected eggs on the rocks. By October the young attain one-third of their growth. An inch long at maturity, they'll mate the next spring.

The Atlantic plate limpet or tortoise-shell *(Acmaea testudinalis)*, long considered the only one found in cold waters as far south as New York, is tan streaked with brown. Found on open coasts, its shape is clearly oval. Those more squarish forms found living among eelgrass were long considered individuals of the same species whose environment caused a modified shape. But it now seems possible that they are a distinct species, *A. alveus.*

Between the old and new gastropods (Archaeogastropoda v. Neogastropoda) lies the order Mesogastropoda. The periwinkle is easily the most familiar member of the middle group. Four closely related species are common along the Atlantic coast. The family Littorinidae, named from the same Latin word that gave us "littoral," is versatile, prolific and collectively insatiable. A square mile of shoreline may have as many as 860 million periwinkles busily moving about by working one side of the foot forward and then the other. Together they'll all eat 57 tons of vegetation while scraping up another 2,100 tons of rock and debris.

The periwinkle's well-developed head has two tentacles, an eye at the base of each and a stout proboscis between them. The male boasts a prominent penis jutting from the body behind the right tentacle. Needless to say, copulation occurs and fertilization is internal in the female who releases egg capsules less than a quarter-inch in size. Some species' eggs are free-floating; others are laid among the algae on which the winkles feed. Another species, the Northern rough periwinkle, gives birth to fully formed young which develop in a special uteruslike portion of the mantle.

The radula, which coils up like a watch spring, is well developed. In one warm-water species with a 3/4-inch shell, it unrolls to a length of more than 6 inches. Depending on species, the periwinkle's tongue may have as many as 300 rows of teeth that wear out at the rate of five or six rows a day. If they were not replaced, the animal would soon starve; instead the radula grows continually from its base to replace the business end.

The common European periwinkle *(Littorina littorea)*, found as far south as Maryland, is grayish brown to black with many fine spiral bands. It browses in the lower half of the tide zone. The marsh periwinkle *(L. irrorata)*, as its common name suggests, lives in tidal marshes from New Jersey to the Gulf of Mexico. Its shell is a creamy gray with brownish streaks on the spiral bands. Both of these animals are about an inch long. The northern yellow or round periwinkle *(L. obtusata)*, ranging from Labrador to New Jersey, is only a third of an inch in size. Smooth and often uniformly colored—an orange or brownish yellow—it sometimes has bands. It inhabits the lower tidal zone and feeds on algae that are rarely exposed by low tides. The northern rough periwinkle *(L. saxatilis)* shares the same geographical range but stays above midtide, often browsing above the high-water mark. A similarly small creature, its shell may be gray, brown, or almost black with spiral ridges.

The slipper shells are hermaphrodites of the protandric variety. This is to say that male and female equipment operate in a single individual at different times of life, which effectively prohibits self-fertilization. Younger slippers are functionally male and more active than their larger sedentary sisters (?) which have anchored themselves to other mollusks (especially other slippers) and arthropods. Frequently these gastropods pile up in small towers of several individuals, ergo with females on the bottom and males on top until they grow large enough to change. Rather than rummage about for food, they trap microscopic particles from the water in their mantles, much as the bivalves do. The arched oval shells are notable for the interior shelf that supports the viscera.

Three species commonly occur from New England to Texas. The eastern white slipper *(Crepidula plana)*, often found within dead moonsnail shells, is white inside and out. The inside of the common Atlantic slipper *(C. fornicata)* is darker and spotted, though the shelf appears very white in contrast. The reddish-brown convex slipper *(C. convexa)* has a hooked apex or tip that may look in profile like an elf's cap.

Moon snails, from the inch-long common baby's ear *(Sinum perspec-tivum)* to the 4-inch common northern moon snail *(Lunatia* or *Polinices heros)* and 3-inch Atlantic moon snail *(Polinices duplicatus)*, are common inhabitants of shallow coastal waters, where they are uncommonly voracious. Eight species wash up along the eastern seaboard north of Hatteras. These carnivores burrow in sand, hunting bivalves—notably clams. They grasp their prey with the foot and bore a tidy hole in its shell with the radula, softening it with an acidic excretion. Some may eat four clams a day. In turn the moon snails are eaten by a variety of bottom-feeding fish, by oyster drills and starfish. Touch a live starfish arm to a moon snail's shell and the mollusk will spread its foot almost entirely over its round shell. Evidently this leaves the predator without enough hard surface to grasp with its suction-cup feet.

Between meals, moon snails fossick about on the surface of the sand, leaving meandering furrows. Since the foot spreads out when extended, these tracks are half again as wide as the shell which is generally quite smooth and almost semispherical. The fragile "sand collar" often found on tidal beaches contains moon snail eggs. (For those who never saw a Victorian gentleman's detachable collar, this is a thin round structure that looks somewhat like a gasket from an odd engine.)

The Neogastropods, or members of the latest snail order, include two carnivorous groups of particular importance and perplexing interest respectively. These are the oyster drills and dogwinkles, which are sometimes included in a single family—sometimes separated into two.

As their name implies, the oyster drills demonstrate a dietary dedica-tion that oystermen and gourmets abhor. Boring through the shells of large bivalves with their acid-lubricated radulae, they specialize in eat-ing oysters in the whole shell, as it were. The most common is the Atlantic oyster drill *(Urosalpinx cinera)*, a snail that grows to one inch in height and boasts a moderately sculptured shell with as many as twelve axial ribs running between the whorls. Found from Nova Scotia to Florida, they may be gray, white, brown or orange.

The dogwinkles are sometimes hard to identify. According to the American Museum of Natural History's encyclopedic paperback in the northern or Atlantic dogwinkle *(Nucella lapillus)* "variations in color, shape and surface sculpture are bewildering." Exploring a low-tide shore of Mount Desert Island, Maine, I once found large numbers of snails up to 1 1/2 inches that defied identification at first. Some looked like periwinkles with low, indistinct spires, others had sharper whorls —but they all appeared to be of the same ilk. Gathering some diverse specimens, I noticed that most of the individuals feeding on barnacle beds were white dogwinkles. The bright orange ones had probably been living on mussels, whose pigmented meat was responsible for the distinct shell color.

THE WHELKS

Two families of whelks also belong to the order of Neogastropods. They are notably carnivorous, eating both live prey and carrion. True whelks of the family Buccinidae number some 2,000 species worldwide. The family name comes from the Latin word for trumpet, possibly because these shells make distinguished signal horns like the true conchs of tropical waters. A Nantucket man who keeps a few daysailers for charter got tired of not being able to keep store-bought horns aboard. He substituted large snail shells, the spires of which he cut off neatly with a hacksaw to expose the internal cavity. Blow into this with pursed lips and it makes a marvelous sound.

The 3-inch common northern or waved whelk *(Buccinum undatum)* is a drab inhabitant of offshore waters from the Arctic to New Jersey. It has between 9 and 18 ribs per whorl and a dull white to brown surface. Its egg masses are clumps of tough little sacks containing embryonic shells. Often washed ashore, these were traditionally called "sailors' wash-balls" because coastal folks used them instead of soap.

The genus *Busycon* belongs to a family that includes the Florida crown conch of southern waters. From Florida to New Jersey the clan is represented by the lightning whelk *(Busycon contrarium)* which, as its specific name implies, is perverse. Put another way, it is left-handed or sinistral; its shell spirals the "wrong" way. To tell the difference, hold any large shell with its aperture toward you and its spire on top. Put it on like a mitten (after checking for occupants). If the left hand fits, it's sinistral; if the right hand fits, it's dextral. If you get bitten, there's a hermit crab inside. Most shells of all kinds are dextral, but mirror images may appear. Some experts classify these as separate species; others say a mutation is involved, perhaps caused by a typographical error in the DNA.

The 8-inch long dextral knobbed whelk *(B. carica)* found from Cape Cod to Georgia commonly has a distinctly orange aperture lining and knobs along the shoulder of the spiral. The slightly smaller channeled whelk *(B. canaliculatum)* has a rounder aperture and a distinct channel or groove running along the spiral between the whorls.

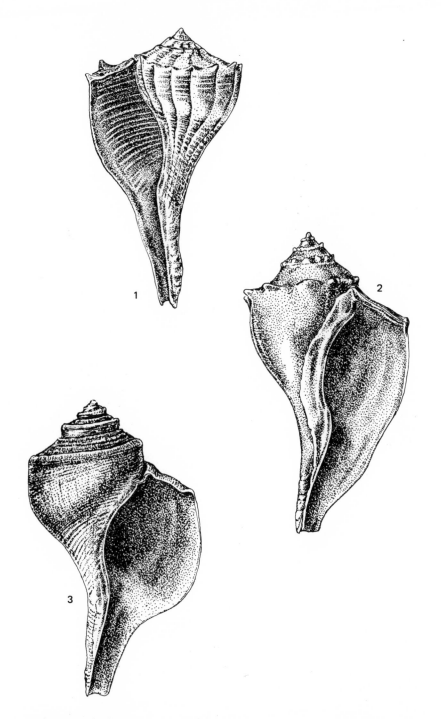

1. Lightning whelk (*Busycon contrarium*); 2. Knobbed whelk (*B. carica*); and 3. Channeled whelk (*B. canaliculatum*).

Whelks (which are considered delicacies by many coastal peoples) feast on clams themselves, although not by drilling through the meal's shell. Instead *Busycon* forces open a bivalve's shell using the lip of its own shell as a wedge. Then it pokes its proboscis inside and eats with the radula.

Whelk egg cases are found on the beach as often as the mollusks themselves. These are the spiraling chains of leathery hollow discs that hang from a tough strand like a necklace. Each capsule, about the size of a nickel but with edges that differ from species to species, contains as many as 100 eggs. Not all of them hatch; many so-called "nursery" eggs are eaten by their hardier embryonic siblings. This is their only food.

Driftwords:

Bang

In the beginning—long before the first mollusk appeared—was the Logos (the word/deed/act), was the "big bang," was the Creation. Take your pick; you name it. Something happened and nothing's been the same since. The Bible allows, too vaguely for us moderns, that "God created the heaven and the earth." The scientific consensus holds that a massive explosion occurred on the order of 15 billion years ago, a burst that is still rending the universe apart. (Science doesn't explain what exploded or how the raw material got there in the first place, wherever "there" was.) Recent calculations suggest that the rate of universal expansion is slowing down; that in time it will stop growing and its component parts must pull together again; that the universe's matter will coalesce into a another single mass which will become so dense and hot as it compresses into itself that it must expand again through another enormous explosion in the unspeakably distant future. To accept these things, add equal parts of poetic insight and scientific intuition to the conceptual pot.

W. B. Yeats: "Things fall apart; the center cannot hold; mere anarchy is loosed upon the world."

Einstein: "The most beautiful thing we can experience is the mysterious. It is the source of all true art and science."

Render unto science what science can justly claim; namely some detailed descriptions of finite things, some hard-won theories about other things and some massive shrugs of shoulders. Whether or not the "big bang" that created our universe was the first or the nth, accept that it happened in the instant which we might as well call the initial one. After the explosion and the first dispersal through space, huge aggregations of matter were mutually attracted to one another by gravity, proximity and happenstance. These pieces eventually formed discrete bodies which fell into dynamic equilibrium as solar systems, galaxies and the bestiaries of our constellations. The sphere that became earth —whatever its origin—found its place in a localized scheme of things orbiting around a rather ordinary star. Molten and spinning through space, it must have been like a drop of mercury on a table or an orb of undulating water before an astronaut's face, like a blob of the stuff one sees in photographs of blast furnace crucibles pouring out their liquid load. As it circled (or ellipsed) the sun, it all responded to physical forces as the oceans respond today, its surface rising and falling hundreds of feet in molten tides.

In time things began to stabilize. Cooling slightly and slowly, the earth began solidifying. In the process volatile gases were released to initiate an atmosphere containing water. Ultraviolet light broke down the water, releasing earth's first free oxygen which, in a cascade of chemical reactions, created more water. Rachel Carson writes:

"The gradually cooling earth was enveloped in heavy layers of cloud, which contained much of the water of the new planet. For a long time its surface was so hot that no moisture could fall without immediately being reconverted to steam. . . . As soon as the earth's crust cooled enough, the rains began to fall. Never have there been such rains since that time. They fell continuously, day and night, days passing into months, into years, into centuries. They poured into the waiting ocean basins, or, falling upon the continental masses, drained away to become sea. That primeval ocean, growing in bulk as the rains slowly filled its basins, must have been only faintly salt. But the falling rains were the symbol of [and the tool for] the dissolution of the continents. From the moment the rains began to fall, the lands began to be worn away and carried to the sea. It is an endless, inexorable process that has never stopped—the dissolving of the rocks, the leaching out of their contained minerals, the carrying of the rock fragments and dissolved minerals to the oceans. And over the eons of time, the sea has grown ever more bitter with the salt of the continents."

This is about where the Book of Genesis picks up the natural history. In the comfortable words of the King James Version, "The Spirit of God moved upon the face of the waters." A more exact translation of early scripture evokes "a mighty wind that swept over the face of the waters." Why quarrel with either? The most fertile germ of truth might lie in the synthesis of the two images. Render unto mystery what is mysterious. Since these are matters whose real beginnings elude scientific description, accept them as manifestations of the inexplicable, or manifestations of "God using that name to comprehend all the great and inexplicable things and the redemptive or destructive powers that lie outside human command and understanding," as Robertson Davies has said. So be it.

As for the prehistoric scribe who wrote Genesis, though he muddled the sequence of subsequent events, he certainly was inspired—whether divinely or intuitively doesn't much matter. For though he couldn't have been there to see it, science confirms there must have been oceans and wind early on. Earth as we know it couldn't have become what it is without them.

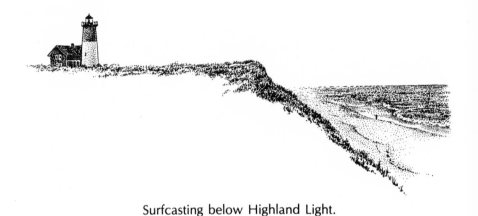

Surfcasting below Highland Light.

Chapter Three

Fishes of the Beach

The title only looks like an oxymoron; it describes this chapter's scope. The sea is full of fish and the beach itself obviously empty of them, except in various states of morbidity. While thousands of species depend on beach-protected marshes for their nurseries, few fishes have any connection with the shore per se; when a connection occurs, it most often involves a monofilament line with hook attached. Nonetheless, beach people with or without tackle encounter a wide variety of these marine vertebrates: the schooling vegetarians that come ashore to escape predators; the strong swimmers like striped bass that can be seen braving the translucent crests of breakers as they feed; the notorious stingray which slashes many an unsuspecting wader's leg with its spined tail; carnivorous species commonly caught by even casual fishermen.

The finned swimmers are fascinating in their biological success, their habits and their diversity. They are also inscrutable in many respects and outrageously complex—compoundly contradictory to the point of chaos. Blame it on the state of the sciences in general and on our limited understanding of evolution in particular.

In ichthyology, as elsewhere, taxonomists are playing catch-up ball. Successive generations of investigators explained things as best they could on the basis of available knowledge, only to have their heirs tear up established theses with new tools, theories or discoveries. While new species are described with some frequency, the worst confusions involve the higher taxa as younger taxonomists explain anew how various genera, families, orders, classes, and even phyla are related.

Consider, for example, the on-again-off-again taxonomic relationships of the striped bass and white perch which have moved in and out of kinship like the offspring of Hollywood celebrities. The striper was christened *Roccus lineatus;* then it appeared that another fish already had that name and the striper's was changed to *Roccus saxatilis;* now it's *Morone saxatilis.* Meanwhile the white perch, formerly *Roccus americanus,* became *Morone americanus.* Charles L. Wheeler, chief of the National Marine Fisheries Service's intriguing aquarium at Woods Hole, observes: "They used to be the same genus. Then someone tore the whole thing apart and switched them out. Now they're in the same genus again. But it's a new one."

In simplest terms, a fundamental goal of systematics is to decide which primitive chicken came before which egg in the primordial slime. It is a matter of considerable frustration that there will probably always be more questions than answers because no solid evidence exists; the early vertebrates were sired by cartilaginous animals, biological softies who left few fossil records.

Nonetheless, some fairly certain notions have been surmised pro tem. The first vertebrate was a marine creature whose descendants became the earliest known fishes. They, in turn, also sired swimmers that used their fins to grope with and crawled out of the sea to become amphibians, whence came reptiles, birds and mammals like us. As one refreshingly plain-speaking fishman at the Virginia Institute of Marine Science tells his students: "You're just Sarcopterygiians"—i.e., collateral descendants of a creature whose other offspring spawned the famous coelacanths, among other things. (Through a forgotten ancestor, even Darwin himself had a distant cousin in the Dover sole.) To put it more elegantly, the Encyclopedia Britannica states: "In a sense land vertebrates are simply highly modified fishes, for when fishes colonized the land they became tetrapod (four-legged) land vertebrates."

That colonization occurred on the order of 350 million years ago, give or take. While it was in progress and terrestrial life-forms began diversifying to occupy niches in the new environment, marine forms also evolved. But specialization occurred at varying rates on land and in the sea. Taxonomists didn't appear until long after the bony fishes had swum into every aquatic habitat and many of the pioneer species had disappeared. Working with newly uncovered shards of the shattered fossil record, with the old clues of anatomical and embryonic similarities and with increasingly sophisticated tissue analysis (including comparisons of DNA), the scientists are trying to put the puzzle together.

To start making some sense of it, take it on faith that sharks and rays (Elasmobranchs in the class Chondrichthyes) evolved from one early ancestor. Many sharks are relatively modern and certainly successful; some of the 200 species bear living young, which is the height of reproductive sophistication. Yet as a group they remain "primitive" in some important respects. Their skeletons are made of cartilage, not bone, and they lack air bladders, organs of interest in the bony fishes. Somewhat later, in evolutionary terms, another primitive ancestor sired another group of marine swimmers. The class Osteichthyes comprises all the bony fishes, including separate groups of fleshy-finned fishes, ray-finned fishes (e.g. sturgeons and bowfins) and teleosts, today's dominant group.

A large plurality of all modern vertebrates are fishes; their species may even outnumber all the living birds, mammals, reptiles and modern amphibians combined. Figures are relatively stable for birds (8,600 species) and mammals (4,500), but as a Canadian zoologist warns: "Amphibians and reptiles may increase significantly (perhaps at a slow rate because herpetologists are far fewer than other vertebrate systematists)." (The remark tells more about scientists than species.) Throwing quantitative caution to the wind, this expert states there are 18,818 living species of fish; another hazards the guess of some 40,000. A few years ago the Senior Principal Science Officer of the British Museum suggested with comfortable, even lyrical poise that "fishes are almost ubiquitous and virtually numberless. In the ocean they live at all levels from boisterous well-lit intertidal regions down to the cold, sunless waters that flow over the sediments of the abyssal plains." Another expert, not wishing to grind anything from axes to hatchetfish, suggests 20,000 as a reasonable round figure for bony fishes ranging in size from the Philippine goby that measures 2/5 of an inch overall to the 60-foot whale shark.

Life began in the sea, but ocean water is not the perfect environment for complex organisms. Witness the salinity problem. The salinity of a fish's body fluids is midway between the salt levels of fresh water and seawater. Hence fluid moves in or out by osmosis, the phenomenon that tends to equalize the salt content of two liquids separated by a permeable membrane. The animal's epidermis surrounding the scales provides mucus which serves as a kind of waterproofing as well as a lubricant to reduce external friction and a protective barrier against microorganisms. But osmosis persists between the fish's body fluid and the external medium. A marine fish loses internal water to the sea this way; it makes up for the loss by drinking as much as 40 percent of its body weight a day. Since the beverage is salty, its salt content must be separated from the pure fluid; excess salt is excreted through the gills and intestine while fresh water osmoses out through the skin. Freshwater fishes, on the other hand, absorb water by osmosis from their surroundings and eliminate it through their kidneys. Some species must do both at various times in their lives. These are the andromous and catadromous species (from the Greek for up- or down-wandering). Herring and bass, which swim up inland streams from the sea to spawn, simply switch water-budget mechanisms, as do the catadromous eels which mature in fresh water before traveling to the mid-Atlantic Sargasso Sea, where they mate.

Sharks and rays solve the problem differently. They recycle a metabolic waste product to their advantage. While most vertebrates expel urea, these retain it in the bloodstream. This keeps the internal salt content about as high as the surrounding seawater—osmosic pressure doesn't distinguish between salts. Hence a shark's body fluids don't seek to dilute the sea water outside the shark's skin. The high urea content is the reason that shark for the table must be well bled soon after capture; otherwise it is unpalatable.

Gills are structures of wonderful design that enable their possessors to extract ample amounts of free oxygen from water. (Fish don't breathe any oxygen that is bound up in H_2O, but only the O_2 that's dissolved in the fluid at a maximum level of about 10 parts per million.) Gills work better than our lungs; fishes typically use 80 percent of the oxygen available to them while people do well to absorb 25 percent of the vital gas in the air we breathe. Two elements are responsible for the gill's efficiency: its surface design and the arrangement of its hematological plumbing. Water entering the fish's open mouth flows over the gills and exits beneath the gill covers. The gill membranes are so intricately folded that a high-metabolism fish like a herring or mackerel may have 70 square inches of oxygen-absorbing gill surface for each pound of body weight. Next, a "countercurrent" arrangement of blood vessels assures the most complete absorption of vital gas. Water and blood flow in opposite directions across and through the gills respectively. Oxygen-poor blood first reaches the rear gill parts across which water with the least oxygen passes. Partly-oxygenated blood flows through parts of the gills exposed to water increasingly rich in oxygen. Blood about to leave the gills passes through parts receiving water with the most oxygen at the front. This arrangement minimizes the difference in oxygen content between the blood in every gill part and the water flowing across that part. The greater the difference in oxygen content, the higher the diffusion pressure; thus the total absorption of oxygen is enhanced. Were the plumbing arranged the other way around, the gill would work less effectively since diffusion pressure would be lower. If blood with the least oxygen were exposed to the most-oxygen-rich water, and blood with the most oxygen exposed to the poorest water, the total transfer of oxygen would be less. By the same token, the actual arrangement allows the most efficient removal of carbon dioxide from blood in the gills.

If fish breathe the same gas that we do, the question arises: Why doesn't a fish out of water take its oxygen from the air? The answer is that many can and do. The walking catfish of the southern United States migrate across land from pond to pond. Primitive African lungfish, the coelacanth's closest living relatives, estivate (i.e., hibernate in warm weather) during years-long droughts, breathing air in a state that nearly resembles suspended animation. Other fishes are "obligate air breathers." The bowfins, for example, must reach the surface and gulp air from time to time.

But these exceptions beg the question. Most fishes die out of water though they are surrounded by abundant quantities of the same vital gas they cunningly extract in meager amounts from water. The reason is simple: desiccation. Their gills dry out on land. Those fishes that survive significant periods out of water have mechanisms for keeping their gills moist. One miracle of unrecorded history is that both animals and plants found ways to survive out of water in the first place, since every living cell requires a moist or wet micro-environment. The statement is not as outlandish as it seems. The bark of a living tree is composed of dead cells; so is human skin. Thick or thin, these dead protective layers blanket wet environments where tissues live. Every land animal spends a great deal of physiological effort keeping its lung linings wet since these living cells must encounter quantities of air to absorb oxygen for the rest of the organism. The ghost crab left the sea to live in the dry sand, but it must return regularly to the water and wet its gills. Most fishes never dealt with this problem; since the medium they breathe is wet, they gave little adaptive energy to the matter of preventing gill dryness. But beached by a wave or landed by a fishing line, they face a condition imposed by the alien environment. Their gills dry out and cease to function.

Like its breathing apparatus, a fish's eye differs from a mammal's. In man's eye the shape of the lens changes to alter the focal length. The fish's lens is of a constant shape and curvature; muscles move the whole lens back and forth (like a telescope) to focus on distant or near objects. Sight is an important sense for both predator and prey species living in oceanic shallows. Because the eyes are at the side of the head—and the lenses usually protrude—most fishes can see aft along the length of the body while they also have a region of binocular vision in front.

Since visibility is limited in even the clearest seas, fishes depend on highly developed senses of hearing, scent and touch as well. A number of icthyological families make audible sounds, evidently to communicate with others of their kind, at spawning time in particular. All fishes sense water movement through a biologically unique organ, the lateral line. Characteristic in each species, it runs generally straight from the tail, then distinctly curves along the body on each side of the fish. Composed of individual sensory hairs set in flexible swivel joints, the lateral line monitors minute changes in water pressure. Toss a pebble into a pond of minnows or snap your fingers underwater when snorkeling among schooling fish and each individual will turn away from the disturbance almost simultaneously. The minute shock wave reaches each fish's side almost at the same time. The lateral line is constantly useful; at night it warns a swimming fish of unseen objects since the water near a rock or another fish responds differently than unobstructed water.

So much for generalities. Consider in turn some of the fishes encountered by people along the beach.

CRAB-EATING SHARKS

Although three sharks commonly appear on the beach, none is a candidate for movie stardom. (And the less said the better about voracious child-, woman- and maneaters, at least along the coast from Maine to the Carolinas. *Jaws* is fiction.)

The smooth dogfish *(Mustelus canis)*, which often takes a hook to most fishermen's disgust, occasionally grows to 5 feet in length though two-footers are much more common. "One of the most common sharks in the United States," according to A. J. McLane's nicely illustrated and straightforward *Field Guide to Salt Water Fishes of North America*, "this species is well known to anglers who catch large numbers during the summer months."

Gray or brown to blend with local bottoms, the smooth dog has long pectoral fins and two large dorsals of about equal size. Armed with keen eyes and low flat grinding teeth set in abutting rows like cobblestones, "it is perhaps the most relentless enemy of the lobster," write Henry B. Bigelow and William C. Schroeder in the definitive *Fishes of the Gulf of Maine*. It eats large crabs and small fish as well. But curiously, according to that Interior Department publication, this shark doesn't attack healthy menhaden in aquaria—only sickly ones.

Like all sharks, the dogfish lacks gill covers. Instead it has gill slits rather like straightened chevrons on a policeman's collar. The shape and number are characteristic for each species. Its skin is rough due to pointed triangular scales that look like microscopic teeth and are composed of similar material. As in the other cartilaginous fishes, fertilization is internal. Male sharks use grooved "claspers"—i.e., modified ventral fins—to inseminate the females. The smooth dog is truly viviparous. Gestation takes ten months; 10 to 20 young are nourished through a placental connection with the mother until they're born live and immediately start fending for themselves.

Despite its common name, the spiny dogfish belongs to a separate family from the smooth dogfish's. *Squalus acanthias* has no anal fin but both its dorsals bear sharp spines in front. The animal uses these defensively. Curling its body when captured, it snaps back and forth to do what damage it can with the spines. And the damage can be considerable, especially when the shark is grasped by an unwary human's hand.

Aristotle was the first to describe the live birth of this fish whose 18- to 22-month gestation is the longest among cartilaginous fishes. As long

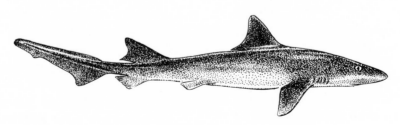

Smooth dogfish (*Mustelus canis*).

as 13 inches at birth, it normally grows to only 3 feet though some may reach 4 feet.

Bigelow and Schroeder note: "Much has been written about the habits of the spiny dogfish, but nothing to recommend it from the standpoint either of the fishermen or its fellow creatures in the sea." Cruising in schools, they prey on everything: worms, crabs, mackerel, cod, haddock. Spiny dogs attack rapaciously, wasting much of their kill, and

> have not been of sufficient value . . . to compensate for a hundredth part of the damage they do. . . . so erratic are their appearances and disappearances that when one has had good fishing today he may catch only dogfish tomorrow and nothing at all the day after, the better fish having fled these sea wolves and the latter departing as a result.

Gray- or brown-skinned, spiny dogfish have small flat teeth with sharp corners that form an almost continuous cutting edge the width of their mouths.

The sand tiger *(Odontaspis taurus)*, formerly known as the sand shark, cruises the length of the Atlantic coast but is most often met between Delaware Bay and Cape Cod. It grows up to 10 feet, though the vast majority are under 6 feet. Its first dorsal fin and anal fin are about the same size; its second dorsal fin is larger. The teeth are slender, pointed and sharp. Despite is formidable appearance, this is a rather sluggish, largely nocturnal shark that eats small fishes, squid and a few crustaceans. Despite its size it has rarely been known to attack man.

The sand tiger's reproductive pattern represents a compromise between more common forms. Normally two fertilized eggs hatch within the mother and, since there is no placenta, the embryonic sharks survive gestation by eating unfertilized eggs.

FLAP-WINGED FISH

Bizarre-looking flat fish belonging to the same class as sharks, the skates are harmless to man despite their appearance and associations. Under water they flap their odd winglike pectoral fins to swim gracefully like circular or diamond-shaped birds.

These are the animals responsible for the black leathery (or brittle) purselike egg cases that litter many beaches. Their four long curly corners suggest something diabolical, but in fact the long pair of "horns" extracts food and oxygen from the water while the short pair expels wastes. Called devil's pocketbooks or sailor's purses ("because they always come ashore empty"), these egg cases are laid with a sticky substance that attaches them to submarine plants. Presumably the glue loses its strength after the young hatch out as miniature adults ready to fend for themselves. Typically they eat crustacea, mollusks and small fishes. In Europe skates are eaten themselves by gourmets. There is little acknowledged market for them in this country although skate meat, punched out with round cookie cutters, often masquerades as scallops in many restaurants.

The little skate *(Raja erinacea),* the most common along the East Coast, rarely grows longer than 18 inches. It is gray, tan or pinkish above, with a thorny body, and white below. (The female has a "thorny" body while the male has thorns only along the fins and tail.) The largest in Atlantic coastal waters is the barndoor skate *(R. laevis)* which occasionally grows to 5 feet in length. It is brown or reddish brown with irregular blotches on top. The smaller winter skate *(R. ocellata)* prefers cold water. It is light brown with round dark spots and grows to about 3 feet.

Among the order Rajiformes, the stingrays of the family Dasyatidae deservedly have the worst reputation. They've been hurting people since colonial times at least; Captain John Smith was stung by one when he explored Chesapeake Bay.

From the human viewpoint the rough-tailed stingray is a very unpleasant fish; even obscene in the sense that it has no apparent redeeming social value—not even as a palatable foodstuff. Big and ugly, it has the sullen mentality of a street thug who jumps unsuspecting passersby on their way home from the movies. It is armed and venomous. *Dasyatis*

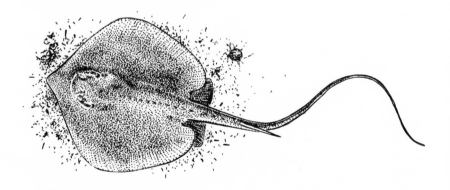

Atlantic stingray (*Dasyatis sabina*).

centroura grows to dimensions of 12 by 7 feet. Like all its family, notably the 10-square foot Atlantic stingray *(D. sabina)* and the smaller smooth butterfly ray *(Gymnura micrura),* its tail bears a sharp spine or two. When bothered or stepped on, it lashes out with the tail, lacerating the wader's leg and often leaving the spine behind. Glands surrounding the base of the spine excrete their contents along its sides. The substance is toxic but sometimes doesn't reach the wound. Some of the estimated 750 to 1,500 annual victims in American waters suffer no toxic side effects— only excruciating pain from the spine which has reverse barbs that make it difficult to remove.

These animals, which prefer warm water but range as far north as Cape Cod, eat mollusks and crustaceans. Consequently they are bottom feeders and frequent shallow waters where they're encountered. A writer who was stung by one suggests scuffling along when wading rather than lifting one's feet since a ray that is nudged will move away without a fuss. A ray that's stepped on fights back. Sometimes hooked by fishermen, they remain dangerous when landed.

An enormous member of a close family is the giant devil ray or manta *(Manta birostris).* The female shelters eggs that hatch internally before birth occurs. These creatures, bearing earlike flaps in front of the lateral eyes, are known to grow to a 22-foot wingspan. Offshore they occasionally leap from the water and soar like giant bats. But they are so docile that scuba divers sometimes hitch rides on their backs. They subsist on small organisms like small shrimps and plankton.

MENHADEN

The first time I visited the Outer Banks something seemed wrong: The high-tide line was not marked with seaweed but with silvery fish for a mile in either direction. They hadn't succumbed to chemical pollution or an oil spill; this fish kill had natural causes. Some of the corpses were whole, others were in parts, while the majority were just missing a clean-cut chunk of flesh from the back or throat. They were menhaden, driven ashore the day before by voracious blues.

The menhaden has more aliases than the polygamous skipper of a coastal tramp steamer: pogy, mossbunker, hardhead, yellowtail shad, greentail, fatback, chebug, whitefish, silversider, pilcher and bug head (for the little parasitic crabs often found in its mouth). One of the true herrings (family Clupeidae), *Brevoortia tyrannus* has silvery or brassy sides fading to dark blue or brown above and no visible lateral line. The head is about half as long as the body from the spot behind the gill cover to the base of the deeply forked tail.

Theoretically edible, but rarely eaten by any person who could find another fish, the menhaden is the unwitting mainstay of the largest commercial fishery on the East Coast. It is unpalatable due to its high oil content, the same characteristic that makes it so valuable a fish. Selling at dockside for $50 million in a recent year, this industrial raw material is processed into fertilizer, fish meal, pet food, soaps, lubricants, leather conditioners, paints and other products. Single offshore catches of a million fish have been recorded in the past, and the annual take sometimes numbers a billion fish. But annual harvests vary widely due to dramatic population fluctuations. In 1890 some 90 million pounds were taken and four new processing plants opened in New England; a year later the catch was down by half.

Like its kin the Atlantic herring *(Clupea harengus)*, round herring *(Etrumeus teres)*, hickory shad *(alosa mediocris)*, true alewife *(alosa pseudoharengus)* and others, menhaden travel in enormous dense schools. Unlike some of the others, it spawns at sea, the specific time of summer probably depending on water temperature. About 3 inches long by the first winter, a menhaden doubles its length in the next year and may grow to 15 inches. Some live nine or ten years, a fact proven by microscopic examination of their scales. (Every fish has a set number of scales. The arrangement is fixed in each species and as an individual grows from fingerling to trophy size all its scales grow apace. Because feeding conditions vary with the seasons of the year, fishes grow at irregular rates.

Menhaden (*Brevoortia tyrannus*).

The scales, which must grow sporadically too, become marked with visible rings which, like a tree's, can be read to interpret age.)

Uniquely toothless, this member of the clan understandably eats nothing but plankton. Swimming close to the ocean surface (sometimes leaping out), it sieves microscopic organisms with highly specialized gillrakers. These internal structures simply protect the gills of some fish; in the menhaden as in some bivalves the gills are food collectors as well as respiratory organs. A single manhaden can filter 6 or 7 gallons of seawater a minute and extract a pint of food an hour.

The reasons for abrupt changes in population are unclear. A scarcity of plankton one year may mean fewer menhaden the next or, overkill by man or other predator may be the cause. An important link in the food chain from plankton to some sea birds and every larger fish in the Atlantic, the menhaden is preyed upon by whales, porpoises, sharks, cods, swordfish, tunas, bass, squid—nearly everything but its own toothless kind. As one sport-fishing expert has written; "In the wilderness, death is a way of life."

BLUEFISH

The bluefish "is perhaps the most ferocious and bloodthirsty fish in the sea"—sharks included—according to one authority. Traveling in schools of like-sized fish (because they cannibalize smaller members of their own race) they often kill far more than they eat and decimate huge schools of prey species. A bluefish will gorge itself until it regurgitates, then immediately feed again. Looking down from a Nags Head fishing pier, the spectacle of these ravenous killers darting irregularly through the water—running amok—is extraordinary. When "the blues are running" they strike anything that looks like a smaller fish including almost every artificial lure dropped in the water. The other spectacle to witness

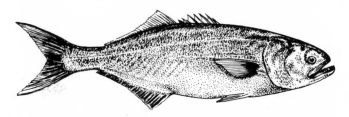

Bluefish (*Pomatomus saltatrix*).

is the fishermen running amok. They'll pack a pier until their lines tangle but continue fishing until the school is visibly gone and the bloody catch lies like split logs around a chopping block.

The solitary member of its family, *Pomatomus saltatrix* has few common names beside "blue," though young specimens are called snappers. The generic name means "operculum cutting"—possibly because this fish will go for its victim's throat in the vicinity of the gill cover (or operculum). It will go for the hands of captors too and frequently bites a fisherman's finger to the bone if he tries to dislodge a hook before dispatching the fish with a "pacifier" or "priest"—i.e., club. Avidly sought for both sport and food, this fish must be handled carefully.

The bluefish is rather marine blue-green in color above, fading to white below. Very simply designed, it has neither fancy pigmentation nor extraneous external structures. Its forehead slopes in a regular curve down to its slightly undershot jaw. Along the East Coast it grows to 3 1/2 feet; off Africa a 45-pound specimen was reportedly caught from a destroyer's fantail during World War II. Its spawning and migration habits are barely understood.

Five-inch snappers appear off New England in August, presumably the year's juveniles. The following year these individuals measure 12 to 15 inches, then start growing at even faster rates. They may eat twice their weight a day, gorging on menhaden, mullet and marine worms, whenever the latter leave their seabottom tubes to propagate.

PUFFER

The northern puffer might not be identified by a weekend angler if it ever kept its cool. But disturbed, threatened or hooked, it inflates itself with air or water like a balloon. The smaller individuals distend their bodies so much that the small fins disappear. This defensive creature, also called swellfish, blowfish, globefish, bellowsfish, is hyperbolically named *Sphoeroides maculatus* in Latin: spotted spheroid.

Regularly found from Florida to Cape Cod, the puffer has the habit of disappearing irregularly from a habitat where it was recently plentiful. At ease it's a reasonably slender specimen, normally less than 10 inches long, with a small mouth and "buck teeth" that aren't teeth at all but modified bones divided by a suture. A bottom feeder, it uses them to assault mollusks and crustacea, crabs in particular which it tries to disable by first biting their well-protected nerve centers. Its scaleless skin is sandpapery due to short, stiff prickles.

Spawning occurs in late spring or early summer when a female lays more than 175,000 eggs. As in many fish, the male is typically smaller than its mate.

The northern puffer belongs to the family Tetraodontidae which includes about 60 species worldwide including *Tetraodon hispidus,* said to be the planet's most poisonous fish. People who eat it may die within five hours from a toxin that has no known antidote. In the past this South Pacific oddity provided islanders with arrow and spear poisons. Other members of the family may be poisonous in one area but deliciously harmless in another—perhaps due to different diet. Nonetheless, lethal poisonings are still common in Japan, where puffer is a very expensive winter delicacy.

Once considered a trash fish in America, *Sphoeroides maculatus* is now marketed to epicures under the toney name sea squab. The flesh along the back is said to be boneless and tasty but the viscera can be extremely toxic. The liver, gonads and roe are especially dangerous. *Bon appétit.*

PISCATORIAL PANCAKES

The order Pleuronectiformes comprises fishes of great economic and culinary importance: flounder, halibut, plaice, sole and turbot. By many other names these bottom dwellers lie as flat on the ocean floor as a crepe in a pan of flaming brandy. While a skate lies just as low on its belly, flatfish lie on their sides—right or left as a matter of each species' preference.

In the process of finding their place in the sedimentary scheme of

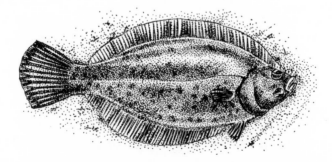

Winter flounder (*Pseudopleuronectes americanus*).

things they didn't give up using the eye on the side they habitually lie. Emerging from an egg two weeks after spawning, an eighth-inch-long flounder swims like any other fish at first: dorsal fin up, ventral down, and an eye on each side of its head. Soon the juvenile begins to list to one side as it swims. The eye peering toward the bottom migrates around or through the head to join its partner on the side that will be uppermost throughout later life. The jaw, however, remains oriented through the face, giving the flatfish a rather sinister sneer as it goes its predatory way. The general appearance, in no way helped by the asymmetrical eyes, is of a two-bit prizefighter who lost a quick decision to a Mack truck. These are not sedentary fishes. While they spend a good deal of time literally lying in wait with only their eyes exposed above a thin blanket of sand, they actively pursue any likely prey that passes overhead or within darting reach of the bottom. The different species have various food preferences, collectively they eat all manner of finfish, crabs, lobsters, mollusks and even sand dollars.

These fish can be described as "right-handed" or dextral if their eyes appear on the right side of the head (and they then lie on the left side of the body). "Left-handed" or sinistral flatfish have the eyes on the left side and lie on their right. They range in size from the delectable hogchoker or American sole *(Trinectes maculatus)*, which rarely grows longer than 8 inches, to the Atlantic halibut which has been known to exceed 700 pounds.

In brief, the more common East Coast right-handed flatfish are the Greenland halibut or turbot *(Reinhardtius hippoglossoides)*; Atlantic halibut *(Hippoglossus hippoglossus)*; American plaice or sand dab *(Hippoglossoides platessoides)*; yellowtail *(Limanda ferruginea)*; winter flounder, black-back or lemon sole *(Pseudopleuronectes americanus)*, and hogchoker.

The common East Coast left-handers include the summer flounder or fluke *(Paralichthys dentatus)*; fourspot flounder *(P. oblongus)* and windowpane or brill *(Lophopsetta maculata)*.

NOISEMAKERS

Cynoscion regalis' generic name comes from the Greek word for dog. In spawning season the male vibrates its air bladder to make a sound like barking. The female, which has a thinner abdominal muscle, is silent. In English this cosmopolitan species is most often called weakfish. That name, perhaps coined by Dutch colonists in their language, persisted because the weakfish's mouth parts are so fragile that hooks often tear out of them. It's also called sea trout or squeteague after an Indian word. Under any moniker *C. regalis* is a slender, bright-looking fish that swims in schools along the coast and into brackish water. In addition to a diet of crustacea and mollusks, it competes with the bluefish for scaled food.

The weakfish is slender and handsome, lightly mottled almost like a Seurat sunrise highlighted with yellow pectoral fins. Usually under 2 feet long, it may weigh about 4 pounds, though a 30-pounder is on record. They spawn near shore from May to September; after 40 hours the eggs produce larvae less than .07-inches long.

Other members of the family Sciaenidae include the banded croaker *(Larimus fasciatus)*, the Atlantic croaker *(Micropogon undulatus)*, the various other sea trouts *(Cynoscion* sp.) and the red drum or channel bass *(Sciaenops ocellata)*, a most reputable game fish.

While some fishermen claim they can smell quarry through the surf, many authorities agree this family's drumming noises can be clearly heard from shore. The fishes must have a better purpose than announcing their presence to human and marine predators, but full explanations have yet to be made.

CANDIDATE FOR EXTINCTION

The striped bass or rockfish *(Morone saxatilis* pro tem) is coastal and andromous; it seeks fresh water to spawn. Traveling deep into Chesapeake Bay's marshy tributaries and as far as 160 miles up the Hudson River, a large female may produce 10 million eggs to be fertilized by a score of small males. (However, she doesn't produce every year.) The young stay in fresh or sheltered brackish water until their second year when they join schools—historically enormous congregations—that migrate up and down the East Coast.

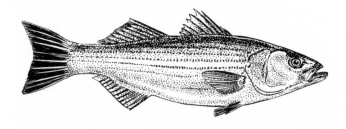

Striped bass (*Morone saxatilis*).

The early colonists valued this fish which appeared in such numbers that John Smith saw shoaling schools "as will load a ship of 100 tonnes." In 1634 a New England apologist wrote of the "basse. . . . It is a fine fat fast fish having a bone in his head which contains a saucerful of marrow sweet and good, pleasant to the pallat and wholesome to the stomach." Before that decade was out, the Massachusetts Bay Colony banned the use of both this noble fish and the adulated cod for fertilizer. It was too good for such a base purpose, which alewives served well enough.

The striper is olive gray above with silvery sides marked by seven or eight horizontal stripes that fade with age. The largest of these perchlike fishes, which are the females and misnamed "bulls," once ran well over 100 pounds. Now a 35-pounder is considered big. Very strong swimmers, though not notoriously fast, they can sometimes be seen feeding in the translucent crests of breaking waves. They feed voraciously on smaller fish and a variety of mollusks and crustacea, notably lobsters. Bigelow and Schroeder note that these fish will gorge on one kind of food, then pause to digest, then gorge again in apparent unison. They are most active from sunset to dawn but also feed by day.

Like many species, stripers' numbers fluctuate greatly. In the past they regularly declined for five years running, then in a single frenzied year rebounded nearly to their former numbers. But in *Striper, a Story of Fish and Man,* Maine journalist and former Long Island hand-seiner John N. Cole warns that the cycle may have been broken. The likely reasons: a combination of freshwater pollution of spawning grounds, offshore dumping of sewage and the saltwater sport fishing craze, now a $3 billion a year industry. His data are alarming. From North Carolina to Maine, catches are dwindling. Numbers of fry in Chesapeake Bay, "the nursery which incubates 90 percent of the East Coast's stripers," were the lowest on record in 1977—and the predicted bumper crop of 1976 has not materialized yet. An annual fishing tournament in Rhode Island used to land thousands of pounds of striped bass; in 1977 not a single striper was caught.

Cole's conclusion:

> We can not utilize the waters of the northeast as chemical sewers without destroying the integrity of those waters. That we have done, and, in the process, we have destroyed that particular and graceful swimmer of the surf, the striped bass. . . . Ten years from now, at its current rate of decline, the striped bass will no longer roam the inshore waters of the Atlantic from

Cape Charles to the St. John. The northeastern migratory striped bass, that creature with its genesis in the great glaciers, will have vanished. . . .

We may just take some bitter satisfaction that this fish was introduced into Pacific waters around San Francisco Bay, where it survives.

RESOURCEFUL OR PERVERSE?

New England fishermen used to predict easterly storms when the goosefish appeared—she's hard to miss when she shows up. This is one of the continental shelf's more grotesque creatures according to human aesthetics. Perhaps as large as 50 pounds, most of that is head, and most of the head is a mouth that gapes to an 8- by-9-inch maw bordered by a jaw fringed with flaps of flesh that look like tatters. The tapering and camouflaged body is rather squashed in appearance, built low to the ocean floor. Goosefish are so ugly that even their mothers don't love them; they often eat their own.

Lophius americanus belongs to the well-named angler fishes, a breed that fishes for its food. The first dorsal spine is adapted for use as a lure. This slender appendage bears a flap of skin at its tip like a little flag—or more like a carrot on a stick. The goosefish or angler attracts its prey by waving the flag and drawing it down in front of its cavernous mouth. When a smaller fish follows the lure, the angler gulps it down. Some authorities say it bites; others say it simply inhales by opening its gills which are behind its paddlelike ventral fins and the prey washes in with the current.

Anglers have been landed under odd circumstances. A Rhode Island fishermen hauling cod felt the line get suddenly heavier and found the cod on his hook had been swallowed by a goosefish en route to the surface. Small goosefish with several fishes in their mouths have been found swallowed by their own larger kin. A Frenchman of the Renaissance reported finding one on the shore holding a fox by the leg—not a Mexican standoff, a littoral showdown. The popular name for this resourceful fish derives from stories of its having swallowed geese. Whether or not that occurs, it is reliably reported to have been found with sea ducks in its stomach. It also eats gulls, diving birds like cormorants, skates and stingrays. Its own flesh is said to boneless and delicious.

L. americanus lays her eggs in veils of mucus a foot or two wide and 10 yards long that may contain as many as 1.25 million ova in a single layer. The sexual habits of the goosefish's deep-sea relatives are unusual to the point of perversity—though biology makes no value judgments. Bernard Ludwig Gordon describes it in *The Secret Lives of Fishes.* In the abyssal darkness

> where courtship could easily prove futile, once the male finds his mate, he attaches himself to her, never to let go. The site of the attachment appears to be a random choice—sometimes on the abdomen, the sides, the head, or even the gill cover. The male grips the female with his strong teeth, and his lips and tongue grow into her skin. His mouth, jaws, teeth, fins, and gills degenerate. Only his reproductive system remains independently active. The two blood systems become fused, and the male is nourished by her blood, literally becoming part of her, his body merging into hers. He never grows; if anything, much of the male disappears into the female. An angler female taken near Iceland was 40 inches long, and the attached male only 4 inches. The female was judged to be a thousand times the weight of her mate.

Why is the goosefish a fish of the beach? Ask Michael J. Ursin. His terse and taxonomically up-to-date *A Guide to Fishes of the Temperate Atlantic Coast* warns that this one "lies on bottom in shallow water with very large, well-toothed mouth wide open and bites anyone that steps on it. Do not allow very young bathers to wade about where large goosefish are common." Beyond that, in winter the goosefish seeks shallow water, and cold snaps sometimes kill these com-

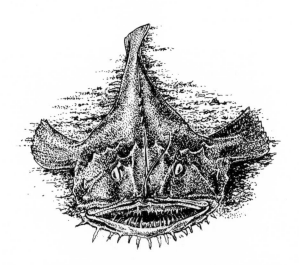

Goosefish (*Lophius americanus*).

mon visitors which then end up on the shore. Their peculiar jaw-bones, with one to three curved rows of pointed teeth, are often found by summertime strollers who mistake them for the relic of some creature too grotesque for this day and age.

Driftwords:

Time

The sun set at 7:13:35 tonight by my watch. I'd left the beach below Zack's Cliffs, parked the jeep and walked back to the berm for a last look at sunset on the rainbow clays of Gay Head. I planned to be early; I was late. Beyond a cloud bank that hovered a pencil's width above the horizon, the sun shone bright orange/red. No doubt geometry has a name for the shape it seemed: a circle with a flat-bottom, as if someone had sliced a slab from a wheel of cheese and set it down on the horizon's shelf. Then it moved, slowly but perceptibly in little jerks, as if a gallactic rat were pulling it down through the slit between the shelf and the wall. (Of course none of this could be true. The sun doesn't set, the world turns. And not in jerks but smoothly. When we see the sun set, it is already below whatever horizon happens to confront us since its light takes several minutes to reach our eyes. It's gone before we see it.) But down it went, or seemed to go beyond the gray horizon beneath the now purple cloud. Then above the apparent flat line of sea there was just a sliver of sun and (blip!) it vanished like a letter in the slot. Yet for a minute or two it kept reappearing—that is the thinnest perceptible crescent appeared *below* that 6-mile-distant line, on the water itself a hairbreadth below the horizon. No doubt the science of optics would explain that the unseen edge of distant cloud beyond the horizon was still struck by direct sunlight and bounced the light off the nearer water toward me. But it looked like a specter of the sun trying to return, gripping at the feeble Gay Head Light which had begun its blinking. That's when I looked at my watch, which always runs a few minutes fast.

A cascade of terns.

Chapter Four

Meet the Birds

They are always there . . . like the poor, the rich and the shore itself.
Birds haunt ramshackle arcades of the incomparable honkytonk along
Salisbury Beach, Massachusetts and hover above the artificially wide
sands of Ocean City, Maryland, and wait out gales on dredge spoil
heaps in Ocracoke Inlet. They animate every island, especially those not
frequented by man. A beach may be so changed by human use that it
lacks even mole crabs and compass grass; it will still have gulls. Winter
may be so cold that spindrift lies in frozen spongy clumps; yet sanderlings still work the swash's edge in comic platoons. Summer's solemn
herons patrol the marsh behind a barrier while on the other side, beyond
the surf, gray willets flash bright white chevrons, shy oyster-catchers

wield their crimson bills and eager terns dive like darts. Birds are the clowns of the beach, the lions, acrobats, roustabouts, barkers, beggars, pickpockets, cops and constant spectators all. There is a type cast for every role in the littoral circus. Without doubt they are the most varied and visible fauna of the shore.

For all their ubiquity and variety, they lack the stuff of many superlatives. As a biological class, Aves are not as old as fishes nor as multitudinous as bugs. Even in an enormous springtime swarm that smudges a distant sky then seems to vanish and reappear, the peeps are fewer than periwinkles in an acre of healthy marsh or coquinas in a square yard of wet sand. Birds are less prolific than the crabs and don't become tame as usefully as many mammals. But count them among the most wonderful animals on earth (when they bother to alight).

Because they inhabit air, and perhaps because they're so visible, birds command our wonder and delight. They always have, invading man's darkest mythology and brightening each summer day. A kind of pigeon led the ark to Ararat; eagles gnawed Prometheus' liver as Zeus' revenge for giving our crowd fire. Gulls saved the Mormons from famine to earn Utah's perpetual thanks. Ancient Egypt called birds their gods. (In contrast, modern America names nuclear submarines after fishes.) I suspect that everything ever written about every flier since Pegasus is at least partly true; nothing is beyond them. Visit Saquish Point off Duxbury, Massachusetts, to see the ruddy turnstone earn its name. On Cape Lookout's 23-mile-long island, which may have more species of birds at one time than people, great blue herons stalk the open beach; they haven't read the literature which calls them denizens of the marsh.

That birds rank so low in what we haughtily call "intelligence" just points up our myopia and conceit. One of the crows, a most precocious bird, can learn to count to seven; even Roy Rogers' horse could pretend to do that. But Trigger couldn't fly and neither man, spider, ape, fish nor any other creature functions so brilliantly in three dimensions. Think about it. Birds soar, sink, hunt, flee, swarm and settle in relentless reference to horizontal breadth, horizontal depth and vertical height in a nebulous medium. By comparison, the other vertebrates work only in horizontal planes with an occasional hop through the vertical. A snake's world, for example, is fundamentally two-dimensional: Crawling on its belly, it depends on the given of solid ground, opting between right or left and forward or around. Man or mountain goat does the same thing and functions more like an asp than an avocet. Certainly we can climb most mountains, one step at a time, so long as there is something to step on. We can leap from crag to crag, like a cocktail party conversationalist, but we barely jump our own height and stay aloft mere parts of seconds, fighting gravity and depending on it to bring us down to earth.

Yet albatross circle Antarctica aloft; Mother Carey's chickens take their living from the ocean surface without touching down. The birds command every physical dimension, willing themselves up, down, sideways and through intangible air free from pedestrian dependence on firm earth. Some shore birds in their pole-to-pole migration flights cruise 3 miles high. A kingfisher hovers, dives, spears a minnow beneath the waves with its bill, then soars up, around and settles on a swaying branch just by using its noodle thoughtlessly.

Only a marvelous brain can order and control such physical agility —yet a brain that resembles a modern reptile's more than ours. (This is because the first birds radiated from reptilian stock. Their feathers, the design and functions of which deserve a chapter in another book, derive from scales.) Despite the aspersions often cast on "bird brains," the cerebral centers that control sight and coordinated physical action are relatively huge. Each bird is a virtuoso of instant reaction to every kind of natural physical circumstance. Yet as Nobel Prize-winning behaviorist Niko Tinbergen points out, a bird is not "a mere bundle of immediate response to external stimuli." Each one reacts differently at different times to similar events depending on what's going on inside itself. Its "internal condition causes the bird to go and search for specific situations which can provide the right stimuli" to trigger reactions which the inner bird demands. "In psychological terms: a bird's 'needs vary,' " Tinbergen has learned.

Of course, over the centuries, the birds' inability to think like us— to change basic habits in a generation—has had tragic consequences. Some species evidently learn with one experience to stay far from a man with a shotgun. An African crow who'd been endangered by a blast will alarm its companions the next time the man appears armed; that hunter will be cogently avoided by succeeding generations of the flock. But North American shore birds didn't learn so fast. Nineteenth-century hunters went out in force every year augmenting their arsenals like Dr. Strangelove until they fitted skiffs with scatterguns too heavy for one man to lift alone. Entire flocks were mowed down as they came to settle and feed in a quiet bay; survivors of the first volley were just nonplused and often tried to aid their wounded kin. The survivors' descendants did the same and some species were shotgunned to extinction.

We say the birds were dumb to fall for wooden decoys, to enter the same trap flight after flight. The real stupidity was the hunters who could reasonably anticipate the consequences of unbridled greed or simple blood lust. The Eskimo curlew was physically and mentally equipped to fly—probably nonstop—from the Canadian and New England coasts to Tierra del Fuego. (This upland member of the sandpiper family "flew in such dense flocks as to remind me of the passenger pigeon" wrote Audubon himself.) Called "dough bird" because it fattened itself so well before migrating and hence was very tasty, the species was gunned away. This despite the fact its fondness for insects kept grasshoppers in check throughout the Great Plains each spring. A gregarious and fatally unsuspicious bird, it was not Machievellian enough to fear man inland or along the coast. William Beebe mourned: "When the last of a race of living things breathes no more, another heaven and another earth must pass before such a one can be again." The Eskimo curlew is probably extinct.

Their learned v. latent brainpower aside, another awesome aspect of birds is their exquisite design. No other group of cerebral animal possesses such practical beauty in the combination of diverse elements from aerodynamic facility to bright-hued or dull feathers that distinguish species. The shore birds' mottled plumages are superb camouflage on their rocky, shell-strewn or grassy breeding grounds. In breeding season a drab marsh drake that boasts just half a dozen eye-catching feathers on each wing displays them like a battle flag with the simple act of preening. A common pigeon's broad-spread tail slows its landing speed by 60 percent. A peregrine falcon, perhaps the fastest creature to ever live, has round nostrils surrounding pinpoint baffles of bone which let it breathe at speeds around 175 miles an hour as it hunts over barrier islands. The wings of gulls are so aptly proportioned for flight that they showed the Wright brothers how to build a machine that flew.

Nor are the niceties of their design all external. Most birds' bones are hollow to limit weight and supplement lung capacity with reservoirs of air. But diving grebes and loons, which hunt fish under water, have solid bones; added buoyancy would be a hindrance when they swim after prey. Unnecessary bulk is literally a drag in flight; most birds' sexual equipment atrophies after each breeding season. When frightened, some birds evacuate the bowels as they flee; it makes them lighter.

But there's not space here to go far afield. Consider the birds of beach and marsh, a rich enough variety. The first problem is identifying these characters. Unlike other fauna the birds don't necessarily hang around while spectators guess their names. You examine a clam in the hand, a fish on a line, or a crab scrambling in a pail at leisure; but not birds which can fly away faster than you can riffle the pages of a field guide. For example, about two dozen basically black and white members of a single avian family inhabit or visit the Atlantic coast from Quoddy Head to Cape Lookout. Nearly twice that number of species from closely related families of the same order also frequent the same neighborhoods.

Part of the identification process is simple elimination. For instance, the first step in recognizing an Eskimo curlew is knowing its common relatives well enough to rule them all out before summoning the American Ornithologists' Union to declare the extinct bird reborn. To recognize a gull or tern not nearly as invisible as that curlew today requires knowing the Laridae family by more than reputation. And with that, it's taxonomy time again.

For the most part, beach birds belong to a single zoological order. Charadriiformes constitute a large taxon based on similar skeletal structures and feather-distribution patterns. The sandpipers and their numerous kin make up the Scolopacidae family. The plovers and turnstones are Charadriidae while the gulls and terns are Laridae or (in English) gulls and terns. We don't have a single vernacular term, so it's syllabically most efficient to call them Laridae, and more euphonious too. This breakdown sounds simple enough but—are you ready?—the bird men are tearing up their taxa too. For a time it seemed the gulls' phylogenetic relationships were carved in stone; now some taxonomists are reshuffling things on the basis of behavior! Pardon my tangent, but the value of systematics is at stake. Taxonomy is a subject nontaxonomists love to hate; no sooner do we get the categories straight than they're all reordered. Perplexed by this, a decade ago Peter Matthiessen complained: "Each bright new nail of information, far from strengthening the taxonomic structure, is now likely to shake and resettle the whole rickety edifice."

I sympathize with the sentiment and share the assumption on which it's based: Taxonomy ought to provide a stable construct. But taxonomists don't see it that way. The purpose of systematics, as it turns out, is not just to serve up all the species in nicely labeled trays. Taxonomic categorization is not simply a matter of Latinate tongue-twisting. The real purpose of it all "is to uncover the evolutionary history of living things," says Richard L. Zusi, a Smithsonian bird man. As that history appears in fragments, episodes and scattered chapters, it illuminates the nature of life itself. Now that contributes to a noble undertaking.

Poring though the scientific literature, it becomes apparent that the people who deal in taxonomics are concerned with matters beyond nomenclature. Yes, they debate classifications, tacitly undermining the "splitters" of past generations who created as many taxa as they could and adding to the "lumping" trend of contemporary science in which categories are combined. They reorganize higher taxa, which seems a little like doing Dewey Decimal over again with the goal of reassigning old subjects to newly numbered shelves. But searching through the bound volumes of *The Auk* and *Ibis,* and reading file cabinets of little monographs on finely focused subjects, something else comes clear. These people are exploring specific problems in physiology, behavior, ecological relationships, genetics, anatomy—the subtopics of living birds. They contribute to taxonomy in passing, as they borrow from it. But most of them use it as a vehicle, not an end in itself. It seems a useful matrix like a printer's type tray—albeit one in which the partitions are constantly being nudged around. It contains a constant collection of items—lead letters or bird species—but no single item has a permanent home.

At times I have been a sailor, and fond of the rule "a place for everything and everything in its place." That implies a system. As a system, Linnean classification is damnably untidy. It seems impossible, just as the flight of a bumblebee is theoretically inexplicable according to the rules of aeronautical engineering. As its wings work for the bee, taxonomy works for taxonomists—though for few other people. Why have I bothered with it at all? Because when writing about something as complex as the biota of the beach, some system of organization is mandatory. One could study and describe all the round animals first, then the black ones, then the soft. One could consider whiffets in alphabetical order. The new Audubon field guide groups its bird pictures by color for easy identification, then groups the descriptive notes according to habitat. But if you want to read further in other sources, you'd better have a Latinate label to compare, so that guide has Linnean names.

If Karl Linné had foreseen what he was creating, he probably would have turned to making shoes instead. He just set out to bring some organization to the chaos that was eighteenth-century man's piecemeal study of the natural world. Perhaps it sufficed in his time. Yet today simply running a complete bibliography on a species can take days. There is no place to simply check some whiffet's phylogentic pedigree and current status, especially if it's been revised or (heaven help you) renamed. There are only serial indices like the *Zoological Record* which fills several library shelves with fine print. With only a Latinate binomial there is no single encyclopedic source that will disclose what kind of animal it is, whether flesh, fowl or good red herring. Tracking down an animal without a doctorate is like going to a music store and being told that the choral scores are in the basement. Period. So much work is going on in every zoological field that even the specialists are hard-pressed to keep current in anything but the narrow confines of their areas. It's an impossible system. Infuriating. Crazy-making. As incomprehensible as a Marakesh bazaar on market day—where you can buy a chicken and cous-cous only after you learn the language.

But biologists, I finally realized, are not so different in a way from the members of my diverse fraternity. Writers, editors, journalists, critics, scholars, poets and linguists consider their work important. We support our favorite dictionaries as avidly as Pittsburgh people back the Steelers. We argue about the serial comma, an obsolete device in my view. We discuss etymology. We use grammar; it is an important if protean tool because our language is a living, evolving thing. Yet very few of us consider grammar an end in itself or consider ourselves grammarians. But getting back to the birds. . . .

The Linnean relationship between our herring gull *(Larus argentatus)* and the European lesser black-backed *(L. fucus)*, which sometimes strays to New England, points up the difficulties in building the solid structure nontaxonomists might like. Richard L. Pough writes authoritatively that both birds apparently descend from one ancestral group in Siberia.

> As this Siberian species pushed out east and west to colonize nearby regions the new populations tended to vary [only] a little from the original stock. These units begat others until finally the two divergent lines met halfway around the world, that represented by the lesser black-back having apparently come from the east, that of the herring gull from the west across North America. Beginning with the present Siberian population (the Vega herring gull) and following each of the lines, one discovers that each group is so similar to its neighbors (often interbreeding with them) that they all appear to be merely races or subspecies of a single species, and yet when the lines meet the end groups breed side by side without interbreeding. This, the surest test of a valid species, poses a problem in nomenclature which some ornithologists have solved by putting all the birds in one superspecies. Why the herrings and the lesser black-backs did not interbreed when they met is hard to determine, but the acquisition by the former of a 2-week-earlier breeding season may have something to do with it.

In behavior and habits the two remain almost identical.

Tinbergen wrote in *Scientific American* a few years back, "Even a nodding acquaintance with gulls suggests that their signaling behavior is just as typical of the family as their coloring and physical conformation." A gull demonstrates its gullishness by being web-footed, white-bodied, stout-billed, and by sharing behavioral traits. Laughing gulls talk to each other and communicate by gesture. To a non-gull such as a behavioral scientist, these vocabularies seem remarkably alike from species to species. (By the same token, the speech and body language of a Cape Breton Celt and a gaucho in the Argentine might seem indistinguishable to a migrating Arctic tern since they derive from a common source that's foreign to the observer in question.)

Genetic and geographic differences aside, ethologists recognize that seemingly identical physical and vocal displays are distinct enough to keep some closely related birds from getting together. Further, it's apparent that a great deal of gull behavior is latent; cerebral programming changes slower than cosmetic plumage. If behavior can be biologically isolating and keep birds of similar feathers apart, behavioral similarities can indicate evolutionary relationships. Hence some taxonomists are now revising the gulls' phylogenetic chart on the basis of behavior. They offer the sensible hypothesis that a species which behaves very much like another but looks quite different may be more closely related than superficial plumage at first suggests. Habitual actions become part of the formula for defining kinship among species.

Only a few scientific generations ago taxonomists compulsively defined species (and genera) according to externals like feather coloring. They split the birds into as many taxa as possible, it seems. Nineteenth-century ornithology decreed, for example, that our two largest herons, the great blue and the great white, obviously belonged to separate species. Later investigators learned that individuals of both colors regularly interbreed. The great white heron occurs only in Florida (for unexplained reasons) while dark birds summer as far north as Nova Scotia and Alaska; they are not "reproductively isolated" in Florida where both appear. Hence they do not belong to separate species. Today the trend is to lump established groups together on the basis of a widening range of subtler characteristics. After all, there is nothing hard and fast about the parameters of a genus or any higher taxon per se. It's an arbitrary category defined by nothing more than scientific consensus, not holy writ.

As in the other catalogues, this chapter will not describe every coastal denizen of its zoological category. It will introduce the birds most commonly seen and offer a short course in instant identification—because an instant is often all one has. But be advised that the first lessons may be the most uncomfortable: Birds are best described in comparison to each other. A great egret is enormous—for a bird. Next to a locomotive it's little. The least sandpiper weighs an ounce, at most, but since the birder can't induce it to sit upon a scale, the species is said to look like a semipalmated sandpiper in miniature. The way to learn birds by sight is to read, watch, remember and compare. First read a bit at leisure. Then simply eyeball individuals of a habitat's most numerous and visible species, like the sanderling and herring gull. Get an idea of each kind's limited variations and fundamental consistencies; then judge every other peep and white-headed gull by comparison in the mind's eye.

Sooner or later get an encyclopedic bird guide. There are four widely used and respected ones. Each has its strengths and shortcomings. Roger Tory Peterson's *A Field Guide to the Birds* is the most famous of the lot, the Steinway concert grand as it were. It has extensive notes but the rather schematic illustrations are bunched in the middle of the book and hard to find. The Golden Field Guide Series' *Birds of North America* by Chandler S. Robbins, Bertel Bruun and Herbert S. Zim is more handsomely illustrated with paintings that face the thumbnail descriptions. But these notes are very brief and the handy paperback edition falls apart after long field use. The latest of the lot is *The Audubon Society Field Guide to North American Birds,* which comes in eastern and western editions. One wag called it "the first pocket-sized coffee table book" since it's illustrated with photographs. Many pictures are stunning but others blurred or fail to show outstanding field marks. Also, the pictures are separated from the interesting notes. Some ornithologists consider Richard H. Pough's old *Audubon Water Bird Guide* the best of the lot. The notes are very extensive, the illustrations attractive and accurate. But this book, first printed in 1951, is hard to find and maddeningly dated in some respects.

Don't even think about rare species at first. Every bird will seem a rarity to a novice, and there are enough common birds to keep even an experienced newcomer to the beach busy for a weekend or a summer. (After that there are enough occasionals, exotic migrants, strays and stragglers to keep a committed birder alert for the balance of a lifetime.)

Something else to ignore at the outset: every juvenile. Whether born blind and naked or precocial (active) and downy, a young bird soon takes on adolescent plumage that differs from its adult dress like diapers from dinner jackets. For its first winter many a bird acquires new body feathers but retains its juvenal wing and tail plumage. The bald eagle doesn't get its characteristic white head until its fourth year. Most of the many gulls look more like their contemporary cousins than their parents until their third year and are very hard to tell apart. Start with their elders, mature *Larinae* within the family Laridae (which also includes the *Sterninae* or terns and noddies).

THE GULLS

From season to season and year to year, these are the most constantly visible coastal birds. (Some wander inland; Franklin's gull is a freshwater bird of the prairies; no matter.) The dominant local species in any habitat from Chekovian drama to Chilmark, Massachusetts, is called simply "seagull." Local folk can often tell nothing more about it than a city man can describe nesting habits of *Columbia livia* (the rock dove formally). As common on a beach as those pigeons in a park, adult gulls have webbed feet, short tails that spread like fans and white plumage except for the mantle and head. (The term "mantle" refers to the top of the wings from tip to tip and the section of back in between.) Not highly specialized, gulls are strong fliers, good walkers and able swimmers. Diving from the air, they catch some food live but find their real bread and butter as scavengers. Without them every beach would be a shambles of dead fish, dead birds and assorted trash—more so than they are today. Gulls eat carrion, garbage, birds' eggs (including their own kin's sometimes), crabs, mollusks, an occasional starfish and their cousins when they can't get anything else.

At times they seem a most cunningly industrious lot. One early November morning on a Virginia barrier island I watched a flock of herring gulls catch Cancer crabs from a falling tide as neatly as embassy wives picking stuffed mushrooms from a chafing dish. Flying into the wind several feet above the water off a point where bay and ocean meet, a gull would stall, bellyflop onto the water stabbing its head beneath it, and come up with a little crab. The gulls rarely missed. That is each one would come up with a crab almost every time but often drop it immediately and grab it again. Sometimes a bird would juggle the same crab like a too-hot hors d'ouvre three or four times before getting it from behind, to avoid the pincers. Then the gull would fly to the beach and prepare the meal. Watching through binoculars and later examining the remains, I became fairly sure the gulls dropped each two-inch crab on its back on the hard damp sand and pecked two or three times to kill it. Then the gull would peck the bottom shell away and pick the crab quite clean before flying out again. Gulls came and went for an hour; only about a dozen worked the shoal at any one time, crabbing with deliberate concentration but not haste. Surprisingly, there was little thievery among them.

When gulls go clamming in Maine the spectacle is a cross between aerial ballet and fruitstand robbery. Working at low tide the gulls snatch small quahogs from the mud flats between rocky points and ledges. A clam in its beak, the gull flies 20 to 40 feet high above a rock and drops it so that its shell cracks. (This is common enough behavior among other bird families that eat other animals. Pliny wrote that Aeschylus departed this life when a European buzzard "mistook the poet's bald head for a rock and dropped a turtle on it," according to one respected ornithological text.)

The American gull's problem is to fly high enough so the clam breaks on impact, but not too high to get the meal before another gull steals it. Some of the best fed gulls in a flock don't seem to bother digging their own clams at all, but simply soar and dart like pirates amid much screaming and flutter. Others seem adept at tossing the clam up when they reach the apogee of the flight, then diving to land on the rock barely an instant after the clam. On Nantucket I once saw a single juvenile go through the same routine most cautiously while other gulls watched idly. This bird was greedy and foolish; it never flew high enough to break the clam, because the beach just there was made of pebbles, not bedrock. It flew up, dropped the clam, chased it to the ground, pecked, picked it up and repeated the routine. Evidently realizing it was doing something wrong, the gull moved off a little way to try another surface for its anvil—and dropped the clam on a wave, which swallowed it. Another time on Nauset Beach a great black-backed juvenile picked up something, flew and dropped it on dry sand again and again without the slightest harassment from other gulls. The object wasn't a quahog, but the clam-sized butt end of a two-by-four. We live and learn.

To distinguish the common gulls, look for the following characteristics:

The great black-backed gull is biggest. It has a white head, white chest and black mantle.

The herring gull, almost as big as the black-back, also has a white head and chest. But its mantle is gray. There is a red spot on the bill and the legs are pink.

The ring-billed gull is slightly smaller than its almost look-alike cousin, the herring gull, and also has a gray mantle, white head and chest. But the spot on its bill is large and black. The legs are yellow.

The laughing gull, the smallest common gull on this coast, has a black head (in summer) and dark gray mantle. In winter it loses the black cap for slight mottling.

Half a century ago Arthur Cleveland Bent, businessman by trade and ornithological essayist by choice, published a remarkable encyclopedia under the colophon of the Government Printing Office. Now reissued by Dover, the multi-volume *Life Histories of North American Birds* is the King James Version of bird books. The nomenclature and some data (like ranges and migration schedules) are understandably dated, but it remains a useful source seasoned with elegant verbosity. Bent never met a bird he didn't like. Take the great black-backed gull *(Larus marinus)*, for example, which has now extended its range from the Maritimes to the mid-Atlantic coast at the great expense of smaller birds. Quoth Bent:

> While cruising along the bleak and barren coasts of southern Labrador I learned to know and admire this magnificent gull, as we saw it sailing on its powerful wings high above the desolate crags and rocky inlets of that forbidding shore, its chosen summer home. Its resemblance to the bald eagle was striking, as it soared aloft and wheeled in great circles, showing its broad black back and wings in sharp contrast with its snow-white head and tail, glistening in the sunlight. It surely seemed to be a king among the gulls, a merciless tyrant over its fellows, the largest and strongest of its tribe. No weaker gull dared to intrude upon its feudal domain; the islet it had chosen for its summer home was deserted and shunned by other less aggressive waterfowl, for no other nest was safe about the castle of this robber baron, only the eider duck being strong enough to defend its young.

Perhaps the eider suffered the big gull's presence because it suited its own purposes. Most gulls are alarmists, the great black-backed not least of all, and raucously announce the appearance of possible predators, particularly man. In Labrador people used to fatten this species for table use, and eggs of all the Laridae were pirated as breakfast food.

Nesting on remote coasts, *L. marinus* remains a handsome bird, predatory or haughty depending on its mood. It frequently permits the company of herring gulls but is much warier of people than its smaller companions.

The herring gull *(Larus argentatus)* is the popular prototype of East Coast seagulls, a most vociferous and prolific bird. It is also remarkably communal. Along the crannied coast of Maine, for example, experi-

1. Ring-billed gull; 2. Herring gull; and 3. Great black-backed gull.

ments show that the herring gulls effectively patrol entire stretches of shore—though only one may be visible from any single cove. If a particle of food appears, the solitary gull will snatch it. But discovering a large supply, whether a garbage truck, a school of herring or an ornithologist testing a hypothesis with a bagful of fish, the gull never keeps it secret. It flies a telltale pattern and issues a loud call. Other herring gulls posted out of sight from the cove but alert to their neighbors' behavior join the feast. In turn, still more distant gulls see and hear the second wave depart and also respond.

This is the bird Niko Tinbergen studied for his landmark animal-behavior text, *The Herring Gull's World.* In it the ethologist detailed many of the subtleties of avian life, as well as some things not so subtle, such as a male gull's nuptial gift. Herring gulls exhibit programmed behavior to a fare-thee-well. One individual's gesture, posture or action—termed a releaser—triggers a specific action by an interacting bird. Consequently a breeding colony of gulls (or terns) is a frenzy of endless counterpoint. Certainly the seasons initiate some internal changes; the lengthening sunlight of spring days stimulates a bird's pituitary gland to secrete hormones which trigger the breeding urge.

The first result is departure for traditional nesting areas, not just latitudes, mind you, but the place where the gull was hatched. Though they winter in loose flocks of individuals—not couples— "herring gulls seem to pair for life," Tinbergen writes, and they re-establish old bonds en route to the nesting grounds again. Once at the rookery, the males establish territories which they defend from other gulls. Often a ritual display is enough. Threatened on its own ground, a resident strikes a threatening pose, whether the uninvited guest is male or female. Another male usually takes the hint and leaves, or else fighting ensues. A female turns her head away in a characteristic, acquiescent posture. Thus the resident male's single act prompts different reactions and those reactions, in turn, provoke different new reactions. Whether the intruder is male or female, a series of point-counterpoint transactions occur before either violent fighting or mating. Some of the exchanges involve only physical posture; others are vocal. Recent investigators have shown that gulls have distinct sounds to communicate various messages—a consistent, cogent vocabulary.

If the newcomer is female, things come to a head when the male walks off a few yards and makes nest-building motions in the sand. She responds with begging signs and sounds.

The male seems to try to avoid her solicitations . . . yet he does not walk away. After a while the male's neck swells, the swelling travels upwards, then he opens his beak widely and . . . evidently with some exertion regurgitates an enormous quantity of half-digested food. As soon as the male opens his bill the female frantically pecks into his mouth and begins to swallow the food with incredible greediness.

Chacun à son goût.

Copulation is highly choreographed and a little awkward since it requires contact between each bird's cloaca, the alimentary/reproductive vent beneath the tail. To make a long story short, the birds toss their heads and take a few steps around each other. The male utters

a rhythmic, hoarse call. Immediately afterwards he jumps on his mate's back, waving his wings and settling down on his tarsi on her shoulders. His feet rest on the female's upper arm, which the toes are holding in their grip. The female continues and intensifies the head tossing, touching the male's breast every time, and even rubbing her bill against his breast. The male, uttering the copulation call all the while, lowers his tail until it touches her tail, then makes a series of sideways rubbing movements and finally brings his tail down at the side of the raised tail of the female, and, waving his wings to keep his balance, brings his cloaca into contact with hers. This is repeated a number of times. Thereupon the male stops calling, folds his wings and jumps down at the side of the female. There is no postcoition display, but usually the birds begin to preen after a while.

This description of avian coupling seems to pretty well apply to most birds except in matters of detail. The differences between species' behavior in all reproductive matters from early courtship to chick-rearing involve fastidious detail. Some gulls copulate for several minutes on the commodious beach. Great blue herons mate on branches or in their treetop nests and take only seconds to conclude this most important business.

The herring gull's nuptial regurgitation may have evolved because it symbolically anticipates later parental behavior. (By the same token, premature nest-scraping motions evoke the possibility of making a nest together. The convention seems to be: "Look what I can do when the time is ripe.") Gulls feed their young regurgitated food. The parent approaches the nest and leans its bill in reach of the chicks. Experiments have shown that the characteristic spot on the bill serves as a releaser for a hungry chick. The chick pecks at the spot and the pecking prompts the parent to disgorge a meal. A chick that doesn't peck hard enough —an experimentally placed chick of a weaker species, for example— doesn't get fed and starves. A chick presented with the wrong kind of spot may not peck at all, but just thrash and cry feebly until it starves.

The two common smaller gulls along our coast are the ring-billed gull *(L. delawarensis)* and the laughing gull *(L. atricilla).* The ring-billed looks much like the herring gull but is smaller, has yellow legs and a spot that seems to circle both the upper and lower bill. A scavenger, like nearly all members of the family, it also forages for live food along the wet beach and flies inland to farms where it follows plows for unearthed worms and grubs.

The laughing gull, which exhibits the most distinctive seasonal change of plumage, wears a black breeding cap in summer but sheds it in fall. This is the bird that follows the ferries between the Outer Banks islands begging for food. A regular vacationer may wonder what's transpired if he returns in winter when these gulls' heads have turned nearly white. It is an agile flier, but seems to be declining, in part because of the growing numbers of herring gulls which rob its eggs.

THE TERNS *(Sterninae)*

These are the more graceful black-capped white birds of the summer coast. "Sea swallows," as they're often called because of their darting ways and usually forked tails, are more specialized than their stockier gull cousins. They fish for live prey, often close to the surf line. Flying parallel to the shore, they adjust their altitude so that a plunging dive

Laughing gulls in winter plumage and black summer hood.

will carry them as deep as the minnows are swimming. (They don't swim in pursuit like loons.) Head pointing down like a granny wearing half-glasses, a tern hovers, folds its wings and plunges sometimes completely underwater to grab a fish with its sharp bill. Body buoyancy brings it to the surface again. Some terns hunt cooperatively in flocks, diving down into a minnow school from the left side of the group, then flying up to the right side and waiting their turn again. But ornithologists use the term "cooperation" uncomfortably; it may just be that members of a flock maneuver for the best position, which is downwind of the schooling fish. After a bird has caught a fish it has little choice but to take an unfavorable upwind position and jockey for a better one.

To distinguish the four terns commonly seen along the Atlantic beach, look for these characteristics:

The Caspian tern, nearly as large as a herring gull, is the biggest of the lot. It has a red bill and slightly forked tail.

The royal tern, almost as large as the Caspian, has an orange bill and noticeably forked tail.

The common tern, still smaller, has an orange bill with a black tip and a deeply forked tail.

1. Common terns standing and flying; 2. Least terns standing and flying; 3. Royal tern standing; and 4. Caspian tern calling.

The least tern, understandably the smallest of them all, has a yellow bill and legs. Its tail is quite broad.

Particularly lively, the common tern *(Sterna hirundo)* has a complicated courtship ritual that begins more than a month before actual nesting. It involves first tentative then extended visits to the traditional rookery, and flights in which a male carrying a fish is accompanied by a partner or series of partners, not all of them necessarily female. Finally after several trial runs, a male with fish in his bill settles down on his territory and makes nest-scraping motions with his breast. When a potential partner or hungry male approaches and tries to steal by, the territorial male pecks.

At that point another male would peck back or retreat; a female keeps approaching and utters a characteristic begging call. Soon the male presents the fish to her; she plays with it and offers it back. They'll pass the fish back and forth several times until it's in tatters. Then they fly off together. One will fish and feed the other; then they'll exchange roles and fly ritual patterns. Usually these nuptial rites preceed actual breeding by more than a week. However, it's worth noting that these terns will delay the first courtship stages if the weather's wrong or if the nesting area is still wet from spring rains.

In a particularly dense territory the nests may be only 12 inches apart and territorial disputes are common. There is inevitable fighting and some birds are killed. Yet settled birds may defend an absent neighbor's nest against unknown terns. There are three eggs in the normal clutch, but incubation doesn't start until all are laid. The eggs hatch together, like a number of inland birds whose unhatched young have been shown to peep at each other before pipping and breaking out of their eggs simultaneously.

Common terns prefer sites with some grass, since the young learn to seek its shade when the parents are away fishing. The precocial chicks quickly learn to recognize their parents and, as soon as they can fly, watch for them to return with food and fly up to meet them. Later they'll accompany the adults and watch while they fish, waiting on a nearby rock or piling to be fed.

When predators approach, the adult terns attack in concert, defecating and striking intruders on the head in flights of two or three at a time. There are old accounts of ornithologists repeatedly having their pith helmets pierced.

The largest of the lot, the Caspian tern *(Sterna caspia)* is also the least communal and the most predatory. It fishes alone, nests in small groups or with ring-billed gulls and often robs the nests of other birds. This tern breeds in Canada and winters only as far north as the Carolinas but frequents the coasts between its summer and winter homes when migrating.

The crested tern with the orange bill is the royal *(Sterna maxina)*, which nests in colonies so dense that the brooding birds are within pecking distance of each other. Very choosy, they seem to have several inflexible requirements for a breeding ground: complete absence of four-footed predators (including man, as usual); general inaccessibility and good visibility; extensive shallows nearby and proximity to an ocean inlet. Hence they colonize remote islands, including new dredge spoil banks. They habitually nest so close to the high-tide mark that entire colonies are sometimes inundated by spring or storm tides. Unlike some terns, they regularly defecate on their nests until the uniformly dense, round colony takes on a "whitewashed" appearance. This waste material hardens the nests rims so they withstand some minor flooding.

Rarely does a pair of royals lay more than one egg in a clutch. If it is destroyed or stolen, they'll lay again later in the season. Throughout the incubation period and during early brooding, royals will abandon their nests at the sight of a predator. They'll flee from gulls, which then invade the colony and break eggs at leisure, returning to eat the contents later. After the chicks are a few days old, however, the adults will attack intruders en masse and "dive-bomb."

The precocial chicks assemble in a "creche" almost as soon as they can walk and stay together. When threatened by man or dog, raccoon or other predator, the creche scurries away, usually onto the water until the danger passes.

The littlest tern, formally called the least *(Sterna albifrons)*, has also flown under the alias of killing peter, little striker and kill-em polly. It has a yellow bill, gray wings and a white forehead patch beneath its black cap. Less fastidious than its cousins, it nests on less remote beaches where it is far more accessible to people. Before the turn of the century this bravado nearly resulted in the species' extinction when least terns sold for a dime apiece to the millinary trade. But the bird has made a strong comeback and is now common on many beaches.

Among its notable habits, the least tern will dive in the ocean, return wet to the nest and sprinkle the eggs with water on particularly hot summer days. When a young bird is fledged it accompanies a parent to the feeding grounds and gets fed there by the solicitous adult. Bent's

Life Histories includes this almost unspeakably charming report from a contemporary:

> Near me were two little young, just hatched and their down hardly dry, yet they were able to run about a little. Nearby were several other youngsters. As I lay there propped up on my elbows, awaiting the return of the mother bird, several of them flitted back and forth. . . Soon the mother of the two nearest little ones alighted, and, running to her charges, settled easily upon them, shading them from the hot sun's rays. Then she turned her gaze upward and called softly in reply to the tender notes of the male, which circled overhead. Soon he alighted and took the mother's place in shading the young, while she flew away, perhaps to fish and bathe. Soon she returned with a little sand eel, which she gave to one of the tiny ones, who ran to her for it. Then she flew again, descended into the sea and returned to her charges which the male relinquished to her care. She stood over them with ruffled feathers, and seemed to shake off some drops of water on their little panting forms, then raised her wings a trifle to shade them from the hot sun. . . . Again the gentle twittering, and the father came down on the sand with a tiny, bright, silvery fish. A little one stuck its head out between the mother's wing and her body, the father courteously passed the fish to the mother, and she fed the chick, which begged for it with open mouth. Again the breadwinner winged his way over the sunny sea and returned with another fish. Now the little ones were asleep under the mother's breast. He offered her the fish. She refused it. He flew away, but soon alighted and proffered it again, only to be refused again. At last, having full assurance that his family did not need food, he swallowed it himself. Where shall we look to find a lovelier picture of happy, harmonious family relations than that shown here on this desolate beach, beside the roaring surf?"

The account is useful for the actual observations of actions and behavior. However, take the anthropomorphic assumptions with a seaful of salt. How did Mr. Edward H. Forbush tell the adult male from female? Nobody else can, except during courtship and breeding.

THE "SHORE BIRDS"

Laridae aside, several other closely related families populate the beach; the taxonomy becomes too esoteric to be generally interesting. There are the Charadriidae (plovers and turnstones), the Scolopacidae (sandpipers and their allies), then separate families respectively for the oyster catchers and the skimmers. The following selection includes just a handful of the scores of birds that casual beach visitors see and serious birders recognize at a glance. The list includes the obvious birds—the ones that stand out clearly—as well as some other very common ones that mass in perplexingly mixed flocks.

Black–bellied Plover *(Pluvialis squatarola)*

An arctic breeder like many shore birds this black-and-white-mottled bird migrates spring and fall along the coast and often winters as far north as Virginia. About as large as a quail, in summer plumage it has a black front and face topped with white that hangs to the shoulders like an English judge's wig. The back and wings are mottled in the standing bird. In flight a black patch appears under the wing. The rump is white. These latter field signs are good all year around. In winter the bird is mottled brown-and-white above and all white below.

The wary black-belly eats quantities of berries, insects and aquatic animals including mollusks, crustaceans, fishes and small lizards. It nests in scratched-out hollows on the tundra where both adults incubate a normal clutch of four eggs. In our latitudes it's most often seen with willets, curlews and its close relative the golden plover. (*P. dominica,* a smaller bird, has nearly the same profile but its mottling is brown and black.) The black-belly is a strong flier; "in time of storm it sometimes seem to be the only bird aloft." With the great skua and arctic tern it's said to be "one of the most far-flung birds on earth."

Ruddy Turnstone *(Arenaria interpres)*

One of the best-named shore birds, the ruddy turnstone eats by turning stones and shells over with its bill and snapping up whatever's beneath: worms, mollusks, crabs. (In case it's escaped anyone's attention, our feathered friends of the littoral are ferocious carnivores.) If it encounters a likely obstacle too big to handle alone, it may cooperate with another of its kind and the two will work together. Also, the turnstone will occasionally dig a hole deeper than itself in pursuit of burrowing food.

Like a majority of the look-alike sandpipers, *A. interpres* is about half the size of the clan's largest cousin, the willet. But the turnstone has a most distinctive look. White-bellied in all seasons, it has an irregular white wig in summer and a splotchy reddish-and-black back. (In winter its folded wings take on a more regularly mottled look and its head darkens.) Roger Tory Peterson describes its in-flight breeding plumage as a "harlequin pattern," a striking design of russet, black, and white. One immutable field mark is the "calico bird's" unusual bill, which is thick at the base and tapers like an asymmetrical wedge, turning up slightly toward the tip.

The turnstone arrives at its Arctic breeding grounds in late May. It will nest in exposed tundra or under bushes, lining a shallow hollow with dry leaves and grass. If its four-egg clutch is destroyed, a breeding pair will not replace it. Both parents brood the eggs. When they hatch, the female departs toward the wintering grounds beyond Virginia. The males leave a fortnight later and the juveniles last of all. The following spring yearlings migrate northward but stop in groups far short of the nesting grounds. I've seen them along the Massachusetts coast in midsummer.

Aside from turning stones on the beach, this bird explores seaweeds for small animals, probes into rock crevices, robs gull and tern nests, and feasts on flies and maggots found on sea mammal corpses that wash ashore. This latter habit can be dangerous; these birds have been known to get serious food poisoning from carrion bacteria as a result.

Semipalmated Plover *(Charadrius semipalmatus)*

More colorfully called the ringnecked plover, this bird has several look-alikes. The most famous, which prefers dry lands to the seashore, is the larger killdeer. (*C. vociferus* is notable for feigning a broken wing and limping in helpless frenzy when an enemy approaches its nest.) The ringneck, as its name implies, has a single dark-colored band like a collar. The killdeer has a double collar; the rarer Wilson's plover has a very broad collar and dark bill, while the smaller piping plover (called the "feeble") has a very narrow collar. Now to ice the cake of congeneric complications: The ringed plover, which breeds no closer than Baffin Island and winters in the Old World, matches the ringnecked plover except for its unwebbed feet. "Semipalmated," a word of certain currency in shore-bird circles, means possessing partly webbed toes.

This busy bird flies fast in large flocks that twist and turn in unison. Breeding on beaches in the Maritimes and in Canadian tundra, it winters along the coast below Connecticut. Like many of its relatives, the ringnecked plover works the swash in spurts, running several steps, stopping, and bobbing its entire body as it probes the wet sand for worms, small mollusks and tiny crustacea.

Willet *(Catoptrophorus semipalmatus)*

There is something of Cinderella—or of the Frog Prince—in this lanky sandpiper. Pacing the swash and bobbing its head, probing for

1. Sanderlings flee the swash; 2. Three dunlins probe the tidal wrack with a ruddy turnstone; 3. American oystercatchers stand and fly; and 4. A black-bellied plover waits for the tide's turn with a semipalmated plover and the smallest shore bird, a least sandpiper.

worms and snatching little fish, it is decidedly drab. A pauper in an old brown tweed coat who used to be called "humility." But when it flies, this wary vocalist flashes beautiful wings, each one bearing a broad white chevron. The marks seem to combine in a **W**, the bird's initial across its 30-inch wingspan.

In flight, the willet frequently sings one of the brightest one-note songs in the avian repertory. The *Audubon Field Guide* describes it as "will-will-willet"; the *Golden Field Guide* as "pill-will-willet"; the same syllables are used by Peterson, who writes its alternate call as "kip-kip-kip." But the Audubon book notes this call as "kuk-kuk-kuk-kuk-kuk." A. C. Bent jots the music down as "wek, wek, wek, or kerwek, kerwek, kerwek, varied to piuk, piuk, piuk. . . . Less frequently another note is heard which sounds like beat it, beat it." All this simply suggests the absurdity of trying to write bird calls; in English they all look like gibberish.

This handsome, flighty bird nests in open areas along the coast from Chesapeake Bay northward. Parents and brood may abandon the nest on the day the eggs all hatch. One willet has been seen carrying its young one by one across a creek from the nest to hide them in high grass. Seemingly solicitous parents, the adults briefly escort the chicks around to feeding grounds but typically abandon them before they can fly. For a willet this is normal behavior; the species thrives sufficiently that the migrating birds sometimes pass in flocks of thousands.

Sanderling *(Calidris alba)*

Weighing in at between 2 and 3 ounces, the sanderling is one of the larger "peeps," a word properly applied to the small sandpipers but widely used for any of the smaller shore birds. What this character lacks in size it makes up for in numbers and sheer energy. Ralph S. Palmer writes authoritatively in the handsome *Shore Birds of North America:* "in a mixed gathering of peeps, those constantly in a great hurry are sanderlings." The *Audubon Guide* authors say: "Practically every day of the year these birds can be found on any ocean beach." Tireless and cosmopolitan, they earnestly play a kind of tag with the broken waves as they run up and down the foreshore snaring small invertebrates. They're particularly noticeable in winter when they're sometimes the only birds in sight, their reddish and brown upper plumage gone a pale gray above their white breasts and bellies. In flight these little birds flash broad bright white wing stripes. Their bills and legs are dark, nearly black.

Leaving nonbreeders behind in the lower latitudes, sanderlings nest in the high Arctic where they subsist on buds and berries until the appearance of fly larvae in the ponds. The breeding display begins with the small male vibrating his wings and flying steeply up, then singing on his downward flight. On the ground he puffs out his feathers, lowers his wings and makes nest scrapes in the barren ground. When the eggs are laid, the male rarely takes a turn on the nest during the 23-day incubation period. One parent attends the hatched chicks, but both leave before the young fly at the age of two weeks.

This bird looks a great deal like the least and semipalmated sandpipers; its larger size is diagnostic. It's about as big as a starling and was once shot in great numbers for human food.

Dunlin *(Calidris alpina)*

A starling-sized sandpiper with a long down-curved bill, the dunlin "gives the appearance of having ballast too far forward," according to one expert. But appearances mislead; this bird has been clocked by a plane at 110 miles an hour.

Dunlins are often seen on winter beaches as far north as Long Island, the upper plumage a dull gray above a pale belly. Also known as the red-backed sandpiper, its name is descriptive only in summer (given that any shore bird's red is an earthy tone). Like least sandpipers, these unwary birds don't flee a human until closely approached, though a mob of them will chase intruders on their nesting grounds.

Willet.

Semipalmated Sandpiper *(Calidris pusilla)*

The most numerous shore bird, the semipalmated sandpiper is a little larger than the least sandpiper, which it closely resembles. When comparison isn't possible, the best field sign is its dark legs. A snatcher and prober, it uses its stubby bill more haphazardly than most peeps, poking into soft sand or preferably mud for insects and larvae. Another Arctic breeder that migrates along the coast, it winters from the southeast United States to Paraguay.

The semipalm nests in the Arctic where one of Bent's correspondents observed:

> It was found that the parents made no effort to feed the young. It was soon seen, however, that such care was not necessary. The young would stumble about and pick up minute gnats and flies with great dexterity, and the shallow algae-rimmed pools furnished them many a juicy "wriggler." The gait of the young sandpipers was a stumbling toddle, while their large feet and legs were all out of proportion to the rest of their slender bodies. By dropping and extending their wings they were able to use them as crutches, which often kept them from falling.

Bent observed that they were fully fledged about a month after hatching and flew south at the age of 5 weeks.

Least Sandpiper *(Calidris minutilla)*

The littlest shore bird is seen most often along marshy mud flats though it frequents the beach when fresh water freezes. The least sandpiper's flying weight is less than an ounce. Similar in appearance to other peeps, it stands out by virtue of its yellow legs and lilliputian stature. The size of the literature describing this littoral sparrow approximates its own size.

Preparing to breed in tundra bogs, the male "ox eyes" faces a stiff breeze for its territorial nesting display. The male also does most of the incubating over the four-egg clutch, but little is known about its brooding habits. It winters along the Outer Banks and southward.

Osprey *(Pandion haliaetus)*

Though rare peregrine falcons hunt the barrier island chains in fall, the raptor most often seen along the shore is the fish hawk or osprey. This bird is a wonder when it cruises the shoreline perhaps 150 feet aloft, its five-foot wings bent at the "wrist" and held motionless as it glides, eyeing the shallows for food.

Like all the falcon clan, it has exceedingly keen eyes. When an osprey sights prey—it lives on fish exclusively—it folds its wings and dives, then breaks with wings spread and feet forward to kill with its talons. Sometimes submerging, it struggles from the water, arranges the fish fore and aft and flies off carrying the prey torpedo fashion. (Sometimes it is mobbed and robbed by several gulls or a solitary eagle.) The feet are remarkable. With lumpy, scaled soles, a hind toe that can clasp from either side and sharp curled talons, they can grasp the slipperiest fish.

It would be dramatic to report that the fish hawk has unerring aim but that isn't the case. Near the mouth of Chesapeake Bay one summer afternoon I watched a juvenile work over a weir. The trap had plenty of fish and the osprey dove again and again, only to come up empty-taloned and perch on a stake, puzzled. Also, an adult sometimes tries to take too big a fish, and the killer becomes victim, too. Corpses of large fish have been washed ashore with a drowned osprey clutching their backs after the wounded prey dove and carried the birds under.

In their way, ospreys are friendly to man. Bent reports that farmers used to build nesting platforms to attract them; they served as avian watchdogs and would cry out whenever strangers approached. Almost any kind of elevated platform would do for their untidy nests which a perennially mated pair will renovate with additional sticks each year. On the Outer Banks they nest on abandoned telephone poles. Along the Inland Waterway they build on navigation buoys. In an eastern shore river one pair returned year after year to a wrecked oyster boat whose bow stood a few feet above high water. In Maine they nest high in live pines and dead hardwood trees.

Like all the birds of prey, ospreys feed at the top of the food chain. These birds, which live into their 20s, ultimately received the largest doses of persistent pesticides which caused them to lay eggs with abnormally thin shells. That malady, combined with a shrinking habitat, combined to greatly reduce the osprey's numbers. With DDT no longer in common use they have made a comeback and do not now seem threatened with extinction.

American Oystercatcher *(Haematopus palliatus)*

An oystercatcher on the beach stands out more than a circus clown at a Quaker meeting. This is the bird in the tuxedo with pink feet and a red nose. Its wings are black (with a white chevron in flight). Its shirtfront is white up to the neck. The face and head are black, the eyes have orange pupils and, yes, the feet are pink, sometimes red. But even Cyrano de Bergerac had no nose compared with the oystercatcher. It is long, straight and bright red. Beyond that, the bird carries itself oddly afoot, as if it were too barrel-chested to stand up straight. Its flight seems surprisingly fast for such an ungainly posture.

Haematopus palliatus is almost well named in English because it eats bivalves, if it doesn't actually catch them. Inspecting a mudflat at an odd pace between a strut and a toddle, the oystercatcher searches for shellfish with their valves ajar in a falling tide. Finding one, it stabs inside with a sharp stroke of the chisel bill. The most popular explanation is that the bird instantly snips an adductor muscle, leaving its prey powerless to clam up. But the bill's end is blunt and it has also been suggested that the bird simply stuns the animal.

Audubon said oystercatchers nested as far north as Labrador in his day. Gunners nearly wiped them out along much of the coast but they've recovered as far north as Massachusetts today. They stay far from human settlements—even from individual walkers—and are only seen in quite wild coastal places. Though they winter in large groups (as far north as North Carolina), they scatter in breeding season, each pair preferring a certain solitude. The nests are simple scrapes on a stone ledge, pebble slope or sandy rise with good visibility in all directions. I've rarely seen an oystercatcher alone in summer. Usually they travel in pairs, sometimes quartets. Spot one and you'll soon see another.

Aside from bivalves, oystercatchers also eat small snails and oddities like the purple sea urchin which they turn upside-down and devour without breaking its fragile shell.

Black Skimmer *(Rynchops niger)*

"You are what you eat," the saying goes. But the black skimmer is what it is because of *how* it eats. *Rynchops niger* is the bird with the enormous underbite. The lower bill grows faster than the upper and is longest by about one-third in the adult bird. Further, the lower bill has compressed sides; it's thin as a knife blade and has a straight, rather sharp upper edge. This fits into a slight groove in the upper bill.

Towards dusk the black skimmer flies low across calm waters with the tip of its lower bill cutting through the water. Then it loops back and flies the opposite course. For years it was rumored that the skimmer stabbed the surface of the water as it passed, then returned down along the line of bubbles snatching up whatever small fish had been drawn to the disturbance. While it sometimes feeds like this, another technique is constantly involved. The black skimmer often catches fish on its first pass even in muddy water, and evidently it fishes at night as well. In fact, it fishes blind. Leading with its chin, it cuts through the water until it strikes something—whether a log or minnow. Without missing a wingbeat the bird snaps its head down and pointing aft, it lets go of a stick or grabs living prey, then brings the head forward again. Hence this bird has found a special niche, catching food it cannot see.

The black skimmer nests in large colonies on open beaches as far north as Massachusetts. It winters along the Outer Banks and further south. This is a black-winged and black-capped bird with white face and underparts and red legs. The base of the unmistakable bill is red which shades into black towards the tip.

MASTERS OF THE MARSH

The way to most beaches crosses marshland and the first remarkable creatures to be seen are the herons—outstanding birds that look eccentric and deserve mention because of their marvelous visibility from the beach road. They are waders, stalkers and waiters with long stilty legs and, usually, sinuous necks. Notably designed to suit their habitat, they live by catching quick prey from the shallow waters: fishes, crabs, amphibians, small reptiles and mammals. Some cunningly shake their toes in the mud to stir dinner out of hiding; the reddish egret spreads its wings in a canopy to shade the murky water. At rest, with the head nestled between the shoulders, or alertly standing in wait for a passing meal, or moving slowly in pursuit, they seem most royally graceful birds. But darting their sharp bills atop those unlikely necks they're invisibly fast. In size and manner they range from the incomparably shy least bittern to the ostentatious great blue heron which is too big to hide. Standing 4 feet tall it greets intruders with a loud squawk and, preferring to be alone, imperiously flies off elsewhere beneath ungainly, comically ponderous wings.

Their common names tend to be self-explanatory, though sometimes so complex that shorter monikers might apply. A sensible kid I know realized that one fisher in particular didn't need a name with four elements that were hard to keep in order. So Jonathan dubbed the black-crowned night heron, unforgettably and suitably, "fat bird." I've heard the cattle egret called "bugger" for its eating habits. (This Old World species, a white bird with tan breast and crown, spread to the shoulder of South America and thence to Florida three decades ago. It has now colonized much of the East, where it's found in lowlands following livestock and eating the insects they stir up.) The snowy egret, a lovely little white bird with black legs and yellow feet, is simply a "snowy," the glossy ibis with its down-curved bill a "glossy." However, some eminences never get public nicknames by virtue of their dignity, or our respect for them: Oliver Wendell Holmes, Martin Luther King or Great Blue Heron.

Driftwords:

Smokey the Beach Bear

By and large, the National Park Service is a godsend. Sometimes controversial, perpetually bureaucratic, nonetheless it is the largest single custodian of undeveloped beaches—391 miles of ocean and bay shore along the Atlantic coast. Debates over specific management policies, long-term master plans and "recreational use" vs. "wilderness preservation" will continue—quite properly—for generations. Nevertheless, without the Park Service, Fish and Wildlife Service and park authorities in ten states precious few wild beaches would remain. Condominiums, bungalow cities, trailer camps, fishermen's eyesores and honkytonks would proliferate along the beach from Quoddy Head to Cape Lookout until the beach disappeared—or migrated in disgust. The Park Service received a congressional mandate in 1916 "to conserve the scenery and the natural and historic objects and the wild life [of designated areas] . . . in such manner and by such means as will leave them unimpaired for the enjoyment of future generations." That says it in legalese. Put another way, as some NPS people post the idea on their office walls: "Parks Are Forever." Amen.

Of course the Park Service is a bureaucracy and suffers accordingly. The cooperation coefficient of any public agency seems to decline with size and age. Some county and town park people act most hospitably while some National Seashore officials enforce policies that appear utterly useless *in situ* "because we have to have rules; we're a Federal agency." On the other hand, inconsistency raises its perplexing head— as it must because different habitats react differently. At Fire Island National Seashore, squatters' shacks are slated to be razed and trucked away. In part, this is because FINS managers believe that burning the shanties in a planned wilderness zone would retard new plant growth; perhaps by incinerating some crucial trace elements in the sand. Meanwhile, at Cape Lookout, rangers say they're putting the torch to fishing camps as happily as Nero because burning adds nutrients to the soil and helps fast growing southern plants. Why the discrepancy? Because different environments and different plants react differently.

Some park people are gifted naturalists, others clever careerists dedicated mostly to climbing the administrative ladder with coonlike agility. Last summer the chief (and only full-time) naturalist at one famous coastal enclave hadn't time to discuss the biota with visitors because he was making lists—not of flora and fauna, but of his summer help to please his superiors. Curiously, many of the most inspiring Park Service people aren't full-timers but "seasonals": Fred Richardson, a veteran high school science teacher who leads informative nature walks around Cape Cod National Seashore every summer; Jill Johnson, a trained botanist who knowingly discusses the plant life in Fire Island's Sunken Forest; Dick Baker, Assateague's lifeguard par excellence. These people, and many other warm-weather rangers, bring impressive professional competence to the forest-green-and-tan ranks and broaden what might become an all too parochial viewpoint. They don't suffer the ennui— an occupational disease—that infects many career rangers. One of the latter confessed to me that by Fourth of July a seasoned careerist really wishes all the visitors would simply go away, taking their persistent trash and environmental impact with them. After all, 24 million people visited the parks and recreation areas from Acadia to Cape Lookout in 1978. This ranger, still on the green side of thirty and facing a lifetime of superficial questions from a ceaseless stream of suburbanites, dreams of a billet in a perfectly wild place free of tourists and campers. Where? In Ranger National Park, of course, which lies halfway between the Happy Hunting Ground and Never-Never Land.

Pothead whales—stranded and dying.

Chapter Five

Snakes and Whales, Among Other Things

No mammal or reptile lives full-time on the Atlantic beach between low tide and the dunes; but many visit there to feed, and some to die. Tending to be variously shy, solitary or pelagic, the live animals themselves are seen less often than their tracks and remains. An encounter is likely to be tinged with fear, delight, sadness or awe. Nonetheless, there's a wide variety of so-called "higher animals," from the great whales and porpoises playing beyond the surf off Hatteras, to the tiny timid rodents that ply the Delaware beach grass by night, and the family of carnivorous mammals that left a Maine beach when I arrived one summer dawn. (There were three sets of fresh tracks—one adult and two juvenile—along the swash of a rising tide and two Cancer crabs neatly pulled limb from limb. Mink or ermine perhaps?) Rarely there are sea turtles; more commonly that absurd actor the hognose snake and the dexterous, resourceful raccoon.

In evolutionary terms all the reptiles, birds and mammals have something in common: an ancestor that branches off from the diversifying fishes to become a primitive amphibian some 350 million years ago. We all spring from the same ancient branch on the tree of life. Phylogeny aside, here's a sampler:

TIDAL REPTILES

The cottonmouth water moccasin, found no farther north than Back Bay in southernmost Virginia, is the most dangerous of the lot. Related to the rattlesnakes and copperheads, water moccasins are pit vipers; so named for the visible pits behind the nostrils which are diagnostic of the family Crotalidae. Wildlife authority Roger Caras calls the cottonmouth the third most lethal snake in the United States after the eastern and western diamondback rattlers. But keep in mind that more Americans die of bee stings than isolated snakebites. Cape Hatteras National Seashore, the most popular area with a notable number of cottonmouths, hasn't had a fatal biting in recent years. According to a Park spokesman, the latest nonfatal incident occurred when an adolescent boy pestered one repeatedly.

The cottonmouth *(Agkistrodon piscivorus)* may grow 6 feet long, though the average is about half that size. It is brown with indistinct black bands; its yellow belly may have dark markings as well, and a dark band runs from the eye to the corner of the mouth. It is distinguished from nonpoisonous water snakes by its deep spade-shaped head, light lips and white mouth. A good swimmer, the cottonmouth lives beside marshes on the bay sides of southern barrier islands. Its diet includes frogs, other amphibians and fishes. The young are brightly marked with reddish brown. Between 5 and 15 are born live after an unusual year-long gestation.

The hognose snake *(Heterodon platyrhinos)* belongs to the wide-ranging family Colubridae, which includes more than half the 2,700 species of snakes in the world. Neither poisonous nor particularly graceful, this serpent comes in a variety of colors: gray, black or reddish brown. The best field mark is an upturned nose with which it digs for toads, insects, moles and the like. I've seen this snake resting in the swash zone— waiting for little crustacea perhaps? Because of a slight similarity to the copperhead, this harmless reptile is often killed by Sunday-afternoon outdoorsmen. A better habit when seeing a snake is to study it from a little distance; the one with the ski-jump snout is a docile hognose. The one with a spade-shaped head and vertical pupils is a pit viper. Leave it alone.

The hognose is one of nature's great fakers—more dedicated to histrionics than even the possum whose famous game of playing dead may be a kind of catatonic state that occurs when the slow-witted marsupial is frightened out of its wits. Threatened, a hognose snake first puts on an impressive fuss, pretending it's a fearsome creature. Hissing and rearing back, this bluffer broadens the flesh behind its head into a cobralike hood and feigns repeated strikes—though it lacks both dangerous fangs and venom. If an intruder isn't cowed by the performance, the hognose falls over and plays dead, rolling onto its back. Determined to put on a convincing act, if turned right-side up it'll roll over again to strike another moribund pose as an encore.

The adult female lays from 6 to more than 40 thin-skinned eggs in soft earth and may coil around them, like a cold-blooded reptilian incubator. Laid in early summer, the eggs hatch six to eight weeks later. Hognose snakes live in open woods, fields and sandy regions. They're the most commonly seen snake on the outer beach, but by no means an everyday visitor.

THE LOGGERHEAD'S LESSON

A rarity worth looking for despite the odds, the loggerhead sea turtle is born on the beach, leaves as soon as possible, and returns only to breed. Pelagic and wide-ranging, this animal wanders the Atlantic at a speed of about a mile an hour, feeding on mollusks, crustacea, a few plants and quantities of jellyfish—including the Portuguese man-of-war. Though this dietary staple is 99 percent water, the loggerhead can grow to a length of 9 feet and a weight of 850 pounds. Once numerous, along with four relatives, the loggerhead owes its declining numbers to man—not only man the predator but man the accidental and continuing intruder. The phenomenon has some important implications that deserve attention.

Caretta caretta, which visits such distant points as Nova Scotia and Chesapeake Bay, is encountered at sea singly and occasionally in great swarms. When Dougal Robertson's boat possibly struck one killer whale and was certainly sunk by another, the adventurer and his family survived for 38 days in life rafts largely because they could capture an occasional solitary Pacific turtle. His memoir *Survive the Savage Sea* describes how man on occasion can be justifiably predacious. Another mariner reported seeing unidentified Atlantic sea turtles swimming together about 200 yards apart in a group that ranged over a distance of 60 nautical miles.

When a pregnant female clambers ashore, she seems quite finicky about chosing a place above the high-tide line to lay her eggs. Finding a suitable spot, she digs a shallow depression in the dry sand with a swimming motion, then claws out a hole within the hole with her hind flippers and drops as many as 150 round, leathery eggs into it. Before completing her 90-minute task, she covers the whole nest with sand again, then beats a hasty retreat to the water. She may mate again immediately in shallow water. The male mounts the female's back and leaves deep scars in the shoulders of her shell from his claws after the three-hour event.

In one to three months the eggs hatch en masse and the young all leave the nest simultaneously. Emerging through the sand, they head straight for the water—even if their view is blocked by a dune or ridge of sand. Their sea-seeking technique remained a mystery for millennia; people just assumed they smelled the water or heard the surf. These seemed the most likely explanations, but modern research proved an unexpected factor plays a key role. Newly hatched loggerheads seek an unbroken horizon and distinguish the brighter sky over the ocean from the darker sky above land. This cunning device sufficed admirably under the best of natural circumstances, and the species survived without its young developing real defenses against larger carnivores. The large number of hatchlings gave a few in each lot a fair chance to successfully run the gantlet across the beach. Despite land crabs on the shore, carnivorous fish waiting in the water and the macabre spectacle of feasting birds described by Tennessee Williams in *Suddenly Last Summer,* the turtles carried on. Evolved instinct made scores of siblings scurry from the hidden nest as fast as their legs could carry them; a highly evolved and subtle sense showed them the direction to flee across exposed sands to the safer water. But man changed the odds, both intentionally and by accident.

For centuries buried turtle eggs were gathered as human food. Adults were taken by hungry men for their meat as well. The hawksbill turtle, a member of the loggerhead's biological family, was hunted for the scales that were seared from its back to make tortoiseshell ornaments. In time, fortunately for the turtles, American landsmen found easier ways to feed themselves and rim their spectacles. But while our habits changed, our accidental influence did not. First, human settlement drove the puma away from the Atlantic coast. With the demise of this big cat, raccoons multiplied in a wild environment free from natural enemies and became major thieves of turtle eggs. Then the belated discovery of how young loggerheads find their way to sea revealed another of man's unintended intrusions into the natural scheme of things. Hatchlings head for the brightest light; the subtle difference between the sky over land or over reflective water is eclipsed by electric power. The halo of a city beyond an inland horizon attracts young turtles at night, which would naturally be the safest time for them to emerge. So does a stream of headlights along a coastal highway, or a few beach walkers carrying flashlights. Quite simply, any human development or presence can shorten the odds that a few newly hatched turtles will reach the relative safety of the sea. The lights we need to find our ways lead them astray. As a result, the once-thousand-mile range of breeding beaches along the Atlantic coast has shrunk drastically. A few islands off the Carolinas and Georgia are all that remain. The northernmost place they still breed spontaneously with some regularity is Cape Hatteras.

Even the short-term loss of a specific beach can permanently affect an entire species because turtles don't gather indiscriminately off any coast. Adults return to the beach where they were hatched. Authorities have tried to induce loggerheads to return to Assateague Island which straddles the Virginia-Maryland border, but the results are not encouraging. Eggs were imported from farther south and allowed to mature in raccoon-proof containers. Some hatched successfully, but few females have returned to nest in succeeding years. In decades of beach browsing I've only encountered four sea turtles: a 300-pounder on a lower Chesapeake Bay beach, another about the same size on Assateague and a hatchling behind a barrier dune a few miles north. All were dead. The fourth—possibly a sea turtle and most likely a loggerhead—was certainly alive when I saw it far out at sea. Sailing from Bermuda to the West Indies, I was at the sloop's helm late one calm night when something appeared in the water. It was only a glowing shape, bigger than a medicine ball but not as round, that rose to hover a foot below the surface of the ocean, then sank out of sight as we passed. If it was a loggerhead covered with phosphorescent growth, it would have had a pronounced beak, at least five scales along each side of its shell and an inability to completely retract its head. (Perhaps because it can't retreat entirely inside its shell, people who know say the reddish-brown loggerhead is vicious if molested.)

The other members of the family Chelonidae tend to be smaller than this one seemed. The green turtle *(Chelonia mydas),* which is brown in the Atlantic, takes its common name from the color of its fat. It grows to 4 feet and has been known to range as far north as Massachusetts. (The female of this species evidently only mates every three years but makes up for the hiatus by laying as many as six clutches of eggs in her breeding year.) The hawksbill *(Eretmochelys imbricata)* grows to 3 feet and has overlapping scales. The gray shelled ridley *(Lepidochelys kempi)* grows to 2 1/2 feet and has five scales along each side of its shell like the loggerhead. (The other two have four.) The leatherback *(Dermochelys coriacea)* belongs to another family and is the only sea turtle with an unplated leathery shell. The sole surviving member of a distinct biological suborder—and a giant that grows to 1,200 pounds—it is rarely seen by man.

However inevitable it may seem, the continued decline of these ancient creatures is deplorable. If we need a simple reason to hope for their return, just remember that they eat the Portuguese man-of-war. The larger reasons are ineffable.

A PROMISCUOUS PEST

In 1613 John Smith noted: "There is a beast they [the Indians] call Aroughcun, much like a badger but useth to live in trees." A century later, a Tidewater Virginia colonist wrote home to England about the same animal: "If taken young [it] is easily made tame but is the drunkenest creature living if he can get any liquor that is sweet and strong." This gentleman said his wild drinking buddy caught crabs cleverly, though whether drunk or sober isn't clear. I've not see this behavior described elsewhere, but pass the account on for what it may be worth. This animal reportedly backed up to a tidal creek and dipped its luxuriant tail in the brackish water. When a crab bit, the crabber leapt inland. Caught itself, it brought its catch to shore, then grabbed it with quick hands, tore off the biting claws and ate at leisure.

Now alarmingly familiar, the raccoon has prehensile digits which it uses to eat. This is only one of its anthropomorphic traits. *Procyon lotor* is one of North America's great opportunists. As noted, it has taken great advantage of the biologically recent absence of natural predators like the puma. With its own numbers largely unchecked, it has become a pest that does more serious damage than raiding campsites and robbing garbage cans. The recent decline in coon hunting as a sport has also undoubtedly contributed to the increase of this cunning animal whose intelligence rivals that of many monkeys. Inquisitive, adaptable and omnivorous, in recent years the raccoon has invaded many cities to feast on any kind of leftovers it can steal from people except onions. Wildlife biologists say the only real remaining check on its numbers is a form of distemper that flares up and thins out the population every few years.

Common throughout the continent (except in the tundra and high mountain regions), the raccoon prefers to nest in hollow trees. It regularly visits every beach within a night's foraging distance of a forest. Largely nocturnal, an adult raccoon unencumbered by young will use several nests and visit several feedings sites each night. Evidently it looks for new sources of food while making regular rounds of a wild (or settled) neighborhood. The notion that the raccoon always washes his food is a myth; many live in deserts. Given a choice, however, it seems to prefer aquatic animals and actively hunts crayfish, minnows, mollusks and crabs. A few raccoons have reportedly been found trapped by large oysters when the unmovable bivalve closed its shell on a coon's paw and the hunter couldn't escape an incoming tide.

Raccoons use their hands in surprising ways—even to block out unpleasant reality. (If the use of the term "hand" seems inappropriate, examine a coon's tracks.) Driving a wild October beach at dusk with a skilled naturalist, I spotted a small raccoon poking around the swash. We cornered the animal in the dunes and he put up a game fight, even lying on his back to bring his hind feet into the clawing action. The naturalist tossed his hat at it and caught the varmit with his bare hands to examine it. When the little coon realized he was captured, he surrendered abruptly, issued a few piteous mews, closed his eyes and covered his eyes with his paws in a parody of melodramatic human fright. Released again, he ran swiftly inland. (A full-grown raccoon may weigh 30 pounds. Despite my naturalist friend's example, even a little one shouldn't be trifled with. Armed with sharp claws and fierce teeth, this wild animal is a ferocious fighter that can disembowel a hound.)

Promiscuous and fecund, raccoons first mate in late winter and bear litters averaging 4 cubs after a two-month gestation period. The mother, who may mate three times a season and live a dozen years, might then produce a gross of offspring, which she raises and trains alone. The boars are solitary.

GREGARIOUS SEASONALS

The most common mammal of the coast is a ubiquitous seasonal migrant found in huge numbers, sometimes hundreds of thousands, crowding a few miles of sand from dune line to the surf zone. Growing as long as 2 meters, it exhibits a range of coloring from pale pink or whelk-foot beige to a brown as dark as the nut clam. Sexual dimorphism is the rule, the larger males tending toward hirsute bodies but glabrous heads while the reverse is found among females. Individuals of either gender may have rich hairy growths on the head and lesser pelage on the four extremities. The female possesses two mammary glands above the abdomen for suckling her young like a cetacean. External genitalia may not be apparent due to the coverings the species acquires much as the spider crab camouflages its carapace with algae. Whether this trait is of defensive or predatory origin has not been determined. It may have a sexual function.

Behavior is as erratic as individual morphology, which ranges from acutely slender to the rotundity of sea lions. Terrestrial air breathers, many of these creatures gambol in shallow waters, apparently in forms of play, like otters. Others are lethargic for entire diurnal periods in the open, though they wake to feed more frequently than the walrus. Sexual and pseudosexual behavior patterns have yet to be satisfactorily explained. Breeding habits are so complex as to defy simple categorization. For example, some pairs seem monogamous, while coupling among others appears almost random after brief courtship rituals. There is no correlation between copulation and seasonal, meteorological or temporal conditions, though mating commonly occurs at night. Despite their enormous numbers and reportedly frequent coupling, actual monozygous reproduction rates suggest high sterility. Sexual activity among individuals of the same gender occurs in highly localized sites. As many as 4,000 males have been observed massing on summer nights along one mile-long stretch of inner dune on Fire Island and engaging in inevitably fruitless behavior. (There is no satisfactory biological explanation for this activity which is rare elsewhere in the natural world except among a few marine mammals like orca and dolphins.)

Their senses are not acute. Poor swimmers and lacking swift mobility even on land, they seem to survive by virtue of their large numbers, omnivorous habits and dominating presence. As architects, the species exhibits a degree of activity surpassed only by some ants and African termites. Outside our range, some of their structures reportedly last for millennia, though nests and habitations along the Atlantic coast rarely survive more than a few decades and often less than a year. The detritus of their building activity—and of their simple seasonal appearance—is enormous. In small numbers their affects on the habitat are negligible. When they mass locally, however, they must be regarded as highly pestiferous. In large numbers they totally dominate a locality, decimating vegetation and driving away other animal species much as the great black-backed will exclude other gulls from a New England cove. They also extirpate prey species—birds, crustacea, fishes, even other large mammals. While some scattered individuals may be seen along the beach in winter, most appear during warm weather. *Homo sapiens* is an evolutionary oddity, the only extant member of its genus.

WHALES & COMPANY

Finally the truly marine mammals—animals to wonder at. Intelligent, even apparently articulate, these warm-blooded creatures live in an environment man can only visit. Some wag once remarked that their ancestors must have had better foresight than ours: Having gone to all the evolutionary trouble of colonizing the land, they looked around and returned to the sustaining sea while our antecedents stayed ashore that we might delight in things like war, gasoline engines and the Big Mac.

We've been acquainted with whales, inside and out, since Jonah's time, but never got to know them intimately. One of the ironies lies in the fact that while the study of marine mammals has mushroomed along with the other natural sciences, we've been hard-pressed to learn substantially more about them—because there are fewer whales to study. Of 92 species, a dozen are on the verge of extinction or worse. The cause of their demise and the extent of our knowledge combine in another irony: For centuries man observed whales in order to kill them. Some of the best de facto treatises on their biology and behavior were written in the cabins of whaling ships a century ago.

Nonetheless, many of the marine mammals' habits have been studied for their own sake—as opposed to the whalers'—in recent years. A few have been explained. Some will never be because their possessors have been exterminated so that people could continue having cheap sources of things like mink-farm food, watchmaker's oil, bicycle saddles and brushless shaving cream! Americans no longer participate in the slaughter though other nations continue. Was it excusable a century ago when folks "didn't know any better?" In his still useful treatise "On

Cetology" in *Moby Dick,* Herman Melville noted c. 1851 that the right whale was hunted as a source of "the oil specifically known as 'whale oil,' an inferior article in commerce." Farley Mowat, author of the extraordinary lyrical tragedy *A Whale for the Killing,* summed up the modern obscenity: "As I became older the whale became a symbol of the ultimate secrets which have not yet been revealed to us by the other animals. Whenever anything came to hand about whales I read it avidly; but the only thing which seemed to emerge . . . was that the whales appeared to be doomed by human greed to disappear and carry those secrets with them into oblivion."

People like James G. Mead, a curator of marine mammals at the Smithsonian, are doing what they can to stem this tide and to learn what can still be learned. Knowledge is where one finds it; in the case of whales, dolphins and porpoises the place is often a beach where these animals become stranded and die. Anyone who encounters such an unhappy spectacle can help science get some good from it by doing a couple of things. First, says Mead, take photographs while the animal is still in reasonably good condition. Include something of known length in each frame, like a yardstick or more likely a fishing rod, to establish an ascertainable scale. Second, send word to some appropriate authority: the National Park Service (if they hold sway on that beach), the Fish and Wildlife Service, the National Marine Fisheries Service, local or state police. Most of these organizations know to contact the Scientific Event Alert Network at the Smithsonian in Washington, D.C. You might remind them to phone SEAN, do it yourself or send a collect wire via Western Union to the Network, Telex # 1776. SEAN, incidentally, is interested in almost any major unusual happenings, like the appearance of sea turtles and other dwindling animals.

Given our limited and slowly expanding knowledge, what is a whale (for the time being)? By biological definition, a member of the order Cetacea, a cetacean. One suborder comprises the toothed whales, including the sperm whale (*Physeter catodon,* i.e., Moby Dick), the narwhal *(Monodon monoceros)* whose single tusk in the male perhaps inspired myths of the fabulous unicorn, and the true dolphins and porpoises. A second suborder (Mysticeti) includes the baleen whales, those enormous filter feeders whose curious mouth parts strain tons of plankton, small crustacea and fish from ocean water.

The earliest sea mammals returned to the oceans from land on the order of 50 to 65 million years B.P., long enough ago to have found ways to use the density of the aquatic medium to their advantage. For one thing, they telecommunicate, speaking across—or rather through—hundreds of miles of water in some cases. For another, they evolved into the largest animals to ever live, since the water itself would support living bulk too ponderous to carry its own weight on land. The largest dinosaur, a swamp inhabitant and vegetarian, approached 70 feet in length. Three whale species just about match or exceed that dimension alone. The 100-foot blue whale weighs about four times as much as any brontosaurus ever did. (The largest on record was a female measuring 106 feet and weighing 150 tons.) But it may be that the blue, one of the baleen whales, is about to become as extinct as the dinosaur. Reduced from perhaps 300,000 to an estimated population of 9,000 and largely confined to the Antarctic, this once cosmopolitan species' numbers may have diminished beyond the point of no return.

If living in water had advantages, it also presented severe problems which these air-breathers solved with remarkable evolutionary inventiveness. The nostrils moved to the top of the head so a whale could respire without standing on its tail. The bronchial tree developed cartilaginous arches (like the human windpipe) down to the smallest branches to facilitate fast breathing. A whale can empty its lungs and inhale 500 gallons of fresh air in 2 seconds. These speeds and quantities are responsible for the larger whales' visible spouts, which differ from species to species. Air compressed in the lungs expands and its moisture content condenses when released.

At first the ancestral whales must have been content to inhabit surface waters. But over time they contrived ways to plumb the depths and reap the benefits of vast new food supplies. The sperm whale, which feeds almost exclusively on giant squid, can dive at least 3,000 feet. (Some have tangled with transoceanic telephone cables at that depth and drowned.) The physiological engineering needed to enable such dives is extraordinary. Blood supplies to muscle tissues are reduced in deep water in order to conserve oxygen for the brain and vital organs. In addition, something had to be done to prevent "the bends." If a large-lunged animal like a human diver rises too fast from oceanic depths, changes in pressure cause formation of nitrogen bubbles in the blood with crippling or fatal results. The diving whales got around the problem by reducing the relative size of their lungs by 90 percent and storing oxygen in muscle tissues. Their flesh contains the same oxygen-binding component as our red blood cells. To increase hydrodynamic efficiency, they shed their body hair. To cope with cold they grew layers of insulating blubber which also provide a reserve supply of metabolic food. Their circulatory systems became arranged so that cold blood returns to the heart in vessels surrounding and being warmed by the arteries. To conserve a whale mother's internal water supply, whale milk came to have the consistency of cottage cheese. This milk, which is pumped out by muscle contractions, has four times the fat content of primate milk. Thus the infant has a high-calorie diet, but not a very moist one. How do the young avoid dehydration? Metabolic breakdown of fats creates large amounts of water as a byproduct.

The physiological marvels go on and on. Yet one of the most startling facts is that these mammals exhibit some of man's best traits: affection, loyalty and humor. They direct these emotions not only to others of their own kind but to us as well, despite what our species has done to them. Since it is understandably difficult to observe these animals closely in the wild, much of the most carefully documented behavioral data has been collected in aquaria and marinelands where several of the smaller whales thrive. But whales' charity to man has been seen at sea as well. There are reliable accounts of dolphins driving away sharks (their own natural enemies) from human swimmers, even of helping a floundering person stay afloat and reach shore. In controlled environments analogous behavior is clearly seen in the way common and bottlenosed dolphins treat their young. All cetaceans are born tailfirst and a newborn dolphin that doesn't spontaneously thrash to the surface to breathe is helped—nudged up—by the mother or an accompanying "midwife." The companion female will swim with the new mother for as long as three months, frequently in formation with one adult protecting the young calf on either side. Active assistance of another individual is not simply maternal behavior; dolphins will also surround an injured adult and physically help it reach the surface to breathe.

These animals talk back and forth in highpitched whistles that clearly communicate information. They can also mimic human speech, which must seem to them a slow and monotonous language since they can make and hear sounds from 150 to 150,000 cycles per second, well beyond human hearing, indeed beyond the aural ken of everything but bats. In addition, they navigate with another kind of sound, a form of biological sonar, emitting as many as 400 curious, highly directional clicks a second and reading the echoes for precise information about what's ahead—food fish in particular.

It goes without saying that of the many cetaceans, only a few are seen from the Atlantic beach. These are the most common:

Porpoise v. Dolphin

Generally speaking, porpoises have blunt noses and stubby bodies while dolphins have long noses and slender bodies.

The harbor or common porpoise is no exception. *Phocoena phocoena* reaches 6 feet in length and a weight of 120 pounds. Not one of the notably playful cetaceans, it doesn't often jump or gambol around boats, although it does enter rivers and come close to the New England shore in summer, searching for bottom fishes and schools of herring, menhaden and mackerel. Generally dark gray or greenish brown, this porpoise has an almost triangular dorsal fin with a sloping rear edge rather than a deep curve.

These porpoises travel in pairs or groups of up to 150 and mate in late spring. The young, born 11 months later, are half their mothers' length.

In contrast, the common dolphin *(Delphinus delphis)* often leaps from the water and plays in the bow waves of boats. Its taller dorsal fin has a curved trailing edge. Also called the saddleback, Delphinus has a black back, white belly and distinctive crisscross pattern along the sides. The snout is slender. A wide-ranging animal, it is the topic of some taxonomic controversy that revolves around a simple question: Do slightly different characteristics represent distinct species, subspecies or races of the same species? At the moment the consensus leans toward including them all in one species, but of course this division is subject to taxonomic change.

Along the East Coast the common dolphin is most often seen not far from the Gulf Stream, which meanders quite close to the Outer Banks and Massachusetts' outer islands some years. The adult may measure more than 8 feet from the tip of its nose to the cleft of its flukes.

The closely related bottlenose dolphin *(Tursiops truncatus)* is lighter colored and larger, growing to 12 feet. Blue-gray above and lighter below, it shows no distinct pattern along the flanks. "Flipper" of television fame was one of this breed. In captivity juvenile males engage in rather lively masturbatory activity. They direct their affections at "almost anything that moves, from fish to turtles to other dolphins,"—even to qualified mammalogists swimming in the same tank, according to one of the latter.

The pothead, blackfish, or pilot whale was hunted unmercifully for meat and blubber. Thoreau saw them stampeded by fishermen into the shallows along Cape Cod in the 1840s. The question remains why they came near shore in the first place, since these are deepwater denizens.

Today their occasional mass strandings are still unexplained. For a while it was suspected that ear parasites damaged their sonar so that they failed to pick up the changing echoes of a gently sloping mud bottom. But later research disproved this notion. In *Globicephala melaena* ear mites are "common as fleas on a dog." Even the healthiest animals have them, or so it now appears. Since they've rarely encountered a stable physical obstacle in deep water, Dr. Mead believes "they're unaware the ocean has sides." The reasons a bull leads his herd ashore remain known only to him.

Solid black except for a white belly mark between the flippers, the pothead or pilot whale has a globular forehead as round as an antique iron kettle. The sloping dorsal fin, much wider at its base than at the top, has a deeply curved trailing edge. At birth the pilot whale is 5 feet long. Females mature at about 6 years, males at about 12. They grow to 28 feet on a diet of squid, small fish and invertebrates. Some authorities believe they live 25 years; others estimate a life-span twice that long.

Call Me Orca

The killer whale does not deserve its wretched reputation. Were it a car, a toothpaste or a movie star, someone would simply announce a rechristening and it would soar in popular esteem. *Orcinus orca* grows to a robust 30 feet of hydrodynamic power; it may be the fastest animal in the sea. Sheathed in an ebony-black skin highlighted by a dashing patch of white behind each eye and a white belly, this noble wolf of the oceans boasts the tallest dorsal fin of all the proud cetaceans. . . . (Get the idea?)

Certainly orca is a killer, but so's a kitty cat when it gets the chance. Like wolves, African lions and primitive men, these whales hunt strategically in packs to bring down prey a single individual couldn't handle. A group will even vanquish the largest baleen whales. Unlike sharks and the highly regarded bluefish, they are not known for wanton killing. Nor is there any documented account of their having attacked a human swimmer. In captivity (where they're well fed), they accept training and peaceably share a tank with dolphins which they'd hunt in the wild.

Killer whales hunt other warm-blooded creatures—not only other cetaceans, but seals and birds. In the higher latitudes, orca will rear out of the water to snatch prey from an ice flow. This takes not only what we consider ferocity, but great agility and sophisticated sight as well.

Consider: From a whale's underwater viewpoint, the apparent position of a penguin on a ledge is skewed by the water's refraction. Like trained dolphins, this carnivore compensates for the distortion to unerringly grasp its quarry.

Killer whales are often seen in large groups, notably at the northern and southern extremes of the Atlantic coast. The sharp, straight-edged dorsal fin, almost the shape of a dunce cap in profile, is unmistakable.

Little is known about orca's reproductive cycle. Recent investigations suggest that these whales engage in episodic homosexual activity. Young males are escorted away from the rest of the herd and apparently "raped" by older bulls. This zoologically rare form of complex hierarchical behavior may be a form of training or a way to establish dominance within a social group.

Great Whales

The fin or finback whale *(Balaenoptera physalus)*, also called the common rorqual, is sometimes seen off our coast. "Rorqual," used to describe all whales with throat grooves, comes from a Scandinavian word for tube, since when they were butchered the throat skin looked like a sliced row of hollow cylinders. Grooved or tubed, the throat skin functions like the pleats in a kilt. Swimming through great swarms of small fish like herring, or shrimplike crustaceans called krill, the whale takes hundreds of gallons of water in its mouth, expanding its throat in the process. With the mouth closed, its two-ton tongue squeezes the water out through the baleen plates that hang in thick fringes inside the lips. The krill are trapped inside the baleen and swallowed. When not expanded for feeding, the throat skin returns to its pleated appearance.

The fin whale's lips are not symmetrically colored. The lower left jaw is gray, the lower right white. The left side of the tongue is not pigmented, the right is. This whale may be 70 feet long. On a calm day its spout may rise 20 feet straight into the air.

The humpback *(Megaptera novaengliae)* is another rorqual that sometimes appears off the beach. Averaging less than 50 feet, it has very long white flippers and many irregular lumps on its head, snout and flippers. The most acrobatic of the great whales, it often jumps out of the water and rolls on the surface. Its spout is described as "low and bushy."

The 50-foot right whale is another filter feeder but not a rorqual since it lacks the pleated throat. It has a very bulbous lower jaw. While its near relatives have small dorsal fins, *Eubalaena glacialis* has none. This was once one of the very common cetaceans but now only a few hundred remain in the Atlantic because it was "the right whale to hunt" for its blubber—hence its common name. Those that survive migrate close to shore early each year, appearing off Florida in January or February, arriving off Cape Cod in April and summering northwards of the Gulf of Maine. Evidently they return south offshore, for they are seldom seen making fall migrations.

The right whale's spout is often almost invisible since when this whale swims along the surface it breathes every minute or two and thus doesn't compress vast quantities of air in the lungs that form condensation clouds when released.

Driftwords:

A Most Instructive Fish

Tomorrow is the equinox. Tonight will be longer than the day, and I am closer to the end of this writing than the beginning. Worse, I'm drowning in information. Natural systems become imponderable in their infinite combinations and permutations. Grab at an idea among so many and it squirms away. Data swarm like schools of fish, finding elusive safety in their very numbers, which is why small prey species swarm —so that some survive their predators. Some days I feel like a red-tailed hawk who can't zero in on a single sparrow in the flock. So he rests a while and is mobbed by passerines. One at a time I might capture every concept, but they're flying at me in flocks: Pheromones. Hypothalamus functions. Ecdysis. Rhizome regeneration. Decapod population dynamics. Percolation rates of sand. Elegant questions like "Are There Any Obligate Halophytes?" Crude ones like "Which taxonomist is right about the mollusks?"

The work becomes mesmerizing in its distractions; the information so diverse there can be no order. I search for similes to describe why I surrender more often every week—then every day—to the notion that there can be no simple explanations, but the metaphors themselves fail. I want something as elegant as the cycle E.B. White perceived on his Maine farm: "The worm fattens on the apple, the young goose fattens on the wormy fruit, the man fattens on the young goose, the worm awaits the man." But life along the littoral isn't that tidy.

The interactions of marine systems are insensibly complicated, meaninglessly complex. Consider the unspeakably extended food chains. They work this way: Microscopic plants (phytoplankton) make living matter out of inorganic material. (That's the textbook definition of a plant, after all, the inherent talent that distinguishes plant from animal: Plants make food; animals must eat organic stuff to live.) Little fishes eat the plankton, a slightly larger fish eats the fry and is eaten by a bigger fish in turn, which becomes dinner for a tuna or an osprey. When that predator dies in turn, it is eaten by maggots and carrion birds which defecate into the sea, returning a few wet particles to the water. They sink, decompose, break down into inorganic components at last, then well up with a current of cold water to be absorbed by phytoplankton again. And so it goes. Cyclical? Not really. There are cycles, of course, but the system depends more on vegetative manufacture of new organic matter from inorganic minerals; a form of creativity fueled by the sun's energy. Yet this all requires so many intermediate steps that it becomes vague as it stretches out.

Yesterday, more out of duty than anything else, I read about an incomparably drab fish. Everybody's heard of the menhaden; nobody cares. Too oily to eat and too numerous to have any more heroic appeal than lemmings, menhaden are like dust motes on the Yellow Brick Road of marine science. They seem something to be washed away by tank trucks filled from fire hydrants while a city sleeps. Beneath contempt, too common to spark interest. Sure, because they are so numerous that they support the largest commercial fishery on the East Coast in dollar terms. Huge nets catch them by the millions and factories turn them into meal, fertilizer, oil. A hundred drab industries depend on them for everything from paint to pet food. I couldn't care less as I took *Fishes of the Gulf of Maine* from the shelf. The book is one of those exhaustive catalogues that tells absolutely everything known (pro tem) about something. Information for the record. Boring facts aligned like cobblestones. Tedious data laid brick upon brick in a Chinese wall of information. Has a scientist said "Eureka!" since Archimedes' day? I yawned and read till the library closed. The epiphany came after dinner; a jot of knowledge emerged like a scarlet butterfly from the cocoon built by a brown worm, like an iridescent scarab out of the dung (a critter the ancients considered holy because it seemed to spontaneously create itself out of manure).

Bigelow and Schroeder noted that no other local fish "has a filtering apparatus comparable to that of the pogy, nor has it any rival in the Gulf in its utilization of the planktonic vegetable pasture. Menhaden feed . . . by swimming with the mouth open and the gill openings spread. We have often seen specimens in the aquarium at Woods Hole doing this. And we have watched small ones in Chesapeake Bay, swimming downward as they feed, then turning upward to break the surface with their snouts, still with open mouths. The mouth and pharyngeal sieve act exactly as a tow net, retaining whatever is large enough to enmesh, with no voluntary selection of particular plankton units. The prey thus captured (as appears from the stomach contents) includes small annelid worms, various minute Crustacea, schizopod and decapod larvae, and rotifers, but these are greatly outnumbered as a rule by the sundry unicellular plants, particularly diatoms. . . . And the food eaten at a general locality parallels the general plankton content of the water, except that none of the larger animals appear in the stomachs of the fish on the one hand, nor the very smallest organisms . . . on the other. The menhaden, in short, parallels the whalebone [baleen] whales, the basking shark, and the giant devil rays in its mode of feeding, except that its diet is finer because its filter is closer meshed."

The menhaden filters phytoplankton from 6 quarts of sea water a minute. This is their only food. Straining the sea with their gills, they live on the most elementary plants. In a year a menhaden grows to 6 inches. It lives and manages to multiply because each school is too enormous to be obliterated by marauding predators, whether other fish or man. In turn it is fodder for every predatory fish in the sea that deigns to snap at it: cod, haddock, tuna. When the rapacious bluefish massacre the menhaden, far more of the little fish are killed wantonly than eaten. (Put that in your pipe; man is not the only wastrel.) They become carrion, food for both "higher" animals and lower ones: for gulls, beach fleas, sand crabs; even fertilizer for beach plants staking out temporary turf at the spring tide-line.

But their living tissues are only a step away from being inorganic matter! Some of the stuff that is a menhaden today lay at the bottom of the ocean floor last night as particles of sodium, phosphorus, magnesium and the rest. A minute plant absorbed these molecules and used solar energy to convert them into living vegetation. Menhaden ate these plants, metabolically converting them into fat and muscle before they themselves became the food for bigger fishes like the crazy blues, for birds like gulls, terns and osprey, for foraging mammals like coons along the beach, even for man's stinking factories. Chemicals naturally became meat. (Eureka?) Here was a food chain small enough to grasp. The drab menhaden—a fish numerous enough to feed a multitude without a miracle—is the missing link, the single connector between an alpha and omega.

Doesn't something else eat plankton too? Of course. It's the nutritional wherewithal of every filter feeder, the bivalves in particular: mussels, scallops, clams, which are eaten by snails, starfish and a thousand fin fishes. Go further. Zooplankton and shrimplike krill eat the tiny plants; baleen whales eat the krill in millions; a blue whale eats 4 tons a day. Now there's a noble link, a nexus of true grandeur: from inorganic molecule to Mysticeti in three easy steps. I love it. It lets me grasp. With the simple examples in hand I could compound it. Phytoplankton feed zooplankton and/or krill which feeds the whale. A larval crab, a barnacle, or a sea clam eats a diatom. A moon snail eats the clam, a starfish eats the snail, a lobster eats the starfish and a cod eats the lobster. As a kid I was dosed with cod liver oil and must have needed it because it tasted good. Phytoplankton fed me! And still does. Tomorrow I'll celebrate with a lobster, thanks to plankton and the sun.

Part II
The Physical Beach

Before the beach became a fertile habitat for countless birds, clams, crabs, insects, fish, worms, amphibians, reptiles and more (and before it became a place for mammals including man to visit) it had first to become—well, a beach. The geological processes that made it began eons ago and, abetted by evolutionary botany, show no signs of stopping. This place, ancient and perpetual, continues to change. Enchanted, man has tried to arrest the beach, to settle here and alter it for his convenience. Yet it continues to grow and change to suit itself. It always will.

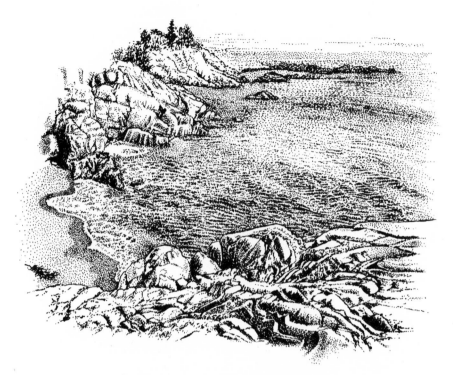

Glacier's legacy: a New England cove.

Chapter Six

$$E = 41\,H^2T^2$$
—Littorally Speaking

Serene as it may seem on a calm day, the physical beach is bewilderingly complex. The forces that made it—and constantly remake it—vary from glacially deliberate to quick as spindrift. Barrier islands may grow and shrink imperceptibly for millennia, then vanish between one storm-charged high tide and the next. Sand spits can lengthen for centuries or appear overnight. The time frame and geographic range of the dynamic Atlantic coast are enormous, yet all change depends on the individual movements of infinitesimal sand grains. And therein lies the secret to understanding the physical aspects of beaches. Things happen grain by single grain or one wave at a time. Each process is simple—even commonsensical—but the combined results are staggering because waves keep coming ashore endlessly. What changes the face of the shore (and what boggles the mind) are the progressions of events, the interactions of diverse forces, the geometrically compounded results of many phenomena. Considered singly they are easy enough to understand.

The bottom line is plain: Every beach changes constantly, even those that appear the same on each visit. Every wave brings sand with it and carries some away. If the amounts are about equal over a day's time or a decade's, the beach looks no different. In fact, it is not the same beach just, as Buddha said, a river is the same and different hour by hour. Composed of a most incohesive material, a beach moves minutely, grows or shrinks with every ripple and tide. Some "accrete" and "erode" in an annual cycle; others build out or recede for decades at a stretch. Some, destroyed in a single hurricane, reappear again by spring or emerge somewhere else.

A reporter for the *Vineyard Gazette* tells this perplexing tale: To the nineteenth-century entrepreneurs who bought it, Skiff's Island, off the southeast corner of Martha's Vineyard, seemed a lovely place for a Victorian resort. They returned the following spring for a site inspection with a high-priced architect, but they couldn't find the place. It was gone. Years later it emerged again and lingered to become a traditional turning-point in an annual sailing race that was won year after year by one yachtsman. Then a challenger finished first and the cup defender cried foul; the first boat had cut a corner and sailed inside that mark. "What mark?" the newcomer asked. The island had sunk again.

That's the way with things made of sand; they come and go. But left to their own devices, an Ivory Soap percentage of the world's sand beaches take care of themselves quite nicely, thank you, for generation after human generation. They are made, unmade, and remade by three things: wind, water and sand.

Since earth's adolescence, wind and rain have eroded the mountains, creating broken rock, boulders, gravel and sand—especially incalculable amounts of the latter. By definition sand is bits of inert material ranging in diameter from .0625 to 2 millimeters on the size of a pin point to that of a pencil lead. We think of erosion as a negative process: It makes a coast retreat; it steals a farmer's topsoil; it makes molehills out of mountains. But it is also creative; sand is its end product, the raw material of beaches. As the mountains were worn down by wind and rain, the smaller stuff which they became was washed downhill. Rivers continue to deliver sand into the oceans today, and the ocean water continues delivering sand to the rims of islands and continents.

The material of most North American beaches is 90 percent quartz, a major component of granite, visibly earth's most plentiful rock. Many trace elements and varying amounts of gemstones such as garnet and topaz are found on any beach. There are also heavy minerals like ilmenite and magnetite, an iron ore especially plentiful on Block Island's Crescent Beach which was mined in colonial times for material used to blot manuscript ink. When strong winds scour a beach, the lighter stuff is blown away and the heavy particles remain. Crescent Beach can turn so black that newcomers suspect an oil spill. Parts of Fire Island turn nearly blood-red in winter, when only heavy grains of garnet compose the surface. Broken shell is another common ingredient of littoral sand. Many beaches below the Outer Banks are composed mostly of the crumbled exoskeletons of marine animals. On St. Croix in the Virgin Islands a short stretch is made entirely of tiny, intact seashells the size of a baby's fingernails.

Since some sand is created in the ocean from shingle or gravel—grist for the ceaseless marine mill—it might seem that all sand is on its way to becoming powder. This is not the case. When each grain becomes a critical small size, it collects a film of water. This wet cushion keeps it from touching other grains and disintegrating more. (The fact that sand grains don't touch uniformly, like a brick wall, has another marvelous result. Spaces between the grains constitute an aquatic habitat for the meiofauna, a multitude of microscopic animals. Too inconspicuous to be included here, they stand on the bottom rung of a zoological ladder, the predator food chain, since they are the smallest prey animals of the beach.)

In deep water, below the reach of surface wave energy, some sand lies still. But anywhere water moves—whether in terrestrial streams or at sea in response to tides, currents and some waves—this material moves as well. This brings up the matter of "competence": the inherent ability of water to transport solid stuff. It is one fundamental mechanism responsible for the beach. The amount of transported material depends on its own particle size and density and on the speed of the moving water. Slight currents transport silt; a 2 1/2-knot current moves inch-round stones. When a given volume of water moves fast, it picks up more material (and bigger particles); when the same current slows down for any reason, it drops some of its solid burden. Coastal waves carrying

sand from an offshore bar and breaking on a beach lose their competence; they drop the sand which builds up the shore. When stronger
storm waves run up a beach, their water swashes back fast enough and
in sufficient amounts to carry sand away. Then the shore retreats.
(Rocky beaches seem more stable than ones made of fine sand. In part
this is because it takes more water moving faster to move stones; it's also
a function of percolation. More water sinks through the surface of a
beach made of big particles. The finer the sand, the slower the percolation rate and more water runs along the surface slope to carry anything
present away.) This, simplistically, is how the edge of a beach comes
and goes. (The upper beach responds to another medium, to be covered
later.) Entire beaches, one expert writes without fear of contradiction,
are "the most dynamic systems of the physical landscape."

The obvious variables of water volume, water speed, and sand size
account for huge boulders remaining in place in the surf off Martha's
Vineyard and for a weeping actress's mascara to smudge her cheek. At
one extreme some objects are just too big to be moved by waves, so
Vineyard settlers could mark their boundaries from offshore boulders.
Old photographs of Gay Head prove that some rocks have remained in
place at least since the last century. However, it bears remembering that
the ocean periodically displays extraordinary force. In *The Sea Around Us*
Rachel Carson noted that Scottish engineers were dumbstruck in 1872
when a storm destroyed a huge concrete breakwater that weighed 800
tons and was tied to underwater rocks with iron rods. They replaced it
with a stoutly anchored pier that weighed more than 2,600 tons. Five
years later another storm carried it away.

Glaciers of the last ice age played key roles in creating today's coastline. During cold phases of the weather cycle, more snow fell each year
than melted and evaporated. This meant an annual increase in the snow
cover of the polar regions. As the snowpack accumulated over Labrador
(in particular), its lower levels were compressed into dense ice. The
Wisconsin glacier, the last of the Pleistocene epoch, grew to a thickness
of 10,000 feet—two miles, or about the height of the *tops* of fair-weather
cumulus clouds today. Its enormous weight made its lower portions
behave in a plastic manner; neither like a true solid nor a liquid, but
something between the two. Acting like viscous, chilled honey, the
lower plastic ice squeezed out around the bottom of the thickening
glacier as new snow kept accumulating and making the whole heavier.
In effect, the glacier grew horizontally in all directions and "advanced"
down across what became New England.

As the ice advanced like a frozen flood, it changed the existing mountains drastically, cutting through them in places, wearing them down, breaking, grinding, polishing, creating sand and raw material for more sand through erosion. The glacier moved "downhill" across inland New England, crossing Maine to carve steep valleys and fjords, including the 1,000-foot chasm of Soames Sound on Mount Desert Island, until it finally ran aground miles offshore. The glacier's leading edge swept the land clean, pushing all loose (and newly loosened) material ahead of it. When the ice began to melt and the glacier to shrink, this mixed debris remained behind in moraines like rows of sweeping compound left by a colossally careless janitor. The Pleistocene's sinuous outermost moraine formed Long Island's backbone to Montauk Point, Block Island, Martha's Vineyard and Nantucket. The glacier melted, then advanced again to push up another moraine. This one made Orient Point (the other half of Long Island's swallow-tailed east end), the edge of Rhode Island, the Elizabeth Islands that run northeast to the armpit of Cape Cod, and the humerus of the Cape itself. Familiar with the Vineyard, I felt a sense of *déjà vu* the first time I visited Block Island. Some cliffs seemed the same; they are composed of the same clays transported by the same glacier.

The glaciers had other legacies as well. They would surround masses of material, then wrench it along as they advanced and drop it when they stopped. This resulted in isolated pockets of debris, "drumlins" like the three dozen islands in Boston harbor. When the glaciers receded they didn't creep backwards of course. They melted where they were. Their water carried finer material downhill, creating outwash plains broken here and there by distinct streams running to the sea. Melting summer after summer, they distributed material fairly evenly across shallow seaward slopes as far south as Delaware Bay. Melting was not perfectly uniform. Blocks of ice broken off the glacier would be isolated. Sand and gravel built up in natural dykes around their frozen forms. When these blocks melted, they left depressions in the new land which became "kettle ponds" if the bottom was impermeable clay. Block Island, only 7 miles long and 3 miles at its widest, has 365 of these freshwater ponds. Cape Cod has dozens more, most of them characteristically round from the action of windblown waves on their once ragged shores.

A secondary result of that ice age was the fall of sea level around the globe as 8 million cubic miles of the world's water was trapped and stored in the glaciers. During the last glacial period sea level fell some

300 feet below its present level. Until as little as 12,000 years ago the Atlantic began a few hundred miles east of where it's found today. Elephant teeth 25,000 years old have been dredged from mud 80 miles offshore. With a warming climate and glacial melt, sea level then rose rapidly for millennia—perhaps 8 inches per century. The modern coastline took its shape between 3,000 and 5,000 years ago, no older age than Stonehenge. When the glaciers melted, sea level rose again. New England coastal valleys flooded. North-south chains of glacier-carved mountains became islands and irregular peninsulas separated by bays and inlets. Maine's labyrinthine coast is the modern legacy of ice-cut chasms which were filled by the encroaching sea.

But the changing relationship between land and sea over the ages is complicated by the fact that while sea level has risen, the land rebounded too. The incalculable weight of ice depressed even the bedrock of the earth's crust. Boston was 600 feet lower 15,000 years ago. Much of the Down East coast is still slowly rising, like the surface of a pillow on an unmade bed after a late sleeper has run off to work. Meanwhile, other coasts seem to be submerging today because sea level continues to rise at the rate of about 4 inches a century. This is particularly important on the mid-Atlantic coast below New England, the stretch composed almost entirely of barrier islands: Fire Island, the New Jersey shore, the Delmarva peninsula, the Outer Banks, Georgia's Sea Islands and the east coast of Florida. Along this enormous reach the ocean doesn't pound the continent itself as it does from northern Massachusetts to southern Maine or from Oregon to Mexico. Rather, the chain of low sand islands absorbs the impact of the seas and protects the low-lying mainland. Being malleable, the islands move and migrate in response to the sea.

There are several theoretical explanations for barrier islands. Less than a century ago G. K. Gilbert suggested that they resulted from sand spits that formed parallel to the coast from corners of mainland or rocky peninsulas. Here water's competence comes into play again since an alongshore current moves up or down almost every beach. If a deepwater source supplies sand, the alongshore current (or littoral drift) drops it wherever the water slows down, like on a shoaling bottom, on a sandbar that impedes the waves or on the downstream side of a point where the current changes direction. Flowing continually, the current brings new sand with it. Shoals grow shallower if they retard the current; spits lengthen. In many places the littoral drift built spits across broad inlets, turning them into landlocked ponds cut off from the sea by a straight narrow barrier of sand. Look at a map of Martha's Vineyard. The ponds on the island's south side were once open bays until sand spits closed them. Some time ago that coast was ragged and irregular. Now it runs remarkably straight for 15 miles from Chappaquiddick to Chilmark.

If a spit didn't completely cut off ocean access, it created a lagoon between the mainland and the new barrier; a prime place for salt marshes to grow. In time the original spit would be breached at random places by storms. Long, narrow islands resulted, as along the New Jersey coast. Where that coast now lacks islands, as at Sandy Hook, it is because the broken sand spits have slowly migrated all the way to the mainland, pushed by the relentless sea.

In our time V. P. Zenkovich, a Russian geologist, proposed the "drowning hypothesis" to explain other barrier island chains. It apparently applies to the Outer Banks in particular, which may be the remains of a huge ancient river delta. This theory holds that when the Atlantic seaboard was farther east, the coastline inevitably featured some lines of earthern hills and river valleys. As glaciers melted and sea level rose, a rising ocean drowned the river mouths and invaded the valleys behind the outermost hills. The results are easy to imagine. Waves began breaking on the old hills' eastern slopes as sea level continued to rise. In fairly short order, inland plants must have perished from salt spray; soil and silt washed away. The soluble matter disintegrated or dissolved, leaving only inert detritus; i.e., sand. As the old hills shrank, waves and tides brought new sand to them from offshore. During gentle weather, the beach built out from the edge of the old hill; during storms the hills were eroded more and sand was deposited on them. This sand would be distributed by wind. Thus the old line of hills gradually changed into a barrier of sand which continued to protect the lagoons and marshes that developed. Though superficially the Outer Banks look like pure sand islands, borings between Wimble Shoals and Ocracoke Inlet reveal layers of old red clay which were deposited during the Pleistocene. The overlying sand came after the ice age. (Elsewhere, notably on the land that became the Vineyard's colorful Gay Head, the glaciers pushed around old clay deposits of previous ages.)

One of the earliest barrier island theories, suggested by a French geologist more than a century ago, held that as waves crossed the shoaling continental shelf, they built up ridges of sand that finally broke through the surface of the sea. An attractive but largely discounted idea, it had a weak point as fragile as the sandbars it depended on. Bars do build up off many coasts as ocean currents bring sand from deepwater lodes. But when these bars rise close to the surface of an ocean or active bay, waves and tides usually carry their sand away before the bar can emerge as an island. This is another function of competence and the energy trapped in ocean water. (The emergent theory can work but most commonly in lakes and calm bays. Skiff's Island is exceptional. That odd island comes and goes due to a rare combination of factors: the convergence of two sand-laden littoral currents; fluctuations in both the weather cycle and the rate of sea level rise; the presence of shoals, and the probability that a glacial island once stood there.)

The rule that undermined the Frenchman's theory brings up a fundamental factor in beach dynamics: waves. They are deceptive things which exert themselves underwater as well as on the surface. Actually each individual wave is part of something larger, a series. An ocean wave is manifested energy. Wind blowing across the water confers energy to the fluid; the water receives energy from the passing air to become kinetic, to have superficial waves. Surprisingly (perhaps), individual particles of wind-driven ocean water do not move major distances as the waves move. Rather, the water particles describe small circular orbits that remain in place while the waves pass. (Certainly water particles move en masse with tides, currents and surf, but those are different circumstances.) If the water isn't moving, what is? Pure energy. The apparent motion of ocean waves is the manifestation of energy borrowed from the wind which disturbs the visible surface of the water. It is much the same as a sound wave, or the energy wave a child in a cowboy suit imparts to a length of clothesline when he jiggles it to make a "snake" along the ground.

An ocean wave is not an independent entity, like a punch in the nose; each visible "wave" is part of the waves before and behind it. Every wave in the ocean is connected to all the other waves that derive energy from the same source. We use the word to mean a single crest; the wave is also the entire stream of energy—the whole series of crests and troughs. The energy imparted by a storm flows through the water until it is released on some shore. Hence, a gale off Tierra del Fuego can be felt by sensitive instruments on the coast of Cornwall 6,000 miles away.

Take it as given that many energy waves pass through the same bit of ocean simultaneously. Some pass obliquely. Some, going in the same general direction, travel at different speeds. Some nearly identical waves, meeting head-on, almost cancel each other out. In mid-ocean, where waves come from several directions and at different frequencies, the water rises to cone-shaped peaks and then subsides—as the high points of several waves coincide at one place for an instant. In a gale, of course, the wind's energy moves across the water in one direction, creating a surface pattern that dominates all the energy waves coming from other sources. Close to their source, waves tend to be steep and irregular; over long distances, they organize themselves, extending the wave length (the distance between crests) to become gentler, more regular swells. They keep going until something interferes; like the sheer Dover cliffs, or a breakwater at Atlantic City, or a low, sloping natural sand beach. This is why waves still wash a coast on perfectly windless days.

When the bottom of a wave runs into shallow water, it "feels" the bottom; some of its energy is lost through friction against the sloping sea floor and the wave slows down. Land changes the course and character of every series of waves. Any obstacle—even a sandbar—alters waves that reach it; the ocean and shore interact, each affecting the other. Along a reasonably straight coast, underwater topography organizes the waves so that they approach the land more or less parallel to it. In turn, the sandy bottom and the beach itself respond to the direction of oncoming waves and are shaped by them. If a coast has points and peninsulas, they receive the brunt of the waves' energy; coves are struck more gently as the waves bend around the points and lengthen. Thus less forceful waves reaching into protected water are not as steep. They bring in sand grain by grain and leave it on the shore, creating a pocket beach.

When waves approach a sheer cliff they bounce back, returning seaward and directing their energy elsewhere. But some of their energy is lost in the collision. In time the repetitive action of the water breaks off pieces of rock which is weakened by chemical action. Rocky outcrops succumb to air pressure as well as to the force of the water. As a wave curls, it traps air beneath it. Breaking directly against a cliff, the wave can force a large amount of air into the rocks' crevices where it is compressed even more. Given enough compression, the air pressure bursts the rock apart at the seams from time to time. Another cause of cliff erosion is the crumbled pieces of rock broken off before. Later waves toss these back at the vertical shore like missiles.

Though water particles don't move far as a result of waves, the effects are dramatic when water itself is transported, rather than just disturbed by energy passing through it. This happens where currents or tides occur or when waves break. Surface tension holds a wave together as it rises—up to a point. But when wave length (the distance from crest to crest) becomes less than seven times the wave height (the vertical distance between trough and crest) surface tension is no longer strong enough to hold the wave together. Then it falls down upon itself whether at sea or along a coast.

When a wave enters shoal water and feels the bottom, the lower part of the wave slows down while the top of the wave continues moving at the same pace. The average wavelength shortens as the waves pile up against the coast; the crests move ahead of their supporting foundations and the waves break as surf. The energy that created the wave carries water physically up the beach face. Since the energy is spent on the beach, the only force drawing the water back down to the ocean is gravity. Because the returning water has less energy, and because there is less volume since some of the water sinks into the sand, the dying wave is weaker.

Consider the matter of water's competence again. Moving briskly up the beach, a wave carries sand with it from the offshore bar; moving more lethargically back to the ocean, it hasn't the strength to carry as much sand away, and the sand remains. This phenomenon means that waves breaking on a beach on calm days leave more small material than they take away. Thus the beach builds up as new material is dropped. Come stormy weather or a tempestuous winter, stronger waves disturb the swash zone more and attack the beach. They bring in larger sand grains; more important, they can carry away smaller stuff because their larger water volumes and higher velocities translate into greater seaward competence. (The steepness of both the waves and beach face complicate these phenomena—but that is an esoteric matter.) Storm waves big enough to carry away more sand than they arrive with steeply erode the beach face and the berm—the part of the beach between the normal high-tide line and the dunes. If the storm waves persist, they may carry the whole old berm away, then attack the dunes themselves.

When waves break across the full width of a barrier beach in severe storms, they entirely remake the place. They remove natural obstructions and push the sand around and level the outermost dunes to create a very shallow, usually quite broad slope. This is the shape of a natural ocean beach, one that hasn't been artificially altered by dunes that build up around man-made fences. Beach grass or sea oats grow from the dunes toward the water and build new dunes that retard and withstand some storms. But stronger surges of water wash them away, rearranging their material. "Permanent" dunes, built by sand collecting around native plants, rise only beyond the reach of normal storms and tides. Yet nothing is actually permanent on the beach; every dune may be touched sooner or later by an extraordinary storm. Undermined, it crumbles; the sea collects its sand and carries it away or bears it inland with the following wave. In sum, the beach is shaped by the ocean and continually responds to its changing forces. Severe winter weather normally robs Atlantic beaches of sand deposited there during summer idylls. Typically, a winter beach is narrower; in summer the same beach will be broader and composed of finer sand grains.

Whether a beach erodes or grows depends in part on the energy of the waves. The energy in foot-pounds per foot of wave crest can be computed several ways. The basic formula is $E = \frac{W\ L\ H^2}{8}$. (E is energy; W is the weight of 1 cubic foot of sea water or 64 pounds; L is wave length, and H is wave height.) This formula uses the *square* of wave height—not a single power of height—because the height of the wave has a multiplying effect. A 2-foot wave has more than twice the energy of a 1-foot wave and can do more than twice the work—whether constructive or destructive depends largely on its steepness. A variation of the formula employs wave frequency (or T for "time period" in seconds) instead of wave length: $E = 41\ H^2T^2$. This is easier to use on the beach since it's easier to count seconds than accurately estimate wave length. Regardless of formulas, a storm wave can pack 6 tons of power to a linear foot of shore.

Pacific coast beaches change dramatically between winter and summer. Winter storms bringing stronger waves in a "fetch" thousands of miles long come from the same direction as summer zephyrs. Where the alongshore current is negligible, sand removed in winter settles in underwater bars facing the beach it came from. When summer returns, the weaker waves pick up this sand and put it back on the beach. So the beach builds until autumn.

On the Atlantic coast it's a little different. Prevailing winds are westerly while storm winds notoriously come from the northeast. Hence the seasonal change is not as distinct—though it exists—as the results of bad weather. Storms at any time of year can make astonishing changes. Early one fall I was at Assateague Island observing a peregrine falcon migration study. Driving up and down this 32-mile island twice a day, we passed through a simple gate nestled against the man-made dune above normal high tide. A modest barrier, it was a single cable hooked to a post at about ankle height. No doubt it had originally been much higher before sand slowly collected along that stretch of beach over several years of gentle weather. That fall a northeaster struck and made the beach a different place. Dunes that had built up around snow fences lost their steep faces where waves reached them. Now there was a ragged line of gentle hummocks instead of the artificial barrier dune. At the south end of the island a growing sandbar, exposed at low tide, hooked for half a mile around Fishing Point. And near the island's north end I was nearly garroted by the clearest index of change—that gate. The cable now hung from a hook higher than my head. The gatepost's apparent growth proved that nearly 6 vertical feet of sand had been removed from the place by a single storm. No doubt much of that sand became the new hook at the south end of the island where it had been carried by the alongshore current and the storm. As the current changed direction to enter the protected bay behind the island, it slowed down and dropped sand stolen from further north.

Year in and year out littoral currents have remarkable effects. Fishing Point has grown 4 miles since the Chincoteague Lighthouse was built more than a century ago. The west end of Fire Island has grown a similar distance. The Cape Hatteras Lighthouse, built 1,000 yards west of the beach in 1852, is now in danger of being undermined by storm tides. The swash now laps less than 50 yards away. (The Lighthouse would have toppled some years ago but for the steel barrier built to protect it.) But the point to the south of that tower, once a mile and a half away, has grown another mile. Given a steady littoral drift, sic transit sand.

The Delmarva Peninsula is growing outward at both ends, toward Chesapeake Bay to the south and into Delaware Bay at the north. Offshore somewhere in the vicinity of the Maryland-Virginia border an underwater "nodal point" causes the prevailing wave pattern to diverge. North of this topographical feature the littoral current usually moves northward. At Ocean City, Maryland and along Assateague Island it usually moves south. It might seem to a first-time visitor traveling the entire peninsula that inshore currents are as fickle as the inscrutable beach which seems to broaden and shrink twice a day. Just about— which is to say not at all. Except under a storm's influence, the currents are quite constant. As for the tides, which rise to cover a foreshore and fall to expose it, they are as certain as death and taxes.

Everyone has heard that tides are controlled by the moon. Pliny observed the phenomenon 2,000 years ago. Newton's theory explained it in 1687. Gravitational force does the work, just as it dumped the apple on Sir Isaac's noggin. (Theoretically, gravity is responsible for every raindrop's attraction to the farthest star. But don't expect any practical results from that, nor from the barely measurable rise and fall of solid earth in response to the orbiting moon's gravity.) Imagine the face of an antique clock representing an ideal "earth" covered with water and orbited by a perfect moon. When the moon is at the top of the diagram it draws earth's water toward it, creating a high tide at 12 o'clock; the water is deepest there. At the bottom of this perfect planet, at 6 o'clock, where the moon's gravity is not felt strongly, another high tide results from the force of the planet's rotation. The water for both these high tides comes from adjacent areas; the water at 3 and 9 o'clock has become shallower and low tides occur there. (Next diagram, please.) When the moon moves to the right of the clock-faced planet it continues to attract the earth's watery blanket and creates a high tide at 3 o'clock. Rotational forces—consider them centrifugal—create another corresponding high tide at 9 o'clock, while low tides appear at 12 and 6.

On our imperfect earth the same phenomena occur, though things are vastly more complicated because irregular landmasses funnel the flow of water between the interconnected oceans. Nonetheless, the moon constantly circles earth, drawing the closest water toward it as it passes; earth constantly rotates on its axis, creating another force most strongly manifested where the moon's gravity is barely felt at the moment. The two high tides that result are fed by water from adjacent seas. Since earth's rotation and moon's orbiting are both continual, ocean waters move up, sideways and down in a constant motion that peaks and ebbs at every point on every tidal coast with predictable regularity. Because the dominant tidal instigator, the moon, circles earth in about 24 hours, 52 minutes, the cycle takes a little longer than a day to complete. High tide and moonrise occur about an hour later every day.

A number of other forces also operate to make the tides vary from place to place and from day to day. The sun plays a particularly important role in counterpoint to the moon; again because its gravity attracts the earth's fluid blanket. The force of gravity increases in direct proportion to the mass of the objects but decreases with the square of the distance between them. Our familiar sun, with a mass 333,400 times that of earth, has less than half the effect on ocean tides as the smaller but much closer moon. Yet when sun, moon and earth are in a straight line, tides range higher and lower than normal because the sun's gravity augments the moon's. The highest and lowest tides of the month, called spring tides, occur when the sun, moon and earth are most nearly aligned; then the moon appears full or as a crescent. Neap tides, when the rise and fall are smallest, occur when the sun and moon form a right angle with the earth. In effect the sun is then at odds with the moon, gravitationally speaking, and cancels part of its tidal power.

Since distance is such an important factor, tide ranges also change as the earth travels in its eliptical orbit around the sun and the moon follows its oval course around earth. Higher and lower tides occur when earth is closest to the sun and/or moon. Add to these variables the fact that earth, like the moon, rotates on a tilted axis, and you have a notion of why some tides are higher than others in a given place even under similar weather conditions and phases of the moon.

In addition, there is the less understood and independent function of distinct ocean basins. A basin holds water like brandy in a snifter. When the liquid moves back and forth in a swirled glass, it rises and falls greater distances around the sides of the glass; the level near the center remains more constant. Liquid in any restricted space, whether ocean basin or brandy glass, has a given period of time in which the liquid naturally takes to move back and forth from one end to the other. This is the container's "resonance." The Bay of Fundy's resonance happens to be about the same as the moon's orbiting time, according to one expert; these two independent factors reinforce each other to cause higher and lower tides. For reasons that aren't fully understood, the difference between spring and neap tides in the Bay of Fundy isn't as great as elsewhere. Nonetheless, tides there range 60 feet; waters rise and fall the height of a six-story building in six hours. Of course that's the worldwide extreme. Some coasts have tides of almost no consequence, largely because of their relationship to the oceanic basin.

Regular cycles aside, tides can vary greatly in a single place in response to several irregular factors that affect the play or torture of surf upon a beach. Onshore wind has an obvious influence as it piles water up along a coast. Atmospheric pressure is another factor. During large storms the ocean is not pressed downward as hard by the air as during fair-weather highs. Warmer water in summer is yet another; higher temperature expands the volume of water in the oceans minutely. Freshwater runoff from the land in springtime is yet another factor as it adds to the volume because it is less dense than salt water.

Variations in tides have been so constant for so long that government agencies publish annual tables and TV weathermen predict them. But before the vacuum tube or even government was invented, the natural world depended on regular tides. Many beach animals rely on periodic immersion though they live on land. Marsh plants that would be defeated by hardy inland vegetation have adapted to saltwater flooding twice a day and would perish without it.

The shore itself must cope with all the variables. It has coped with them; it has survived. The extraordinary thing about it all is that shores persist with their repertoire of self-effacing actions in response to the bludgeoning sea. It would be silly to attribute intelligence here, as if a coast had a choice to do anything but persist, even though the practicalities are so ingenious. Suffice it that the physical beach is a creative thing and its creativity is helped along by its biota. If that idea sounds outlandish, consider two examples: Beach grass collects sand around its stems to build the dunes; the sand in turn stimulates the grass which grows more and collects more sand. Many mollusks live in or on sand along the littoral; after death their pulverized shells become part of sand-poor southern beaches. In any event, there is a nearly organic tenacity in the aggregation of sterile, organic and inorganic elements that make a beach.

Driftwords:

Sic Transit Homarus?

The little town of Woods Hole on Cape Cod's triceps is to marine scientists what Capistrano is to swallows. The preeminent Marine Biology Laboratory is there, and the National Oceanographic and Atmospheric Administration's Northeast Fisheries Center and the Woods Hole Oceanographic Institution (WHOI, pronounced "Hooey" by the irreverent). But when it comes to finding the lion of practical lobster biologists, take the ferry across the sound to a shingled building no bigger than a boat house in Vineyard Haven. John T. Hughes, director of the Massachusetts State Lobster Hatchery since its founding thirty years ago, has the steel-gray crew cut of a World War II minesweeper skipper, a single full-time assistant and an international reputation.

Fulfilling the hatchery's mandate—to raise lobster hatchlings and return them to depleted state waters—didn't turn out to be an overwhelming task. Once discovered and mastered, the techniques of encouraging "berried" females to shed their eggs in a tank and then nurture the larvae through four molts could be done with one hand. With the other, Hughes studied the animals and became the first to breed them in captivity. Though he's released literally millions of infant lobsters, he's never found a way of following his progeny; a lobster sheds any biologist's tag with its molted shell. Hughes must rely on empirical evidence of success. Early on he sowed the waters of Orleans, then devoid of lobsters; a few years later mature ones began appearing again in numbers. Now he's breeding odd-colored mutations: blue lobsters, bicolored lobsters and albinos for release in the wild where their genetic presence will make itself obvious for tracking purposes.

In the course of all his work, according to a Woods Hole colleague, Hughes has come to know "more about lobsters than any man on the East Coast." He's published scientific papers with the mandatory data graphs and qualifying verbiage. He admits his advice has been sought by European visionaries who dream of *Homarus* in the Mediterranean, by Turks who sell lobsters to oil-rich Arabs for $35 a pound, by Marlon Brando who was thoughtfully discouraged from transplanting *H. americanus* around his Polynesian island. When Hughes talks lobsters people listen. He says flatly "it's an endangered species—there's no doubt about that." Some fishery experts quibble with the phrase but agree that a crisis is coming. Even if the American lobster isn't threatened with biological extinction, its commercial future as a commercial creature is dim.

In the historical past these animals washed up on New England beaches in foot-deep windrows after northeasters. They were so common, cheap and disdained that legal limits were set on how often seventeenth-century masters could feed them to their bond servants. Once "a scourge to be abhorred," less than a century ago they were still commonly used as bait for cod and striped bass. At one time a Yankee lobsterman caught 225 pounds of lobster per pot each year. As recently as 1960 Maine watermen averaged 32 pounds per trap and caught a total of 24 million pounds. In 1978 they were hardput to catch 18 million pounds with 2 million traps for an average of 9 pounds per pot. In other words they're lobstering harder with better equipment and catching less. While the national catch hovers around 31 million pounds, the poundage "per unit of effort" has been steadily declining by 7 percent a year.

That datum aside, the very nature of today's catch spells disaster. John Hughes says 90 percent of the lobsters caught "have just reached the legal limit" and of these barely "ten percent have reached sexual maturity." In the Gulf of Maine, for example, half the lobsters don't mature until they've grown to 3 1/2 inches along the carapace from eye socket to first shell joint. But a lobster measuring 3 3/16 inches is a keeper in Maine. (Even smaller animals are legally taken in New Hampshire, Rhode Island and New Jersey.) Furthermore, according to various estimates, at least 80 percent and perhaps as much as 95 percent of all legal lobsters in near coastal waters are harvested each year. This leaves only one in twenty or one in five to carry on the race. The unhappy fact: We're eating juveniles and the vast majority of the breeding stock, which is akin to roasting the golden-egg laying goose.

In Gloucester, Mass., Tom Morrissey looks after lobsters for the State-Federal Management Partnership, an adjunct of the National Marine Fisheries Service. He tells me that regional authorities have approved in principle the urgent need to raise the minimum carapace length to a uniform 3 1/2 inches for animals taken from all state and federal waters. (Each state has jurisdiction of its coastal waters to the 3-mile limit; NMFS oversees the fisheries 200 miles out.) Obviously this would increase the breeding stock and allow most lobsters the chance to mate at least once before coming home as dinner. It would also result in greater poundage at dockside by as much as 30 percent since growth would be greater than natural mortality. But lobstermen oppose increasing the keeper size because it would cause some temporary belt-tightening even though the increments would be on the order of a thirty-second of an inch every year or two.

Politically it's naive to expect any one state will place new restrictions on its own lobstermen while their competitors in the next state continue to reap juvenile harvests. John Hughes hopes a major lobby will take up the cudgel in our increasingly parochial Congress to force executive or legislative action on the national level. Without it he predicts *H. Americanus* will go the way of its eastern Atlantic cousin, *H. vulgaris,* once the mainstay of thriving fisheries in the North Sea countries. But those nations ignored the warnings, failed to cooperate in conservation programs and the fisheries died from over-fishing. Closer to home the yellowtailed flounder and halibut fisheries are threatened by the same disease. If the striped bass isn't the next to go, the lobster could be. It's a shame; it's also avoidable.

Inner dune.*

Chapter Seven

The Starring Roles of Vegetables

A barrier beach without plants is like a ship without a sail, like a boat without a rudder, an egg without salt, dinner without wine, is like a politician without a pressure group. But a plantless beach has even less future. Once sand comes ashore, the pawn of waves and currents, it becomes the slave of a new medium—dynamic air. A breeze as slow as 9 miles an hour blows sand away. Even wind that gentle picks up dry grains and moves them significant distances to start the process of saltation: As each grain falls to the surface of the beach again it jars others up into the wind. The net result is leeward dispersal of the beach. Hypothetically a gale can carry a naked barrier island away as fast as it builds up and dries out. The fact that beaches and barrier islands don't all blow away inland every year is largely due to plants. Even heaps of dredge spoil, the byproduct of deepening a ship channel, become stabilized in the course of a summer as airborne seeds colonize them and take root. Islands survive because of plants. Viva vegetation.

*Among the plants of the upper beach: a slanting swatch of wild rose, round spreading patches of poverty grass, spires of seaside goldenrod and wide-leafed beach pea.

Certainly a beach is a constantly dynamic, moving thing. But there are degrees of dynamism. Islands move and migrate—slowly, thanks to plants. Normally the sum of undramatic vegetable growth is almost equal to the sporadic forces of meteorological events that do most of the dramatic work in a natural scheme of things. The relationship between vegetation and beaches is like some good marriages: slowly productive, fundamentally stable through small accommodations by each party, and occasionally but not fatally tumultuous. To overstate for the example's sake: An established island fails when things get too rough for the ever-accepting plants, or because the vegetation doesn't hold up its end of the bargain and lets things fall apart.

To outline one more overall observation, muddle the marriage metaphor and consider a *ménage à trois* of sea, shore and salt marsh. The material of the beach itself—grains of quartz—is sterile. But it snuggles between two of the most botanically fertile swingers on earth: the oceanic shallows and the marsh. The party to windward, the ocean, is largely responsible for the beach's ability to support life at all, indeed for its great, if selective, fertility. Having carried the sand there in the first place, the ocean provides a variety of nutrients from drab minerals in its spray to bouquets of organic debris and armies of voracious bacteria. In turn, the vital barrier beach cradles the leeward marsh, the nursery-and-garden upon which most higher marine life relies. (By one expert estimate, 95 percent of Virginia's commercial and sport-fish species depend exclusively on marshes and bays for shelter or for food during at least one phase of their lives.) Marine vitality demands healthy marshes, which rely on protective barrier island beaches, which need the strapping ocean. Of course it didn't start out that way. These responsibilities were not ordained in any contract, and opposing forces also operate continually. The surf erodes and salt spray kills many plants. But this threesome settled in and carries on. The fabulously creative (if metaphorically bizarre) cohabitation of sea, shore and marsh depends on the constant support and contribution of vegetables.

First and fundamentally, what is a plant? An autotrophe as opposed to a heterotrophe (an animal). Most plants—and there are 350,000 species of them—produce their own sustenance from inorganic materials. Everything else must consume food that's already organic, whether vegetable or animal. Scratch a carnivore and you'll find that its food supply originally derives from plants. Peregrine falcons thrive on flickers, which eat insects, which live in grass. The cod eats sea snails, which eat algae. Man eats potatoes and steaks from steers fattened on corn. But whether the original food source was a diatom or an ear of Silver Queen, the vegetable survived on a diet of water and "essential elements": carbon, hydrogen, oxygen, phosphorus, potassium, nitrogen, sulfur, calcium, iron, magnesium, copper, zinc, boron, manganese and molybdenum. With these it created its own organic sustenance through photosynthesis, a process of Gordian entanglements. Oversimplified, the formula reads $CO_2 + H_2O \xrightarrow[\text{Chlorophyll}]{\text{Light}} CH_2O + H_2O + O_2$. (Carbon dioxide and water in the presense of light that's "fixed" by chlorophyll become a carbohydrate; i.e., a starch or sugar, plus water and oxygen.) But like all other things biochemical, the process turns out to be more complicated, so much so that even the biochemists haven't sorted it all out to their satisfaction. For one thing, water goes in and water comes out—but not the same water. The plant breaks down the original fluid, uses its constituent elements to make carbohydrates for its own use and, fortunately for our entire biological world, releases oxygen as a by-product. New water, reconstituted from leftover hydrogen and oxygen, is another by-product. Chlorophyll, the visible green pigment found in plants, is the agent responsible for perhaps the most important aspect of the entire proceedings. This substance absorbs energy from sunlight to bind the inorganic raw materials into new, more complex carbohydrates. Without this binding energy, these organic materials couldn't survive. Vegetative things proceeded differently, and much more slowly, before the evolutionary advent of chlorophyll. But the bottom line now, according to expert testimony is simply this: "Photosynthesis is the source of all living matter on earth and of all biological activity." It provides the nutritional wherewithal for all life here; lowly plants are the repository for that awesome process.

Though beaches and their environs support a vast variety of vegetation, these places are hostile habitats at best. Sand is sterile, inhospitably dry and too porous to hold water well. The sea is far too salty for most plants and fraught with the constant motion that would make a mighty oak cry "uncle." Guarded by the barrier, the marsh is frequently calm enough but experiences daily tides which drown its flora's roots, then leave them drying in the sun. Further, brackish marsh water is too salty for most vegetation. Yet the plants are there, thanks to some remarkable evolutionary adaptations. These are the halophytes, plants that can survive salty environments, usually by absorbing extra water or by expelling salt molecules.

Begin with the plants of the beach itself and American beach grass in particular, a well-named plant as energetic as Manifest Destiny. It occupies the beach as aggressively as nineteenth-century Americans claimed the West and clutches its territories as tenaciously. First, it keeps the beach from being blown away by stopping saltation in its tracks. Though a healthy stand of *Ammophila breviligulata* covers less than 8 percent of the surface area, its simple presence inhibits the wind, greatly reducing its speed at the surface to reserve the sand already there and collect newly-dropped grains. A gale may whip spray from the surf and blow sharp sand in someone's face until walking into the wind along an open beach becomes painfully impossible. But the wind at ground level among the dune grass is a zephyr or less. Collectively the blades of grass create a barrier that dissipates the wind, which drops its sand on a surface which is less disturbed. The stems trap grains that would otherwise roll past. Called "compass grass" for the circles its bending leaves make in sand on a windy day, it inhibits sand movements in any direction, gathering grains around its shoots. Obviously any roots anchor both the plant and the material it grows in—even sand —but this plant's above-ground stems also collect sand, to the advantage of both the beach and the grass.

Beach grass's major stems run horizontally beneath the sand. These rhizomes have characteristic nodes every few inches. Most nodes have only roots, which are thus distributed widely beneath the beach surface to absorb as much fresh water as possible when it rains though the green plants above seem sparse. A fraction of the underground nodes grow vertically as well to produce short, sharp stems which develop more roots. Tall, slender leaves grow up around each stem, leaves that in dry bright weather curl around the vertical stem like corn husks around the ear. While the convex outside surface of a curled leaf is smooth, the inner surface is composed of ridges and grooves that run the length of the leaf. (These features are barely visible to the naked eye but can be seen through a hand lens.) The plant's gas exchange pores lie along the bottoms of the grooves, which close when the leaf curls around the stem in dry weather. Working like the squeezed side of an accordion bellows, the ridges effectively seal the grooves shut to conserve vital moisture within the plant and, as botanists say, retard desiccation. Furthermore, the grooves are so narrow that particles of salt cannot invade them but instead adhere to the higher ridges when the leaf is not curled. This prevents the killing salt from entering the plant's pores.

Where do salt particles come from? Salt spray, of course. When air bubbles in the ocean (or surf) burst, tiny droplets of sea water explode from the surface to be carried by the wind. Whether they evaporate en route or wherever they happen to land, they transport particles of sea water's dissolved components. These include some botanically "essential substances," notably magnesium and potassium. Dissolved by rain and washed down through the porous sand, they're absorbed by the grass roots. Other of these airborne particles—common salt (sodium chloride) in particular—kill or retard most vascular plants. But they don't harm beach grass because of its leaf design. Hence beach grass benefits below-ground from growing close to the spray-giving sea but protects itself from the spray above the sand's surface by the same ingenious device that keeps it from drying out in this often arid place.

A. breviligulata thrives in sand; nay, it depends on it. For reasons that remain unclear, sand grains collecting around its stems actually stimulate the plant's growth. It may be that these roots are short-lived and that the only way the plant stays vigorous is by sending out new rhizomes and growing new roots with them. Beach grass bears seeds, but a classic American study revealed that it spreads most actively through rhizomes. Indeed it regenerates at its fastest rate from dormant rhizomes in springtime. Its phenomenal reproductive methods are crucial to a beach's persistence. Its talent "for potentially unlimited horizontal and vertical rhizome growth" is extraordinary, according to a Dutch authority. (*Ammophila arenaria,* a plant of the same genus, grows along European beaches and stabilizes them.) "One *Ammophila* or the other is responsible for the birth of impressive beach dunes wherever they appear around the world. As sand collects around these plants, the grasses grow up through it. They can be buried deeper than one yard and still emerge. The Dutch botanist writes, "The stabilization of sand surface by vegetation differs from other forms of stabilization [i.e., man-made ones] in that the plant cover can keep pace with the accreting surface." And if sand fails to collect, *Ammophila* becomes less vigorous. Where *Ammophila* remains healthy, dunes continue to rise. "There are two major phenomena that enable maritime dune formation to proceed. The first and most important is a supply of sand together with wind to move it." (Sand washed up into low-tide flats or onto the beach face is enough.) "The second is plant colonization"—by plants that can survive burial—under new layers of sand.

Beach grass typically covers the inland side of a dune and may run down the face of a gently sloped dune to colonize the foreshore to the point where spring tides or storm surges drown it. When storm waves attack and erode a vertical scarp in a low dune, the tangled web of subsurface rhizomes is strikingly visible—as on the point of Plum Island on Massachusetts' northern coast. But even then the tangled rhizomes hold the sand far longer than would otherwise be the case. Scarps in grassless sand tumble as fast as sand castle walls. When plants along the ridge of a coastal dune are trampled by thoughtless walkers (or wildlife), the dune doesn't regenerate—because beach grass won't take hold if sand is removed. A little path through the edge of a grassy dune soon becomes a "blowout."

Here the particulars of aerodynamics come into play. Wind blows sand away from the slope wherever it's not held in place by grass. (I've stood on a 200-foot Cape Cod cliff with an eroding face and been blinded by beach sand riding a strong onshore wind up the bare slope.) Gravity adds to the loss and a mobile dune takes the shape of an airfoil. The greatest wind pressure is felt near the top of the dune; sand loss is greatest there. Since sand is lost from this area, this is precisely where beach grass won't regenerate to repair the break. Instead, as wind continues to sweep sand up the dune face, the little blowout becomes a major breach in the barrier.

South of Chesapeake Bay, beach grass gives way to the dominance of sea oats, a very long-stemmed grass that bears plumes of flat-cased seeds like little flags. A hardy plant that can survive both sand burial and exposure from erosion, it has a slender grace that belies its toughness. At Shackleford Banks below Ocracocke, North Carolina, 90 percent of the vegetated dunes support *Uniola paniculata.* In turn, the sea oats support the dunes. This grass stabilizes enormous stretches of southern barrier dunes because of its extensive root systems. Though it also sends out rhizomes, they are not as robust as *Ammophila's.*

The spikelets of the sea oats' plumes fall in autumn and early winter. Many animals feast on them: mice, rabbits, song sparrows and redwing blackbirds. Only the seeds that are swiftly buried in new sand survive to germinate the following spring. Slender new stalks appear annually for several years, frequently growing 6 feet tall and arcing away from the wind with their heads of tattered-flag seeds.

Both beach grass and sea oats, which are perennials, survive uprooting by storm surges and fragmentation. In fact this is one way they disperse. Broken up by waves, the pieces wash up on another beach and take root where they land, frequently along the high-tide line which is fertilized by decaying vegetation that didn't survive the passage.

The beach pea *(Lathyrus japonicus),* which grows as far south as New Jersey, approaches dominance in some locations. Resistant to salt spray and desiccation, it fixes nitrogen in the soil and helps fertilize the dunes.

Its stems creep along at ground level supporting slender branches with pointed heart-shaped leaves, curly tendrils and blue flowers. Settlers in Newfoundland are said to have staved off starvation with beach peas while some nineteenth-century Cape Codders preferred them to garden peas, which their pods resemble. (Lee Peterson's *A Field Guide to Edible Wild Plants* recommends boiling beach peas at least 15 minutes, then serving them hot with butter and pepper. But this useful and careful book warns that other members of the same genus are poisonous.)

Dusty miller *(Artemisia stelleriana),* a perennial, also grows on exposed growing dunes. A complex-looking plant found in low clumps punctuated with flowering stalks in autumn, it survives fragmentation particularly well. Hence an area reached by last winter's storm surges is likely to have a few clumps almost as soon as the first shoots of beach grass appear through the new sand. Dusty miller's name derives from its appearance; the leaves are covered with a pale blue-gray cuticle that looks dusty and helps it resist desiccation.

Sea rocket *(Cakile edentula),* a fast-growing annual, grows on the berm and disperses easily. Bearing lavender flowers from midsummer to early fall, it has rocket-shaped seed capsules. Particularly well suited to dispersing seaside progeny, these capsules fall off and roll down the beach to the swash. Surving saltwater immersion for long periods, the seeds germinate when washed up on another beach. Or, when an original site is inundated by a storm tide, this succulent's capsules float inland and colonize the inner dunes.

Behind a barrier dune, low beach heather and bearberry take over. Throughout the swale on Fire Island these two plants grow in great provision, preferring, as they do, eroding sites where beach grass can't survive—but requiring some protection from salt spray. Vast carpets of these plants are found north of New Jersey. Lilliputian beach heath, "also called 'poverty grass' because it grew where nothing else would," according to Thoreau, goes formally by the name *Hudsonia tomentosa.* Bearberry *(Arctostaphylos uva-ursi)* grows in somewhat bushier stands of small, shiny dark green leaves and hard red berries. These are said to be edible, but I'm told that no less a forager than Euell Gibbons tried fixing them every way he could think of and found each dish less palatable than the last.

Wild or salt-spray rose grows in impressive clumps on Maine's rocky islands and along the rims of Cape Cod cliffs where its exposed briary roots clawing the empty air prove the swift pace of erosion. *Rosa rugosa* has ostentatious blossoms with large but delicate petals and hairy thornlike growths along the stems. The fruits, rose hips, turn from orange to red as they ripen and grow as large as Ping-Pong balls. In Maine, trapped by the tide on a wild island one hungry day, I found them delicious. But some picked from a plant beside a cement walk in one of Fire Island's towns seemed pulpy and tasteless. Dominating some natural sites, these plants seem as native as poison ivy. But this rose is an exotic introduced as a garden shrub from Japan in 1872, according to a New England account written a century after the fact. A botanist reported that cuttings were carried "aboard the ship *Franklin,* wrecked on Nauset Beach in the spring of 1849, and that this rose was introduced to the Cape" with the flotsam. The substance of that story has spread with the wild rose itself and is repeated just about every place the plant occurs. I don't doubt that there were disastrous and tragic wrecks along every stretch of coast—only that so many of the ships carried rose hips and cuttings.

As for poison ivy *(Rhus radicans),* it too dominates large expanses of high dune, inner dune and bayside uplands, often running down to the tideline of a marsh. I can't think of a place I haven't seen it and thanked my stars for immunity to the stuff that drives some folks mad with itching rash. (Alas, such immunity doesn't last a lifetime.)

The swale behind a barrier dune often also has a number of trees, many of them stunted beyond easy recognition. On Assateague Island mature loblolly pines stand no taller than a man but spread out their branches three or four yards in every direction. On Fire Island runty half-century-old pitch pines sprawl like the caps of Chinese mushrooms in a chicken dish. These deformities—adaptations really—show the effect of salt spray on species with little tolerance for it. The inner dune is often stable enough to hold deciduous and evergreen trees. Despite superficial appearances, a barrier island may have ample fresh water floating atop the heavier saltwater table in a convex "lens." A mature swale has sufficient chemical nutrients for trees to grow too. At first the nutrients came from salt spray, then as the first inland plants colonized the place, their leaves or needles (and finally all their remains) decomposed, contributing chemical constituents back to the sand. In this way the live and dead flora of a maritime forest represent a rising organic spiral; the dead nourish the living as old nutrients are recycled and new ones arrive with the wind. But trees only grow as high as they can reach before sea spray salts their leaves or needles. Unable to exclude salt from their pores, as Ammophila does, exposed portions of the tree are constantly pruned by the aerosols. As a result, they take contorted shapes that indicate the sweep of wind over a dune and down its lee.

Back at the beach the seaweeds, algae all, are among the most productive plants on earth—or in the water. Members of an ancient and successful group, some reproduce both sexually and asexually; one grows a few feet long but can muster the anatomical wherewithal for only two layers of cells. Lacking distinct veins, they also lack true roots. Instead they attach themselves to rocks, empty mollusk shells, pilings and almost any other hard surface (including live spider crabs, as noted) with characteristic holdfasts. These organs, shaped like fingers or disks, develop from fully half of the original embryonic material; the other half differentiates into stems, fronds, reproductive organs, bladders and other structures.

Growing from the high-tide line to as deep as sunlight penetrates, these algae are as important to their own habitat as land plants are to barrier islands. In some submarine locations a single species dominates the aquascape as thoroughly as beach grass dominates a dune. Diving or snorkeling in such water, it seems that they and the rocks that anchor them *are* the habitat; a mesmerizing, undulating marine jungle that sways with the waves to reveal every kind of animal—fishes, mollusks, crustaceans—and then hide them again.

The seaweeds are undeniably plants of the beach. Many of them, like the rockweeds along Maine's stony shores, appear as soon as the tide begins to ebb. A walk at low water reveals an entirely different place than the perpetually aloof land. At night especially, many rarely seen creatures forage along a rocky littoral without fear of their most traditional predators, the diurnal gulls. But one can also find green crabs, Jonahs, limpets and scores of snails on every boulder during a daylight ebb tide. They hide in the rockweed waiting for the water's return. Seaweeds are also high-tide beach plants—albeit dying ones—because so many of them come ashore, their stems or holdfasts broken. With them come multitudes of invertebrates and banquets of nutrients which seep into a sandy beach as the algae decompose, creating a ragged line for some of the hardier vascular plants to colonize. Or, as on the stony south coast of Block Island, they seem a permanent feature lying along the base of a cove's cliff in dense mixed carpets 2 or 3 feet deep.

Botanically classified by pigments, the seaweeds are supremely useful plants. Some were traditionally used to pack shellfish for market, or even fragile household goods. Some are harvested for food—but far less in America than Europe and the Orient. Many more are gathered for chemical and industrial processing.

The brown algae include the family Fucaceae which is well represented along the Atlantic coast. Ten-foot bladder wrack (*Ascophyllum* sp.) is not one of the most diaphanous marine plants. It has fairly thick stems, irregular flexible branches that are round or oval in cross section, and two forms of air bladders. *Ascophyllum* is a source of many substances: iodine (in concentrations more than 200 times that of the surrounding water), soda, potash and half an alphabet of vitamins. The *Fucus* genus comprises the closely related rockweeds, which are flat in cross section and have distinct median ribs. They too branch randomly and have visible air bladders that keep them afloat. Generally only 1 to 3 feet long, depending on species, some can double their weight in a week's time if they are thinned out regularly by harvesting.

Kelp *(Laminaria)* is another genus of brown algae with several species common from Maine to New Jersey. The fronds are not branched. Instead they're like leathery straps that grow in various widths and in lengths from 5 to 10 feet. Their ancient common names outshine the Latinate: oar weed, tangle, devil's apron, sole-leather, and ribbon weed. Depending on species, the single flat fronds may be wrinkled *(Laminaria agardhii)*, smooth *(L. saccharina)*, ragged *(Alaria esculenta)* or perforated *(Agarum cribresum)*. Some are annuals and some perennials that live as long as a dozen years.

Despite its common and formal names, sargassum *(Sargassum filipendula)* doesn't come from the fabled mid-Atlantic Sargasso Sea. Rather, this

Probing for small animals among salicornia shoots, a glossy ibis feeds in a patch of Spartina grass. Bayberry (far right) grows taller than marsh elder.

brown alga thrives offshore along the warmer parts of the Atlantic coast. Easy to identify, its fronds resemble bayberry leaves and it bears berry-like bladders that make it seem like a terrestrial plant that lost its way.

Irish moss *(Chondrus crispus)* contains chlorophyll, although that pigment is often entirely masked by deep purple coloring. Dried, it turns white to look like tattered Kleenex. Growing in dense patches and coming ashore in handfuls, its leaves resemble kale or collard greens. Like the other red algae, it grows in slightly deeper water than the browns, to be exposed only during some low spring tides. Offering a dense, complicated cover, Irish moss shelters as many as 50 species of invertebrates down to depths of 60 feet or so. Traditionally this has been the most marketable seaweed in many parts of the world. Eaten in Europe, it is a common source of agar and gelatin and has been compounded into an anticoagulant drug. Its euphonious common name shows up on supermarket product labels since it is an ingredient of cosmetics, lotions, toothpastes and ice cream (as an ice-crystal inhibitor).

Dulse *(Rhodymenia palmata)* another edible red alga, also grows below the normal low-water line. Dark red, it is flat, broad and ribless. Its dark red frond separates into wide segments that sometimes have distinct leaflets.

Ulva lactuca is the bright green undulating stuff known from Florida to Hudson's Bay as sea lettuce. Like so many other algae, it's edible but recipes call for chopping it fine—probably a tedious task because of its unusual toughness. This is all the more surprising since it's only two cells thick. Nibbled on a beach, it seems an unlikely salad green. Slightly irregular like stretched crepe paper, its inch-wide fronds grow 2 feet long.

Eelgrass *(Zostera marina)* is not an alga but belongs to a family of 50 flowering marine grasses (as opposed to true grasses). On soft bottoms from Cape Lookout to Campobello, it may be the dominant underwater plant down to depths of 150 feet. Its branching rhizomes have nodes as close as every half-inch, from which six or eight 3-foot leaves rise. Ephemeral shoots bear as many as 1,000 seeds—food for innumerable fish and water birds, especially brants. Eelgrass beds shelter many shellfish (especially scallops) and may support 200 species of algae. In 1931 a disease wiped out 95 percent of the eelgrass along the East Coast and caused ecological havoc. Fortunately the species seems to be making a strong comeback at last.

Behind almost every barrier beach there is (or was) a marsh. It may be barely visible, as in parts of New Jersey's asphalt jumble; it may be extinct, as along the Norfolk docks, but marshland is as much a part of the total beach as dune grass and gulls. In the classic text *Life and Death of the Salt Marsh,* John and Mildred Teal state:

> Two-thirds of the value of the commercial catch of fish and shellfish landed on the East Coast of the United States comes from species that live at least part of their life cycle in marsh-estuaries. . . . It is estimated by fishery experts that 80 to 90 percent of the fish gathered for market throughout the world come from shallow coastal waters. . . . Experiments . . . have shown that marsh ponds can produce 250 to 400 pounds of fish per acre per year, 100 pounds of crabs and from 300 to 400 pounds of shrimp.

Economic and household food budgets aside, it's horrible to think what kind of biological apocalypse might occur if all the marshes were summarily filled and paved. The oceanic biota as we know it would immediately change, perhaps like a clock without its small hand. And the world, as we and every other animal know it, would change too.

The vegetative wealth of a salt marsh is proven by an unlikely source: the petroleum industry. A coastal geologist who once worked for an oil company describes gathering seismic data in order to map ancient barrier islands. After these islands sank thousands of feet beneath increasingly heavy layers of sedimentary rock that formed, the weight on them became enormous. The pressure turned much of the vegetation into oil. The oilman's problem, then, was to plot the location of the erstwhile marsh, then locate the former barrier island itself. This is because the oil wouldn't stay put as it formed, but would be squeezed into the porous sand nearby. Thus, today's living marshes may turn the Outer Banks into rich oil fields—in a million years or so.

Driftwords:

Beach Manners

For decades a certain Cape Cod beach (unnamed here for reasons that will be clear) was a naked haven. Visitors interested in bare sun- or surfbathing could learn where it was if they thought to ask around. Those offended by nudity knew to stay away from the short stretch and easily found other—in their terms, better—environs.

After the beach became part of the national seashore, a reporter identified the place in print. Things changed almost overnight. The number of buff buffs doubled. The number of voyeurs armed with binoculars multiplied exponentially. The results were appalling and predictable. A bit of beach that had known limited use became the most heavily trod turf that side of Harvard Yard. The beach grass died; birds fled; car traffic became perilously congested. In response, the park authorities banned nudity there—not on "moral" grounds, but for the legitimate reason that it caused environmental damage. Explicitly the bare bathers weren't the problem, but the hordes they attracted had to be dissolved.

Park Service officials dislike talking about the subject for the record. Privately some frown on it; others are disinterested. I've seen a few engage in it out of uniform (perforce) and on their own time—though they were hard to recognize without their ranger hats. As far as enforcing "dress codes" goes, the Park Service seems disinterested so long as nudity doesn't cause a problem of some kind. Some employees of the more rustic public agencies abhor nudity anywhere and harass (or arrest) anyone clad too scantily for their taste. (Note: The legal requirement of clothes on a wild beach is dubious. However, on developed "protected" beaches, clothes can be mandatory according to the well-tested rule of law. Local ordinances can be pretty strict and vigorously enforced.)

In my youth nude beaches were considered bohemian bastions. Times change; beach nudity has become common. Last summer I stumbled on a nude beach bordering the summer estate of a recent cabinet secretary, another adjoining an aloof celebrity's retreat, and a third within a Frisbee's toss of a former White House hostess's residential club. This isn't to say these elitists romp with the naked neighbors; an interesting phenomenon involves invisible boundaries. Ordained by local custom or consensus, the lines can be rigorously observed with little fanfare. On many islands east of the Hudson, the clad and unclad congregate 1,000 yards from each other in perfect if distant harmony, wading in the same waves and tanning in the same sun to only slightly different degrees. (However, the sighting of a man-of-war or stranding of a whale will prompt them to intermingle without bloodshed.) Common sense and the fundamental democratic rule apply. Given a cultural tradition that goes back to bearskins, clothes in public are still the rule. But individuals who like to shed theirs aren't criminal perverts and shouldn't be universally restrained by a tyrannical majority. Nor should the minority tyrannize or drive away less conventional folks from every beach. So a modus vivendi emerges along the shore, and an avant-garde of slight significance goes its happy way getting tanned all over.

As with smoking these days, there are places where you can sunbathe nude and places where you can't. So be it. Everybody wins; the practitioners and the abstainers, if they'll accommodate each other. There is a larger principle here: A public beach is common ground. The important matter of open access aside, except for characters rich as Croesus or egotistical as Napoleon, nobody tries to own the littoral. People visit and have a sense of shared occupancy. An informal place, a beach inspires relaxation of many inland habits and preoccupations, clothing aside. City folks who never talk to strangers at home chat with people they've never met—about the tide, the passing of a migratory bird, the discovery of a strange animal. People whose winter lives are filled with crowds and committees seek the beach for solitude and don't talk to anyone. They "vant to be alone" and are entitled to their physical privacy; the beach is big enough for all. Cold-weather recluses grow gregarious along the common shore. Sedentary people jog along the beach and workaholics nap. Avid sports fans read books. Some women who wouldn't be caught dead at the supermarket without makeup wear nothing but cocoa butter here. Some men who bare their navels in discos wear terrycloth robes at the beach. To each his/her own.

Regarding clothes, don't be a minority of one. If everyone in sight is clad and you'd rather not be, find a more congenial place. If everyone nearby is in the altogether, don't march around all buttoned up like a penguin in a sauna. You'll be uncomfortable, and that's a contagious condition. If no one else is in sight, there's nobody to care what you wear or what you don't. (As for exhibitionists and voyeurs, I think there ought to be a special beach set aside for them—preferably in some place like Madagascar.)

One man's summer castle—after the storm surge.

Chapter Eight

The Onimod Theory
or
Something There Is
That Doesn't Love a Beach

. . . I have seen the hungry ocean gain Advantage on the kingdom of
the shore . . .   —Shakespeare
SONNET LXIV

An idea returns to mind like a forgotten song: That the inanimate
elements of the beach act in ways that are almost organically creative.
Combined, they enable the beach to persist, as if a sterile strip of sand
had an interest in continuing to be. Not that inanimate things have will
or cognizance; they do have some inherent bent toward organization per
se. A chemist won a 1977 Nobel Prize for mathematically describing a
kindred fact: that biological life arose out of inorganic chaos, i.e. that
natural systems "create order out of disorder." Gaseous hydrogen and
oxygen combine to become palpable water; in the unspeakably distant
past inorganic compounds combined and became the first amino acids,

186

the building blocks of life. The very nature of gravity encourages cohesion, often the first step toward organization. Without gravity the stuff that went bang so enormously would have all simply dispersed. Instead, parts of it coalesced as objects with relationships of dynamic equilibrium, namely orbits.

These seemingly tangential ideas relate directly to the beach. How so? Very simply, because when left to their own dynamic devices the beaches take care of themselves. But they do it with little regard for humankind's hard-won "kingdoms of the shore"—whether any sovereign state along the Atlantic coast, or one man's summer castle in the sand. The shoreline is a moving thing. While it grows outward at specific times and places, most stretches of coast continually recede. University of Virginia geologist Robert F. Dolan, an authority on barrier island dynamics, recently finished plotting the recent movement of the entire coast from beyond Atlantic City, N.J. to below Cape Lookout, N.C. His measurements, taken at 100-meter intervals on the basis of aerial and satellite photographs, indicate an *average* recession rate along the entire 400-mile stretch of 4 1/2 feet a year; in places the seaward land vanishes as fast as 35 feet a year. Yet the islands guarding the continent's eastern edge seem permanent and self-perpetuating; they don't apparently disintegrate when man stands idly by. A case in point:

The Outer Banks curves from below Norfolk, Virginia, out into the Atlantic, then turns sharply at Cape Hatteras to cut back toward the mainland near Beaufort, South Carolina—a total distance of over 200 miles. In 1958, part of Bodie Island and all of Ocracoke and Hatteras Islands—the 70-mile central portion of the slender chain—became Cape Hatteras National Seashore. A decade later, the islands south of Ocracoke (Portsmouth, Core Banks and Shackleford Banks) were designated to become Cape Lookout National Seashore. Thomas Morse was named superintendent of the park that would not become a park for another decade until Bicentennial fever swept the country and the Congress. Now retired, he recalls assigning a part-time Park Service botanist to "study the history of the natural history"—to determine, if possible, what the islands would be like if they hadn't been settled and altered by man. The botanist, Paul J. Godfrey, is now a tenured professor at the University of Massachusetts and one of the young graybeards of beach ecology. Today he says he owes his eminence to the lucky stroke of being at the right place at the right time. Barrier island ecology was a relatively young science still; "dig a hole and there was data," he says.

Digging innumerable holes, Godfrey and his wife, a marine zoologist, learned a great deal about the past and present of one island in particular. Core Banks, which terminates at Cape Lookout itself, was the 23-mile long centerpiece of the park-to-be. Unlike the Hatteras Seashore islands, it had never been developed in realtors' terms. Furthermore, it appeared to be in better shape than Hatteras because it had been left alone. Naturally low with a wide bare berm between the normal high-tide line and the natural dunes, it didn't suffer much when violent storms occurred, storms that destroyed human lives and property elsewhere. "Unimproved" by roads or expensive buildings, it could sustain brief flooding without anyone objecting and having it declared a "disaster area." The plants and animals living there had evolved to cope with such events and soon recovered. In their 1976 landmark study, *Barrier Island Ecology,* Paul and Melinda Godfrey described the sustaining dynamism of the island in detail. Certainly Core Banks has some unusual characteristics; for one, it lies parallel to the prevailing winds, not across them like most barrier islands. But this island demonstrates some important lessons about the relative competence of man and nature to extend an island's future.

In a word Core Banks is well designed to cope with the particular rigors of its environment. When attacked by a severe storm it surrenders rather than tries to withstand the onslaught. In surrendering, the Godfreys demonstrated, the island actually benefits over the long term from passing tempests: "The berm is the 'elbow room' for the storm surge. Whatever dunes or vegetation build up in the active berm during quiet periods are usually destroyed by the surge. Those dunes that survive are back far enough to escape the main wave force." When seas wash up unusually high they carry sand across the berm to the island's interior: "Winds then blow the fine sand into dunes. . . . As sand is moved into the interior of the island by overwash, and on dunes by wind, the height of the island increases and tends to keep pace with the rising sea." During the 1950s and early 1960s moderate storms brought significant amounts of sand to the island. "Natural vegetation and new dunes have developed on these terraces during the past decade. Thus much of the island consists of a series of quite recent overwash terraces. New dunes form on the terraces only to be buried or eroded by overwash in their turn. The sand, however, is carried further back into the island during an overwash instead of being lost to the littoral currents, and so it is conserved." As sea level rises slowly and the seaward side of Core Banks erodes, the island grows upwards and moves like a caterpillar toward the mainland as well. Nutrients provided by periodic overwash enrich the entire island; new sand stimulates the growth of native grasses while it also drifts into the bayside marsh, extending the island toward the distant mainland. Overwash also assures that only the hardiest seaside plants will survive—not faster growing inland species that can crowd out salt-resistant vegetation. Consequently the island nurtures plants that can quickly recover and rebuild dunes after storms, while the entire island migrates at such a leisurely pace that it appears to be a permanent place.

But to the northeast "on the islands of Cape Hatteras National Seashore, these natural processes have been greatly altered by the heavy hand of man," the Godfreys observed. Settled centuries earlier and heavily developed for decades, Ocracoke, Hatteras and Bodie Islands had been "protected" by a line of steep dunes that collected along man-made fences. The mechanics were simple enough, even "natural." A fence made of brush or wooden slats checks the wind which drops the sand it carries. Grain by grain the sand collects until it buries the fence. Plant another fence along the top of the dune and the sand rises even higher. This creates an imposing barrier against common storms and a sheltered lee that folks find comfortable. Dune building "in past years was done in good faith." Park Service experts then believed that artificial dunes would help preserve the Hatteras seashore and heal the scars of past abuses, like wholesale cattle grazing which destroyed the grasses. "However, this approach has led to attempts at total stabilization, the desire to hold everything in place, and to prevent the sea from washing over the islands. Such a program has come about to protect roads and buildings and with this development it has become necessary to hold all the sand in place and prevent dune movement, overwash and the opening of inlets. A continuous artificial dune line has been built the length of the Seashore. . . . The man-made dune is effectively a dyke which stops all ordinary overwash. The beach has become very narrow and irregular. . . . Therefore storm waves impinge directly on most of the dune, since they cannot roll over the island, and rebound from the dune faces, eroding beach and dune sand into the littoral drift and out into deep water." One thing leads to another.

Examining the erosion process from a geological viewpoint, Robert Dolan had published similar conclusions earlier. Writing in *Science,* the journal of the American Association for the Advancement of Science, in 1972 he had recommended an overall reassessment of dune building programs:

"In the early 1930s the barrier islands of North Carolina were in what might be called a natural or equilibrium state. Changes were rapid, but the system was well adapted to accommodate powerful natural forces. . . . Although intuition suggests that by stabilizing the dunes one succeeds in stabilizing the entire beach system, the dunes are, unfortunately, a response element of the system, not a forcing element. . . . If the dune areas are stabilized, the new system must adjust to any changes in the barrier itself. That is, if the sea level rises and the beach zones shift landward, the dunes must also shift, or the beach sector of the system is reduced in width, the energy dissipation process is changed, and the entire system is forced out of equilibrium. . . . In the 13 years since the National Park Service initiated its major effort to stabilize the dunes and beaches along the Outer Banks . . . a process of beach narrowing, relative to the original dune system, has been underway. Originally the distance from the dune fields to the shoreline was about 100 to 125 m(eters); since then erosion has reduced this distance by 30 to 40 m(eters), leaving beach widths of 70 to 100 m(eters) in most areas."

Dolan argued that since the width of the beach became progressively narrower "a greater amount of [wave] energy is being dissipated per meter of beach profile." This, he said commonsensically, contributes to a vicious cycle that might have been triggered by building artificial barrier dunes. Since they did not naturally migrate toward the mainland as the beach itself moved, the foreshore must grow steeper as it grew narrower. He suspected that when the beach reached a certain critical angle it acted like a sea wall and reflected wave energy back into the shallows—energy that normally would have been harmlessly released on a broad beach face. This wave reflection could steepen the underwater swash zone profile, too, and hasten erosion.

The specific mechanics involved remain a topic of esoteric debate. If this was happening along Hatteras, it might not happen elsewhere because the tolerances for any phenomenon are narrow while island characteristics vary widely. But geologists, botanists, island managers and ecologists agree on one thing at least: The chances of artificially stabilizing most dynamic islands are slim at best. The natural forces are simply too quixotic for that. Consider the Ash Wednesday storm of 1962. Dolan was completing his graduate work along the Outer Banks when that historic storm appeared.

This was a so-called 100-year storm, one that is statistically likely to occur every century through a coincidence of various conditions. The center of the low pressure system lingered 700 miles off Hatteras, Dolan recalls. Hurricane force winds built up waves that must have self-destructed at sea as they rose too high to support themselves. Even then the wind's energy remained trapped in water that reached across the continental shelf. Steep waves built up in ever shallower water. When they reached the shoals their force was compressed more and the kinetic chaos became enormous. Dolan watched the sea work on the barrier dunes that had been built with the best intentions—to employ jobless men during the Depression and later to preserve valued life and property within the Seashore. Twenty-foot crests 200 to 400 feet apart came ashore at 6 to 8 second intervals. "The actual record showed twenty-one foot waves . . . just before the pier on which the guage was mounted was destroyed." As the storm grew the shore retreated. Barrier dunes were levelled, their sand carried to sea or strewn 120 feet inland. Buildings were battered down and washed off their footings; roads were buried or their surfaces broken into pieces like peanut brittle. The shape of the coast was reordered, rendering recent maps obsolete. Watching that storm, Dolan decided man-made barrier dunes weren't all they were cracked up to be. Had they not been there these islands might have sustained less damage. Certainly there would have been fewer "improvements" to be damaged.

A more recent example of a fierce ocean storm's impact occurred in February, 1978, when a two-day northeaster remodeled New England shores and paralyzed Massachusetts. Boston reported 27 inches of snow and 79 mile-an-hour winds. Cape Cod communities were ravaged. In Chatham the wind rose to 92 miles an hour. The storm surge at Eastham rose 4 feet above spring tide level. Along the coast 10,000 residents fled. Nearly 12,000 private homes were damaged or destroyed at a cost of $172 million. The toll in damage to *public* property in "mostly coastal" towns rose to $213 million. Stephen P. Leatherman, director of the National Park Service's Cooperative Research Unit which has facilities in Amherst and Wellfleet, writes: "Property losses in several Massachusetts towns, located on barrier beaches, totaled in the $100,000 category . . . The nearshore breaker heights exceeded 5 meters" or 16 feet. Dune erosion on Coast Guard Beach, the keystone of Cape Cod National Seashore, amounted to more than 16 cubic meters per meter of beach and dunes receded 9 meters. The parking lot was destroyed. A few miles south at Nauset Beach, a place called "three cabin hole" implicitly became "two cabin hole" when a storm surge swept through the dunes and knocked one fisherman's retreat down like a house of cards. Nearby, a National Literary Landmark was swept away. This was the dwelling Henry Beston inhabited and remembered in his classic *The Outermost House.* Along the length of the Cape, cliffs were scarped back. But the beaches reappeared when the tide fell.

With a four-foot storm surge and 92-mile-an hour winds, that winter storm displayed the intensity of a Category 1 hurricane on the Saffir/ Simpson Scale used by the National Hurricane Center. In the first 75 years of this century 45 such hurricanes struck the Atlantic and Gulf coasts. As tropical storms go, these cause "minimal" damage. The one that destroyed George West's Virginia island home was a Category 2 hurricane, one with a storm surge 6 to 8 feet above normal and packing 96 to 110 mile-an-hour winds. These cause "moderate" damage, but West's remark haunts me. "I owned a thousand acres right about here. This was an island," he said while porpoises played around the boat. "All got in safe except my grandfather and old Mr. Cobb. We didn't know anything about hurricanes then—called them northeasters. Nobody could conceive a tide could come that high."

Though much of his land vanished, the ecosystem and the habitat survived, albeit a little farther west. "The real conflict is not between sea and shore, for theirs is only a lovers' quarrel, but between man and nature," as one writer points out. Along the coast and "on the beach, nature has achieved a dynamic equilibrium that is alien to man and his static sense of equilibrium. Once a line has been established, whether it is a shoreline or a property line, man unreasonably expects it to stay put." Historians believe they can pinpoint the spot on Roanoke Island behind the Outer Banks where Sir Walter Raleigh founded the first hopeful English settlement in America. Archaeologists have searched for it repeatedly until Bob Dolan concluded "The Lost Colony" site has probably slipped beneath Albemarle Sound in the normal course of littoral events. An Athenian observed 25 centuries ago "Change is the nature of things, all is flux, all things are in alteration." Especially the beach, whether stormy or calm.

Fortunately even bureaucratic policies can change.

Responding to investigators like Godfrey and Dolan, the Park Service has adopted a program of noninterference with natural processes along its barrier islands. Park people are manfully trying to manage each enclave in its own best ecological interests. But for various unecological reasons the heritage of past interference persists. For example, the developments within Cape Hatteras Seashore will certainly not be abruptly abandoned. But rebuilt with public money after the next hurricane? That's a different question. Elsewhere it would be absurdly callous to think beachfront owners from Carolina to Campobello won't mourn the loss of treasured land to ubiquitous erosion and try to preserve what they can, however they can. But ironically, natural economic law makes restitution in some places which littoral law has condemned. A Martha's Vineyard summertimer told me he'd bought 16 clifftop acres 20 years ago as both a retreat and an investment. Storm seas undermine the foot of his cliff and rain erodes its brow. In places you can watch glacial stones tumble down the sandy face continually—even on calm days—making furrows and tiny sand slides as they come. That man said his parcel has dwindled to half its former size, but rising land values make it worth many times its original price, if he should sell before it vanishes.

"Each man kills the thing he loves," Oscar Wilde wrote. People who love the shore—and insist on living there—sometimes kill it by building there. A variety of local, state and federal agencies have done their parts through well-intentioned but ultimately misguided efforts to stabilize this protean place whose vitality and survival depend on constant change. Folks who love the more removed parts of the beach and travel there in four-wheel-drive vehicles, kill it with their tires. A buggy track crossing a dune can change an island; driving along a berm changes the subsurface moisture regime, Paul Godfrey has learned. While some plants colonize ruts along the berm, and in a marsh, the evidence suggests that traffic does more harm than good. Certainly more people visit a beach if they can ride instead of walk and more people mean greater impact. (Mea culpa. I was among the drivers while researching this book.) And yet the beaches persist, a fact that is part of their miraculous nature.

Some of the dirtier deeds are done out of shortsightedness so extreme as to border on the criminally stupid. As one angry Long Island official said after the locally devastating winter of 1978, "People who built glass houses on exposed beaches violated nature. They bulldozed dunes to see the ocean from their houses, and the ocean wiped them out" because the dunes weren't there to protect them. The irony is as plain as the facts. The shore attracts people with its wildness and constant, dynamic change. Answering this Siren call, people move there bringing all the comforts of home, making everything apparently secure and hoping to settle peacefully. But the dynamic forces can take away everything they bring, especially if they change the place. The syndrome has been going on so long that folks are finally beginning to accept the Biblical injunction against building on sand. While strict preservationists support restrictive building codes on philosophical grounds, a financial impetus prods the growing trend toward restricting development. People are getting tired of seeing public money spent to fight losing battles with the sea. Others rankle at the hidden public costs of beach development: tax breaks on construction loans for beachfront speculators; Federal loans and disaster relief when the inevitable occurs. It seems the taxpayer has paid coming and going whether or not he got to use that stretch of beach which (as often as not) became sacrosanct private property after its federally encouraged development. As the president of a local Audubon Society wrote after a series of storms washed several Long Island homes away, "We are made well aware of this ownership during the summer months by posted 'private property' and 'keep out' signs that litter the dune area. However, in the case of disaster we can all share the burden of the owners' misfortune with our tax dollars."

Attracted by the natural beach, ingenious man has learned to manipulate natural forces to a degree so that folks can live within sight or earshot of the surf. Consider it on a small scale first. The beach householder's popular method of preserving his precious bit of strand involves a groin, a low wooden wall going out to sea. He builds it from the boundary that is downstream in relation to the alongshore current. The water loses speed when it encounters this solid obstacle and drops its sand. But the obstacle interrupts the current. On the down-drift side of the barrier, the current picks up speed again. Moving faster and gaining competence, it also picks up sand—from the downstream neighbor's beach. Never say a groin doesn't work, a long-time denizen of the Hamptons told me. The board chairman of one of the nation's largest corporations built a private groin that worked beautifully. "It built a lovely sandy beach on his property. But the house next door, where one used to play croquet on that gorgeous lawn, is under the waves." The littoral drift methodically and inevitably washed it away.

Almost every time someone manages to increase his precious acreage, someone else's "kingdom of the shore" pays back the debt. In a letter to his brother, E. B. White spun this sad yarn from his Florida retreat fifteen years ago. "One of the Ringlings, years ago, owned a key near town called Bird Key and his deed included the right to fill. When a promoter finally got possession of Bird Key, he went right to work with a scoop and scooped up about half the bottom of Sarasota Bay, substantially increasing the size of his holdings by just spreading sand in all directions. [In broadening his island he narrowed the waterways around it, unnaturally.] A side result of this brilliant real estate operation was that the tidal current in Big Pass jumped from something like 3 knots to something like 7 knots, washing away beaches all the way from the mouth of the Pass halfway into town and causing a real beaut of an erosion problem. All the property owners along the Pass had to build groins, so that what was once a lively little stretch of natural beach, complete with dunes, sea grape, and Australian pine, now looks like a broken-down docking facility."

Francis P. Shepard, an august coastal geologist at the Scripps Institute of Oceanography has written that "South Cape May (N.J.) has virtually disappeared during the past 50 years due to jetties to the northeast and to the southerly current. . . . Most of the vacationers fail to realize that the works of man are doing far more to eliminate their valued heritage than to preserve it."

Groin or jetty, man-made obstacles all look alike to the ocean. One drastically changed Assateague, the island that straddles the Maryland-Virginia line. The hurricane of 1933 carved an inlet where none had been before, right below present-day Ocean City. A year later the new inlet threatened to close up naturally as the littoral current dropped new sand. But fishermen liked the cut and it was secured by a breakwater. The littoral current, less than half a knot, dropped sand on the north side of the jetty as it slowed down to negotiate the obstacle. Soon it broadened the beach above the barrier at the south end of Ocean City, creating all sorts of room for ferris wheels, french fry stands, penny arcades and assorted honky-tonk. But where the current returned to its normal course and speed it picked up sand—from Assateague's north end which was once a straight extension of Ocean City's island. As the seaward side of Assateague eroded, the marshy inland side grew toward the mainland with sand carried by overwash and inlet current. There were once serious plans to develop that island; house lots were laid out and some roads built. Fortunately the plans were cancelled by the creation of Assateague National Seashore. Since then the north end of the island has moved toward the mainland more than its original width. Viewed from the air Assateague's outer beach is clearly to the west of Ocean City's bay shore, though the islands were once aligned. Many of the Assateague house lots, if measured from a spot on the relatively immobile mainland, now lie beneath the open Atlantic. Yet barrier island systems being what they are, Assateague looks pretty much intact and in place, as if it's always been right there. Certainly it's been an island for a millennium or two, one that's moved around all the time. The Ocean City jetty just modified the movement in a matter of years.

"Confrontation engineering" means building things to stop waves: breakwaters, jetties, seawalls. These can only offer short-term solutions to what people consider a problem. The tide giveth and sooner or later taketh away. Witness the north end of Assateague; witness several erstwhile estate homes in the Hamptons and the houses on Fire Island that once stood atop dunes but are now propped up with crutchlike pilings, the bottoms of their livingroom floors exposed to bathers along the open beach. Witness Salisbury Beach, Mass., which was wrecked in the winter of '78. By summer a piledriver cast its shadow across shooting galleries and burst-the-balloon stalls to build another pavilion on the open beach, replacing one that had been destroyed. "Mother Nature took the sand away," the Chief of Police told me. "Then she gave it all back." For how long remains to be seen.

Island migration is inevitable. Some experts concede that a shoreline can be anchored right where it is—if enough money is spent to turn a sand beach into something else. Seawalls usually work, but can cause wave reflection and erosion elsewhere. They also create a vertical shore; then a walk on the beach is a hopping march along enormous stepping stones. Sandbags are even more unpleasant, and the bigger they are the worse they look and feel underfoot. To preserve a shore absolutely *in situ*—if the sea means to move it—requires turning the strand into a "hardened surface" of one kind or another. Beach "nourishment" works in places that have a convenient supply of surplus sand and bottomless public coffers. The sand is pumped (or hauled) to where the people want it. It's dumped there for the waves to continually wash it away. Effective, yes, but the labor is as Herculean as cleaning stables and the costs are perpetual.

The experts are pessimistic about any man-made structure remaining indefinitely on most barrier islands. Certainly some sites are better than others; and the open beach worst of all. But ironically that is where many people most want to build or buy—with little thought about the inherent insecurity. "In recent years, development of the Atlantic coast barrier islands has been inversely related to the hazards characteristic of the shorezone," Robert Dolan writes. "The most intense developments have been located dangerously close to the sea while more stable landscape areas have remained undeveloped. This inversion stems from the desire to be near the water's edge, even when this location introduces a degree of risk." In a special survey of Ocean City, Md., he found 25 buildings costing more than $100 million that have been erected since

1970. All stand within the reach of the 1962 Ash Wednesday storm surge and within "the predicted inland boundary of the storm-surge penetration zone for 30 years in the future." Certainly some buildings will survive the next storm, as some survived Ash Wednesday. But, as Francis Shepard writes, "Predicting whether a house owner is likely to lose his property during his lifetime is a little like predicting when a war is going to end."

Not only are islands subject to constant frontal attack from the sea, they are also vulnerable to "the Singapore scenario," says J. W. Pierce, a Smithsonian geologist. This occasional phenomenon is named for the supposedly impregnable British fortress which fell to the Japanese from the rear. It works this way: When a hurricane moves north from the Caribbean the first winds felt along the mid-Atlantic coast may come from an eastern point of the compass; whether from north-northeast or south-southeast doesn't much matter. These winds force water into the bays behind the barrier islands and hold it there, abnormally high perhaps for an entire tide cycle. When the storm center passes the wind shifts 180° quickly. The new wind blows all that bay water back, flooding barrier islands from the inland side where its natural "defenses" are weakest and man-made ones often nonexistent.

This has happened innumerable times over the millennia in many island chains with understandable results. North Carolina historian David Stick writes that the phenomenon is responsible for most of the "inlets" along the Outer Banks; they're really "outlets" formed when high waters rushed back to the ocean taking the shortest courses they could find or create. There are eight breaks in the island chain today; in the historical past, 30 such inlets were named and there is physical evidence of another 18. They come and go, most of them filling up again naturally in a few years. Barden's Inlet would have vanished soon after it opened a few decades ago. But fishermen in the vicinity of Harker's Island liked it and federal money was appropriated to dredge it. As a result of currents through the artificially maintained cut, the island of Core Banks is eroding toward the lighthouse, which must be moved or protected by new engineering works.

No discussion of dubious beach development, coastal meddling and human myopia would be complete without mention of the people who dredge Barden's Inlet and almost every other: the U.S. Army Corps of Engineers. Striding around the beaches with an unquenchable sense of mission, the Corps assures anyone who'll listen that engineering can cure almost any natural problem. A shore moves inconveniently? The

Corps will cement it in place, one way or another. They've been doing it for years and show little inclination to stop—even though their results are at best temporary and local. Think of them as coastal Crusaders out to conquer the Infidel sea. The group's Coastal Engineering Research Center once went so far as to declare: "Our campaign against the encroachment of the sea must be waged with the same care that we would take against any other enemy threatening our boundaries."

At this writing the Corps is ambitiously proposing more coastal works despite a wealth of unhappy experience. Somehow they have aggressively refused to recognize what can be called the Onimod Theory—domino spelled backward: Put one engineering marvel in place along the littoral, whether a jetty, seawall or inlet, and soon something else will have to be erected nearby. One groin begets another. The reason: Anything built along the coast causes unexpected side effects because littoral systems are so complex and have so many delicately balanced factors. The absurd history of Fire Island's west end was spelled out by Francis Shepard in his definitive catalogue of America's coastlines:

> When Army engineers built the Democrat Point Jetty (1939–1941) several changes resulted. The westward growth of the point was temporarily stopped. Sand built the outer beach of Fire Island out to the end of the jetty in a few years; [behind the island] a new projection grew northward from the point across half of the inlet. [A new bar appeared in the channel between Fire Island and Oak Beach on the island it overlapped.] The strong current in the channel increased as a result of this bar and attacked the western point of Oak Beach, cutting it back variously from 150 to 200 feet . . . Consequently the beach was built out artificially and a new channel was cut by the State of New York at about the middle of the inlet. This channel soon filled, necessitating more dramatic action, so a jetty was built across the north channel. The erosion has stopped; but according to the 1960 chart, no adjacent channel now enters the bay. The future of Fire Island inlet will depend . . . on how much the shore is controlled by man.

Shepard also reports on a portion of Connecticut shore. The engineers were

> called upon at several Connecticut beaches to check beach erosion where it was becoming harmful to the beach-resort character of the community. In several places, groins have been erected along the shore to trap sand. To replace it on the beaches where erosion has occurred, sand has been dredged from offshore deposits. This sand transfer has oversteepened the subaqueous profile, causing accelerated beach erosion, and a few years later the dredging processes have had to be repeated.

Still, the Corps loves building groins and recently renewed its proposals to construct them along stretches of beach where erosion threatens real estate. After the tempestuous winter of 1978, the chief planning engineer for the Corps' Fire Island Unit testified: "Our studies to date indicate that it is feasible to stabilize the barrier beach, but as this is a dynamic coastal environment, subject to coastal forces of varying intensities . . . there is going to be some loss." Give him credit for a modicum of candor. "You are therefore going to have to periodically nourish the existing formations. Our plan . . . calls for using sand to armor, to build up and act as a buffer [along] the forebeach, berm and dunes to specific levels." But " 'if deemed necessary'. . . if all else fails," the Corps anticipates building as many as 13 massive groins along a 32-mile stretch between Morishes and Fire Island Inlets. The Park Service is up in arms. Part of its mandate is to preserve natural places "for future generations" and rangers say the best way to do that is to let the seashore take care of itself.

Mind you, groins work. But they are expensive and only protect their immediate environs—usually expensive private property—while they make unpredictable havoc elsewhere. Their temporary, local effectiveness is unquestioned. But their long term value is debatable and their long distance effects unpredictable.

In Ocean City, Md., like Miami Beach, "the ocean front hotels are just that," says one coastal wag. Long series of groin fields were built all the way to the Delaware line and the beach grew seawards for a few decades. As the beach grew wider it grew more popular until on any summer weekend its sands were covered with groin-to-groin sunbathers. Once a sleepy shore town, Ocean City became a summer metropolis. Scores, possibly hundreds, of high-rise motels and condominiums now stand in ranks sometimes several blocks deep from the beach—as of this writing. But after three winters of severe northeasters, high tide arrived below the old boardwalk and washed the footings of several new condominiums. However, architects assure me that beachfront condominiums are designed to stay erect in totally saturated sand. So if the sea invades here and makes this island much narrower, the condos might survive. Residents would just have new parking/commuting problems since the parking lots would be several feet underwater at hightide and the buildings a trifle offshore. Ocean City's mayor had other ideas and hired bulldozers to ply the shoals, shoving mountains of sand into steep dunes guarding the buildings. At this writing he seems to have "saved" the city. But there is no reason to believe that these results will be long-lived. Like Miami Beach before it, Ocean City has been treating a symptom for decades but cannot touch the basic condition. The island wants to go west.

Still, the citizens of Ocean City were well pleased with the mayor for making mountainous sand hills between their buildings and the surf. In the fall of 1978 it seemed his dykes had held and in apparent gratitude the voters rewarded him with a fifth term in office. He garnered 3 out of 4 votes, though a proposition to raise his salary was defeated. There are ironies to spare in all of this. It's possible that any effort, feeble or Herculean, might succeed for a few years—depending on the weather. Just as the meteorological oddsmakers hedge their bets on the date of the next thirty-year storm, resort entrepreneurs can put their money on short-term predictions of idyllic summers and easy winters for a few years in a row. The developer who builds out, lucks out and sells out before a northeaster strikes can make a small fortune. And let's face it: The fast buck is *primo mobile* for most beachfront development.

The ocean constantly erodes every beach; even the ones that build out are constantly losing minute sand grains as more take their place for a net gain. Those that seem stabile are constantly replenished from a natural reservoir of sand (which itself may be replenished in the natural scheme of things). The source might lie offshore or in inland mountains. Coastal currents or rushing rivers naturally carry it to the beach. The supply can run out or, more often, it can be cut off—by inland dams or by another groin field. Then sand on a specific beach, continually taken away, will not be replaced. To a human observer it will seem as if erosion suddenly quickened; in fact natural replenishment stopped. The net result is the same: less beach. J.W. Pierce once identified hydroelectric dams high in the Italian Alps as the culprits that summarily changed an ancient bathing beach on the instep of Italy. He'd never seen the dams nor been told about them, but one look at the beach and he knew something was amiss upriver. The dams had been built to provide electric power to a region that Italian planners decided should become a modern Mecca for foreign tourists (who must have power-hungry amenities, of course). Pierce told the Italian government they could easily get their beach back by levelling the dams to release the mountain sand that had fed this strand year in and year out since Grecian times at least. Rather than give up the electric power, Italy decided to truck sand in every winter (when the tourists were away) and dump it on the beach—the crudest kind of beach nourishment.

It goes without saying that individuals and government agencies will continue to take extraordinary steps to preserve "permanent improvements." And these measures will often work, for a while.

Obviously some building near the sea is reasonable and houses on sand spits may be inevitable. It would be nice, though, if builders would recognize the risks, act responsibly and take their lumps or rely on private insurance instead of a federal bailout when the inevitable occurs. As George West said, "Any man says he can build something the ocean won't tear up is is overlooking a whole lot. He's a damn fool pure and simple." Beyond that, some places are best left alone—especially when their natural mechanisms take better care of them than we can.

Driftwords:

The "Obvious" Imperative

When all is said and done scientifically, mysteriously, esoterically, things of the shore often boil down to common sense. Some examples:

At a scholarly meeting, the senior scientist discussed in elegant detail the abstruse physiology of cypress trees in southern salt marshes. After his learned paper was read, a respectful junior botanist asked about the gas exchange on which every cypress tree depends. Swamp mud is anaerobic. Yet the botanical solon seemed to assume that oxygen enters the roots through a medium where none exists. Q: "How can this occur?" A: "It must."

Pale, pink, and a little plump, the young couple from South Boston bought eels in Tony Chiarappo's Bass Run Bait and Tackle Shop halfway up the forearm of Cape Cod. Then they asked directions to the nearest bridge they could dangle their lines from. Tony: "If you like bridge fishing, better go back to Hyannis. There's not many bridges up around here."

Camped under pitch pines after a long day trekking beaches, my friend concocts an extraordinary dinner from the Jeep's rude larder (an old wooden wine crate) and a flounder that was happily scrounging its living from the sea floor just yesterday. Was it the al fresco atmosphere that makes it so delicious? I asked. Or the French culinary technique? The pinch of garlic and dollop of jug wine? Or the freshness of the fish? Mary: "Who cares?"

Part III
The Arts of Beaching

Like Everest, but far more accessible, the beach "is there." For better or worse, millions seek it out today as some have for ages. Remember that Indians who wintered inland spent their summers on these shores, though Europeans didn't discover the delights of warm-weather beaches until the eighteenth century. The early colonists, of course, settled the coasts for practical reasons; few gamboled on the strands before barging west with a "Bible and jug in one hand and (like as not) a native tomahawk in the other," as Faulkner put it. Americans didn't start going to the beach in playful earnest until the 1850s, when a group of New Jersey boosters convinced a railroad to serve Absecon Island. Thus Atlantic City was born. It came of age in 1870 with its first boardwalk, which was built because hotels complained about guests tracking sand in from the beach! An ominous beginning. Now Orrin Pilkey Sr. and Jr., primary authors of the well regarded *How to Live with an Island,* warn about "the New Jerseyization" of the coast as far south as the Carolinas. Somehow the motive behind the first New Jersey boardwalk and the latest seaside condominium city anywhere recalls a famous fictional pair:

> The Walrus and the Carpenter
> Were walking close at hand.
> They wept like anything to see
> Such quantities of sand:
> "If this were only cleared away."
> They said, "it would be grand!"
> "If seven maids with seven mops
> Swept it for half a year,
> Do you suppose," the Walrus said,
> "That they could get it clear?"
> "I doubt it," said the Carpenter,
> And shed a bitter tear.

I find myself on the oysters' side. The beach is better off without people who dislike it as it is. May some beaches be saved from sweepers, carpenters, builders of boardwalks, and others who would change it into a different place.

It is beyond this book's scope (and its author's ken) to discuss high-rise resort living. When I want all the comforts of home, I stay there. When I want a sense of the real world, an adventurous rest, or just a thorough airing, it's beach time. When the hunger grows for a few self-reliant days—a sense of the need to know how to handle natural hazards alone—I find an island. When the city closes in and I need the perspective of being apart, I face an overwhelming ocean. Tiring of the urbane, I watch shore birds. I tend to go where and when other people don't. Some years I've spent more time on the shore in January than July because the easy-to-reach places are empty. For several years running I swam in the Atlantic off the Delmarva peninsula within a week of Christmas when the water still held a hint of summer's warmth and almost every summertime visitor stayed away. Between July 4th and Labor Day I generally walk an extra mile or drive an extra day to find some kind of solitude.

Why go to the beach? For reasons touched on before and hereafter. To see the critters, to taste the rose hips, to let a child reinvent castles in the sand again, to find a whale's jawbone. For isolation and the challenge of elemental living. For superb sea-fresh food simply cooked outside or in a cottage kitchen. For a lover's constant quiet company. For the contrasts of a sweating run and then a surf swim; of a freezing day-long walk, then hot chowder. For the slow, sensuous roller coaster of searing noons and sleep in salty air. For the certain fury of a gale, the glory of the burning sun's rise out of a calm sea, for the miracle of diving birds and the rare wonder of walking naked in moonlight. For the itch of sand between the toes and glimpses of infinity.

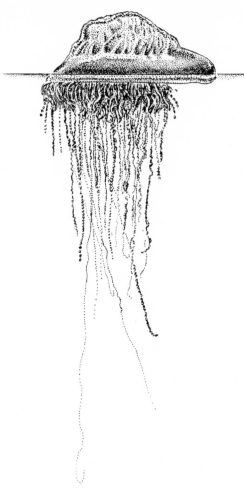

Justly notorious: the Portugese man-of-war.

Chapter Nine

Adolph's and the Lion's Mane

The beach, like Rhett Butler, frankly doesn't give a damn. It doesn't care whether folks visit or not, even whether a visitor lives or not. This is not to say that the beach is a maliciously deadly place. It is impersonal, remote (and in another sense, the more remote the better). Since wild beaches lack telephones and First Aiders behind every dune, people visiting them are on their own and had better know what they're doing.

Anyone going beyond the boundaries of a "protected" beach must be alert to the kinds of pitfalls that can appear. Of course it's best to avoid physical problems, but once encountered they must be addressed directly and on their own terms; you can't con a wave.

Urban sophisticates are adept at verbally resolving all sorts of difficulties, like talking cops out of traffic tickets. But the sun's ultraviolet rays have no interest in extenuating circumstances. They just burn, and seem to burn hotter in spring than autumn, though that appearance is misleading: It's a matter of one's having gotten used to sunshine. By the same token, because the body's temperature-control mechanisms function best after steady use, a winter's layoff means that sweat glands simply don't work as well the first week of summer as they will after Labor Day. Even fatigue is a matter of conditioning—not of one's imagination or moral laxness. Keep in mind that the beach is a physical place and can be dealt with only in physical terms. The problems it presents cannot be disarmed by personal charm or pleas for sympathy: A Portuguese man-of-war has no ears.

This chapter will not deal with general first aid—like how to treat a flesh wound—there are specific manuals for that. Rather it will describe the special hazards of the beach, the various mechanics they involve and ways to anticipate them. These hazards involve matters as general as one's salt/water balance and particulars as nettlesome as jellyfish stings. First, the business of the surf itself:

Born and raised on Cape Cod, Richard T. Baker has guarded lives on beaches facing at least three oceans. He is presently hatching plans to elevate lifeguarding from an informal part-time business of whistle blowing and macho showmanship to a nationally recognized profession that involves tested standards and universal principles. Very strong and almost pathologically fit, Baker stays that way by respecting the powers of the sea. During ten years at Assateague National Seashore where he is chief lifeguard, he has seen arms broken, thighs fractured, vertebrae cracked, and both shoulders dislocated in people who were "just dumped by a wave." His first rule when entering the surf is simple: Don't do it yet. Wait a minute—wait five—and watch what's going on. With a little practice and experience, simple observation can show you a great deal about the water and the surface of the shallow ocean bottom.

First, estimate the height of the breakers and, hence, their power. There's no need to compute foot-pounds of force; just visualize the strength of their impact if one should break over you at shoulder height

—or catch your child across the knees. Anticipate just how far out you (and others with you) can safely wade or swim. Keep these limits in mind.

Next, look for currents and underwater sandbars. That sounds as if it requires clairvoyance or X-ray vision, but in fact it's easy to spot the location of unseen bars. Harkening back to the mechanics of waves, remember that they steepen dramatically when the water gets shallow. Obviously waves break in the surf zone near the beach (where the water depth becomes less than one-seventh the wave length, the distance between crests). Breaking waves are the ones to watch out for because they physically transport water and whatever's in it—including people.

Waves undulating up and down simply demonstrate the passage of energy through the water; you can float among non-breaking waves and bob around like a cork—even beyond the closest surf line. But look farther out as well; there's usually another line of cresting waves. Its location betrays an underwater sandbar, a fairly abrupt shallowing which is responsible for the water's visible disturbance. Study that line of cresting waves which keeps appearing at the same place: It indicates the shape and extent of the bar which lies roughly parallel to the beach. Since bars mean shallows, the water there may not be over your head, should you need to touch bottom after swimming through the deep water beyond the close-in surf zone. Often a bar offers a place to stand and rest.

Regardless of whether the tide is rising or falling, the water breaking on the beach must go somewhere; it seeks its own level in the sea. Thus it rushes away from the land to create a mythological "undertow." Baker says there's no such thing in fact. Call it "backwash." Certainly this rush of water can be strong enough to nudge a wader's feet out from under him, especially at certain tide phases on the steepest slope of a summer beach. If that happens and the wader falls down, more backwash tumbles him farther downhill. This is a simple phenomenon, but folks promote it into the fiction of a malevolent force apparently bent on dragging them the breadth of the continental shelf. It's simply backwash: the flow of water going its own way, when new waves arrive. Farther out is where things can get really perilous.

As waves cross a sandbar they can create discrete inshore currents, occasionally becoming alarmingly strong. Flowing between the surf and the sandbar, these currents are sometimes dangerous, especially to unsuspecting swimmers. They are strongest where they break through a bar since physical openings in the bar act like funnels. The currents move seaward surprisingly fast, especially in relation to the nearby land-bound waves. Misnamed "rip tides," the most dramatic and disarming of these currents occur when they run perpendicular from the beach, heading straight out to sea. This is rare, says Baker, but when it happens the results can be terrifying. An unwary swimmer paddles happily on an oblique line toward the surf, then finds himself suddenly being swept away from shore. The swimmer panics, understandably, and tries to make shore via the shortest route: i.e., by turning right around and swimming straight back. The result can be swift exhaustion and possible drowning since few organisms besides fish swim faster than these currents.

Baker's suggestion—study the surf before entering it—can keep a swimmer out of a rip current in the first place. By observing where lines of breakers end, one can anticipate the location and direction of these currents. A sharp break in a surf line parallel to the beach means that's where a rip current can pass seaward through the bar. It has scoured out a deeper channel in the underwater sand; hence incoming waves don't crest or break the way they do in the shallower water above the intact sandbar. Ergo, Rule One: Stay away from such currents by staying away from gaps in lines of breakers. They are rarely more than several yards across and they are widely spaced. Swim somewhere else, within an unbroken sandbar.

Break Rule One and your life can depend on assiduously observing Rule Two: When you get caught in a rip current, don't fight it head-on because you'll probably lose. Stop. Tread water. Get your bearings. Then move at right angles to the current; swim across it (even though it's still carrying you seaward) until you are outside its influence. This will take only a few strokes since these currents are narrow. Alternatively, if you passively let it carry you past the bar, you'll find that a rip current dissipates beyond the line of cresting waves. Then drift into the crest line and let the breaking waves push you back toward shore; use the ocean's energy to your advantage.

Instructions like these are easy enough to codify in my comfortable study on a quiet night in Washington when most locals are away and even the tourists have taken their groaning Winnebagos off to bed. It's an entirely different matter on a windy day in brisk surf 30 yards from an East Coast beach that threatens to vanish over the western horizon. Please remember anyway: Don't panic. Turn right or left 90° and *swim across the current* to slower water that's moving the right way. And if you do get into trouble in sight of people on shore, don't try to wave both arms violently to attract attention. That just wastes energy and makes you sink besides. Tread water and raise one hand; it'll be obvious that something's amiss—should anyone be willing and able to help in time.

Rip currents running straight away from land are rare. Currents running obliquely through a surf zone are more common. They're more insidious too; more subtle and longer, they move away from the land less dramatically. But the same rules apply. If you see a surf line slanting away from shore, recognize that a current probably goes the same direction and avoid it. If you forget and it starts carrying you the wrong way, don't try to swim against it. Swim across the current to easier water before heading back to the beach.

Closer in, when you start playing in the water, notice which way you're being carried. The surf pushes everything a little distance along the beach with each wave. Almost every working day, Baker sees a parent bawl out some innocent kid: "Didn't I tell you to swim right *there?*" It's an impossible order to obey. The slight slant of the surf will always carry a swimmer or wader up or down the beach. It takes a conscious effort to stay in one place, or to return to Point A. Better tell a child to walk back every few minutes, explaining that the water will naturally push him astray. For yourself, pick a reference point: a pile of driftwood, a blowout in the dune, a beach towel, and keep in sight of it.

While rip currents dissipate beyond the offshore sandbar, seaward winds don't. This doesn't affect swimmers, but it can play havoc with people riding air mattresses. In fact, if the wind is blowing off the shore, don't even bother to inflate a raft. It can be a killer. The reasons are simple. Swimming out, most folks are aware they'll have to swim back and budget their energy. But with the crutch of an air mattress, there seems to be a greater degree of safety, longer mobility and willingness to venture into deeper water. Then a moderate wind can push the raft and rider farther out to sea, taking them into very deep water indeed. Next stop Spain!

Naming the exotic place recalls the Mediterranean beaches of the Costa Brava: Ruby sangria on snow-white sand; cold prawns and sweet clams no bigger than a thumbnail; hot sun and brisk water. It also recalls a drowning off Costa del Sol—the Coast of the Sun—twenty years ago. The train had brought hundreds of Madrilenos to Malaga for the weekend. One young man wired his mother that he'd arrived safely: "Dios me guarde. Tu hijo." The public beach, bordered on the south side by a high outcrop of fossil-filled stone, was wide and hot. The underwater profile sloped very gently. The young man from Madrid waded out a hundred yards or more to the surf off the point, slipped and went under—perhaps hitting a rock. His friends and a score of strangers had a slow time carrying him to shore. A Scottish dentist offered artificial respiration by-the-book, but not speaking Spanish, he was turned down. An American student climbed the cliff barefoot and ran for a doctor who had portable oxygen equipment, but the doctor wouldn't come without payment in advance. With everybody in charge and nobody in charge, the Spaniards tried to revive the anonymous swimmer several different ways. None worked, and now covered with foam-flecked sand he was dead. It was frustrating; all our efforts had been vain. It was frightening; any one of us could have been the victim. It was infuriating; the doctor should have come. A pall fell along the beach. The Catholics crossed themselves. The Scot cursed. I shuddered in the sun. That evening the text of the young man's telegram home went round the quiet outdoor cafés. Bartenders repeated it and passed it on. People crossed themselves again and drank to the memory of that dutiful son.

In America nearly 8,000 people will drown this year. It's the third leading cause of accidental death, which is to say the third most common cause of avoidable tragedy. The cause of death in most drownings is asphyxiation from water in the lungs. (The brain's oxygen supply is cut off and death follows fast.) However, perhaps 10 percent of drowning victims die of simple asphyxiation because a spasm in the glottis (part of the larynx) cuts off the air supply and prevents both water and air from reaching the lungs. Authorities beg statistics on near-drownings, but medical experts warn ocean swimmers about a particular peril: Near-drownings can kill after the victim's apparent recovery from the immediate event. Aspirating salt water is twice as dangerous as inhaling fresh water because of different physiological effects. Quantities of fresh water can be inhaled and actually absorbed by lung tissue without too much harm if the victim starts breathing again (with or without artificial help). But ocean water, due to its salt content, behaves differently in the lungs. It extracts vital fluids because of differences in osmotic pressure. When a semipermeable membrane separates salt water from fresh, pure water particles pass through the barrier until the two solutions are equally salty. It's the same problem marine fishes face. When this phenomenon occurs in the lungs, the secondary effects on blood chemistry as well as lung function are complex and dangerous. Anyone who survives a near-drowning episode in salt water should be hospitalized, medical authorities say, and placed under intensive pulmonary care until both the blood and lungs return to normal.

Underwater swimmers ask for trouble if they hyperventilate before testing their distance. Voluntarily breathing in and out hard seems a good idea before taking that last deep breath and diving. But it's really a bad idea because it abnormally rids the system of almost all carbon dioxide. The normal impulse to breathe is triggered by a need to expel CO_2, not to get fresh air. Oxygen hunger is only a secondary cause of the breathing reflex. Hence, hyperventilation before swimming underwater any distance risks exhausting the oxygen supply before enough new CO_2 builds up to warn that it's time for another breath. A submerged swimmer can suffocate that way.

Other dangers at the beach have equally simple origins, causes that are purely physical. A U. S. Navy installation once geared up for an impossible epidemic when an alarming number of recruits displayed an irreversible eye condition that was supposed to be rare, according to the textbooks. The problem, which led to permanent blindness in too many cases, involved tiny water blisters on the central retina, the rear inner surface of the eye. Fortunately it turned out that no new contagion was involved. Rather, these recruits had been taking LSD. Then, under its numbing influence, they'd do what normal reactions usually prevent: stare in fascination directly at the sun. Under ordinary circumstances, this quickly becomes intolerably uncomfortable. But LSD (and drugs like alcohol) can desensitize or raise the pain threshold. The result for the recruits was sunburn and blistering of the inner eye. Ophthamologists suggest that people other than acidheads should be alert to the problem. Tired vacationers lying on a beach under a light overcast are apt to stare at the dim solar disk, risking retinal damage from visible and invisible rays. The longer one looks directly at the sun, the worse the damage.

Sunburn is well named. The slower effects of ultraviolet light on human skin are akin to that of a flame. Exposed skin reddens as blood rushes to it; blisters develop to protect deeper tissues; and under rare circumstances skin can actually burn. Destroyed cells release organic components that irritate sensory nerves which carry a message—"Pain!" —to the brain. A suntan is the natural protective reaction to sunlight. Biochemically it works this way: Special cells containing a brown or black pigment called melanin are distributed evenly in the skin (or unevenly in people with freckles). The amount of pigment is genetically determined and is responsible for every individual's normal complexion. In theory a person could spontaneously turn dark overnight since melanin production is usually in a kind of suspended animation; the potential for making more melanin is always there but held in check. Sunlight results in tanning but it doesn't create it directly; rather, solar radiation relaxes natural controls. In summertime doses the sun's rays neutralize inhibitors that control an enzyme; unhibited, tyrosinase then stimulates the production of melanin. This has a biological purpose beyond human vanity: Melanin absorbs harmful radiation, protecting deeper tissues beneath the skin. The inhibitors remain active in skin areas protected from the sun; in exposed areas they become active again with less exposure to sunlight. Thus a suntan fades over the winter in people with normally light complexions as skin cells slough off revealing new layers containing less pigment. In addition, body chemistry breaks down some pigment after it forms.

Blacks and other people with dark complexions obviously have a protective head start and can sunbathe longer before burning than people endowed with less melanin. But everyone can suffer side effects of too much sun. Commercial lotions—the so-called sunscreens—effectively filter out ultraviolet rays. Another way to avoid burning is with progressive exposure. Start with short periods of sun and gradually lengthen them as tanning proceeds. Most people know their tolerances, so detailed suggestions would be gratuitous. But a couple of caveats bear mentioning: Chronic sun-worshippers—especially affluent Caucasians who coddle deep tans year after year, flirt with skin cancer from cumulative overdoses of solar radiation. In most forms this is the easiest kind of cancer to cure, but it can lead to serious disease.

Beyond that, even healthy people get burned in the damnedest places at the beach. I knew a golfer who played year-round and had the tan to prove it. Her arms, face and calves were dark, so she didn't use sun lotion at the beach. But she forgot her feet, usually protected by cleats and socks. Not so when she followed a high-tide line looking for shells. After that barefoot walk, she couldn't put shoes on for a week—whether to play a quick nine or even to go to work.

People sunbathing nude for the first time should also take special care. Patches of skin that have been covered by a bathing suit in previous summers have no residual tan from past years and are apt to burn fast. An allover tan can be attractive, but a localized burn can be very painful.

A far more serious problem caused by exposure to the sun, is called "heatstroke" by the American Red Cross and "hyperpyrexia" or "heat prostration" by medical texts. In the classic study of hot-weather health problems, *Physiology of Man in the Desert,* Edward F. Adolph defined it as "disorganized thermoregulatory ability." (Zoologists aren't the only specialists with nomenclature problems.) This condition can kill by any name. It involves a malfunction of temperature-control mechanisms which cannot reinstate themselves spontaneously. Once excessive heat throws a victim's thermostat out of kilter, he is apt to die unless artificial means are used to reverse a runaway heating trend.

Like the bimetal gadget on a dining-room wall, the human thermostat has two controlling elements. Both are located in the hypothalamus, a portion of the forebrain, but they are distinct and each responds to separate stimuli. When a person feels cold, a message goes from the skin to the brain, which then signals surface blood vessels to constrict in order to conserve body heat. Other signals then trigger shivering, which paradoxically helps warm the body. When a person gets too hot due to exercise or environment, the other brain center responds directly to internal temperature without the intervention of sensory organs. Then the hypothalamus signals surface vessels to dilate in order to let more blood flow through the skin, enabling the body to eliminate more heat through simple radiation. At the same time, the brain activates the sweat glands to help cool the body by excreting liquid which evaporates on the skin. For every gram of water that evaporates .58 calories of heat can be released. Evaporation of any liquid releases heat and has a cooling effect.

Normally the human thermostat is set at about 98.6° F. But a number of substances in the bloodstream can pathologically readjust the setting and delay reactions until a higher temperature is reached. These include some bacterial toxins and viruses; hence fever accompanies the common cold or flu. Alarmingly important, excess body heat affects the hypothalamus and interferes with its normal function. This is when the trouble starts—trouble that can compound itself into a fatal vicious circle. If the body gets too hot, the hypothalamus works less effectively; then cooling mechanisms like surface blood vessel dilation and sweating are delayed or weakened. Then the body gets hotter and the hypothalamus works even less effectively. As the body heats up, it inhibits the brain from turning on the cooling equipment full blast, which results in the brain getting hotter until the cooling systems shut down entirely. This can continue until higher body temperature kills brain cells and causes brain damage. Needless to say, an overdose of sun can start this runaway reaction.

Heatstroke symptoms may include any or all of the following: vertigo, unconsciousness, very flushed face, a strong rapid pulse, elevated blood pressure and dry skin, since the sweating mechanism is blocked by the kaput body thermostat. These symptoms may lead to convulsions, coma and death. First aid—or better yet, fast hospitalization—is needed to reduce body temperature so that the hypothalamus can start working properly again. The experts recommend trying almost anything to reduce body temperature if it reaches 105°:

Take the victim to the coolest available place where humidity is low. Strip him to increase cooling.

Aim fans at him to increase air circulation and evaporation.

Wipe him with cold, wet towels.

Sponge the body with rubbing alcohol which evaporates (and cools) faster than water.

Apply ice packs.

Put him in a cold bath. One standard medical text prescribes ice water baths; the Red Cross manual specifies cold water without ice.

But then the Red Cross also suggests that after undressing the victim the First Aider should use "a small bath towel to maintain modesty"— whether the victim's or the First Aider's remains unclear. (Gentle reader, dear friends, passing strangers: If anyone ever finds me felled by heatstroke and wastes any time on "modesty," I'll expire from apoplexy at such rank stupidity. Don't worry about fig leaves in potentially fatal situations. If a spare cloth is available, use it as a sponge. Delay meaningful treatment too long and the victim will have a sheet over his head soon enough.) Concentrate on lowering the body temperature and keeping it below 102°, since it can quickly "rebound" to higher levels.

Adolph writes: "One of the peculiar features of man's metabolism is that when he is sweating rapidly he does not take enough water to keep up his body water content; in other words, his sensations of thirst are not strong enough to demand sufficient water intake to replace water losses." This phenomenon can cause heat cramps and heat exhaustion.

Though less serious than heatstroke, these common conditions can lead to it if ignored. Both involve the sweating mechanism and the body's salt/water balance. The cramps come first, typically in the legs and stomach muscles. They result from too little salt in the body; nerve control of muscles depends on electrical connections made by salt ions in the blood. When an unacclimated person sweats profusely, he expels salt in unusual amounts. This robs the body of sufficient salt to make neurological connections; brain messages don't get through, muscles go into spasm, and the person gets cramps.

Salt depletion is most common when unacclimated people encounter unfamiliar heat. Like the skin's ability to cope with heavy doses of sunshine, sweating improves with time. Disused sweat glands excrete such quantities of sodium and chloride that the sweat itself may be nearly as salty as blood. But once these glands get used to summertime work, their ducts reabsorb much of the salt constituents and recycle them. Hence, someone getting used to hot weather may add extra salt to food for a few days. After getting acclimated, the extra salt should be stopped because excess salt retains water, inhibits sweating, and creates other problems. Remember that a normal diet usually contains ample salt; when more is needed, people develop a special taste for salty foods.

When someone in a cool climate encounters the first heat wave of the summer he simply can't sweat as freely at first; each sweat gland is like a rusty pump and takes time to work up to maximum activity. An acclimated person can excrete nearly 5 quarts of sweat an hour; a new-comer to the heat does well to expel a quart and a half an hour. Obviously, the extent of perspiration depends on ample water in the body. Loss of that water through sweating means a lower supply until it is replaced by drinking. When cells in the brain's thirst center—again, another part of the hypothalamus—get dehydrated, the person gets the message to drink. But the message may be repeated after drinking since it takes time for the water to be absorbed. As a result you can drink too much and experience "water intoxication." This occurs when body fluids become too diluted and there aren't enough salt ions to perform the body's electrochemical work. Thus, muscle cramps can be a symptom of salt deficiency in the form of dilute body fluids.

Heat exhaustion can occur after a few days in an unfamiliarly hot climate. First blood rushes to the capillaries in order to dispel excess body heat through radiation. This can rob vital organs of sufficient blood, so the capillaries then constrict leaving the skin pale and clammy (since sweating has been copious). The net result is a drop in blood pressure. Fainting occurs when not enough blood carries oxygen to the brain. The fainting spell itself can revive a victim since after falling down the head is lower than before and lower blood pressure suffices to supply the brain. Here the body takes care of itself.

The lessons are simple enough: Overexertion and overexposure at the beach should be avoided until you are thoroughly acclimated. And unless you are absolutely fit, pamper yourself when planning to spend more than a few hours on a remote beach. If you intend to walk a few miles, pack along plenty of water or fruit juice and some salty snacks. When sweating freely a quart of fluid an hour is not an excessive amount to drink. Remember that the last half of the distance may take a good deal longer than the first. For one thing, fatigue has set in. For another, if you set out with a falling tide, the walking will be easy along the wet sand; but return with a rising tide and footing is difficult in dry sand above the swash. If your tan isn't complete, carry some cover-up light clothes: a wide-brimmed hat, long-sleeved shirt; long pants; socks and sneakers. Loose, light-colored cotton fabrics are best because they reflect rather than absorb sun and permit air to circulate over the skin.

Don't sneeze at the idea of shoes on the seashore. For one thing, surface sand gets hot enough in the sun to blister bare feet. For another, rocks and broken shells found on some beaches can inflict nasty wounds. There's something in the combination of an irregular curved object and a sharp broken edge that makes a cruel cutter. Step on a sea clam shard and it penetrates; apply weight and it twists in deeper. On wild beaches broken shells tend to collect in shallow drifts along the scalloped foreshore; avoid them by staying out of low parts of the swash zone. But at a place like Townsend's Inlet, New Jersey, broken shells litter the entire beach. This is because dredge spoil from the boat channel has been pumped all along its length to replenish the eroding sand. Alas, the channel was where shells naturally collected and where beach people never walked. Now boats have easy access to the bay and everybody wears shoes on the broadened beach. Elsewhere shoes are necessary so you can choose the surest footing. Exploring a breakwater barefoot at Salisbury Beach, Massachusetts, I couldn't step on the tide-bared barnacles and so instead stepped on green algae and slipped. Falling on a patch of the barnacles that looked no bigger around than matchheads, my arm was raked from elbow to wrist. The minute cuts, too shallow to hurt (at first), measured 15 to the inch and didn't heal for a month.

Aside from mollusks, dead or alive, and stingrays described in Chapter Three, a variety of other animals can hurt—the cnidarians in particular. Call them jellyfish, members of a particularly ancient phylum which includes corals, sea pens and anemones. Formerly known as coelenterates along with the sponges that later found their own phylum, these are a varied group of radially symmetrical animals. (To confuse the issue a bit more, some apparent jellyfish—the comb jellies—not only belong to yet another phylum, but are harmless to humans. Nearly transparent or luminous, they may have a single pair of long filaments with short branches to snare their prey.) To avoid a tangle of zoological distinctions, let a simple rule suffice: Beware of jellyfish with many tentacles. They're the ones that sting.

These animals' notoriety depends on a tiny, fundamentally mechanical structure called the nematocyst. Typically it is a hollow cylinder containing a toxin and a long, coiled, microscopically barbed thread. When anything touches its closed aperture, the thread springs out like a sharp, diabolical jack-in-the-box. One nematocyst doesn't do much damage, but in the Portuguese man-of-war *(Physalia physalis)* each tentacle may have 750,000 nematocysts. The cumulative effect of several thousand minute poison-dipped weapons is extraordinarily painful and debilitating.

Notably sluggish and delicate, a jellyfish spends its life drifting through the water pulsing its dish- or umbrella-shaped bell and trailing its tentacles. Small animals get entangled in the tentacles, immobilized by the nematocysts, and engorged in the central gut. Able to stabilize itself to some degree, and to sense light, the jellyfish cannot distinguish between likely food and anything else. Its nematocysts simply explode at the touch—even if a tentacle has broken off from the rest of the animal. In his readable encyclopedia of zoological horrors, *Dangerous to Man,* Roger Caras analyzes the general problem and offers sensible advice:

> Jellyfish don't swim around attacking men, they pulse and float along their own stupid, blind way waiting patiently to bump into something they can eat. They sting anything they encounter. They are never in a hurry and have been floating around this way for untold years. It is obviously a successful way of life since billions of them are still around. While they can't very well make a meal of a man, they don't know it. They just bump and sting, bump and sting. To avoid the sting, man has only to avoid the bump. While he may be able to depend on the fear, quiet good nature, or the escape "reflexes" of other potentially dangerous animals, he cannot do this with the jellyfish. He must learn to keep out of the way.

When one has failed that and bumped into a cnidarian, the next problem is to remove the tentacles "as they continue to discharge venom," according to Bruce W. Halstead's enormous, lavish and definitive *Poisonous and Venomous Marine Animals of the World.* Wipe them off with a towel, sand or anything handy, he says. Then apply alcohol, household ammonia, vinegar, lemon juice, boric acid, hand lotion, sodium-bicarb paste; these are the standard salves. Ray Manning, a Smithsonian crustacea man and veteran of beaches around the world, recommends another: Adolph's Meat Tenderizer. He regularly carries a shaker of it to sprinkle generously on jellyfish (or insect) stings. It acts on the foreign body the same way it softens chuck steak: by breaking down the proteins. (Returning from North Africa, Manning brought back a homely solution to the tar-on-the-feet problem as well: Wipe it off with any kind of salad oil.)

In East Coast waters, jellyfish are not often lethal; usually they just plain hurt. Because the larger varieties have geometrically larger numbers of nematocysts to hurt with, they can be very painful indeed. In addition, the toxin can be a real danger when delivered in large amounts. (A related sea wasp of the Pacific Ocean packs a disastrous wallop; its sting kills humans in minutes. Fortunately it doesn't inhabit the Atlantic.)

Popular sources disagree about many details of specific East Coast jellyfish. Rachel Carson, in *The Edge of the Sea*, says one member of the *Cyanea* genus has 50-foot tentacles. Zoologist Donald J. Zinn writes of the same jellyfish that its "more than 800 trailing tentacles may extend 200 feet." More important, various authors differ in assessing the danger of some species to humans. The question is whether a particular animal has sufficiently strong nematocysts to penetrate skin. Differences of opinion may depend on the stingee; whether the individual is thick- or thin-skinned. In addition, some people are more susceptible to the toxins which can have anaphylactic effects: hypersensitivity resulting from previous exposure.

One of the most common jellyfish from Greenland to the West Indies is the moon jelly, *Aurelia aurita,* a milky white, short-tentacled specimen often distinguished by red horseshoe-shaped internal structures: the male gonads. In the fall, moon jellies release gametes in the water. Miss Carson wrote:

> At this season the adults are carrying the developing larvae, holding them in flaps of tissue that hang from under the surface of the disk. The young are little pear-shaped creatures; when finally they are shaken loose from the parent (or freed by the stranding of the parent on the shore), they swim about in the shallow water, sometimes swarms of them together. Finally they seek bottom and each becomes attached by the end that was foremost when it swam. As a tiny plantlike growth, about an eighth of an inch high and bearing long tentacles, this strange child of the delicate moon jelly survives the winter storms. Then constrictions begin to encircle its body, so that it comes to resemble a pile of saucers. In the spring these "saucers" free themselves one after another and swim away.

This is a classic example of an organism whose generations alternate between sexual and asexual reproduction.

Small specimens of *Cyana capillata* commonly drift into shallow water as far south as southern New England. This is the lion's mane—a.k.a. arctic jelly, sea nettle, hairy stinger, hair jellyfish and snotty. Halstead describes it as "large, repulsive . . . a mop under a dinner plate." Carson rhapsodizes about its behavior:

> Young cod, haddock and sometimes other fishes adopt the great jellyfish as a "nurse," traveling through the shelterless sea under the protection of this large creature and somehow unharmed by the nettlelike stings of the tentacles. . . . Its offspring are the winter plantlike generation, duplicating in almost every detail the life history of the moon jelly. . . . Little half-inch wisps of living tissue represent the heritage of the immense red jellyfish. They can survive the cold and the storms that the larger summer generation cannot endure; when the warmth of spring begins to dissipate the icy cold of the winter sea they will bud off the tiny discs that, by some inexplicable magic of development, grow in a single season into the adult jellyfish with 50-foot [or perhaps 200-foot] tentacles.

The Portuguese man-of-war, or bluebottle, is actually a colony of specialized, mutually dependant organisms, not a single individual. A warm-water oddity, it is most common along southern coasts but drifts from the Gulf Stream to the Outer Banks, Nantucket and the Vineyard. When they're seen near shore, word spreads fast. For one reason, the man-of-war's reputation for inflicting pain is deservedly widespread. For another, it is undeniably pretty. The long-tentacled animal stays afloat by means of a triangular balloon that rides the surface of the ocean. The gelatinous balloon or "sail" is an astonishing pale translucent electric blue, often with almost iridescent pink highlights. Surprisingly, the animal manipulates its sail to a degree in order to catch the wind and move in a chosen direction—like a skillful windsurfer. However nice they are to look at, a man-of-war is a drifter to be avoided in the water. One swimmer stung by *Physalia* off Florida died after the encounter— of heart failure, perhaps induced by the pain of several thousand nematocysts which leave large welts. Many other people have been scarred and hospitalized by the mindless creatures. Nonetheless they are not without merit. They shelter some fish; they are fodder for sea turtles and the giant sunfish. (I've even seen a calico crab make a meal of a little red jelly off Fire Island.)

Another animal to beware is the spiny black sea urchin that haunts the rocky New England littoral. Stepping on one barefoot will prove the point. It's like walking on a porcupine. The purple sea urchin *(Arbacia punctulata)* is the most visible on our coast. It lives on shallow rocky bottoms and avoids sunlight. Like its starfish relatives, this five-part radial animal siphons water through a madreporite ("mother of pores") on its upper surface and pumps it through tube feet. In this manner it can move an inch a minute. What it lacks in speed it gains in mobility, moving in any direction with equal ease.

Certainly the greatest potential hazard to human life and health—in numerical terms—is the easiest to avoid: a hurricane. The problem is that most people have never encountered one and so are not likely to take timely warnings seriously. First, consider the strength of these tropical storms. A Category 1 hurricane is of the intensity of the February 1978 northeaster which paralyzed New England and swamped Cape Cod. A Category 2 hurricane devastated the Virginia coast in 1933 and opened the Ocean City inlet. Hurricanes in these categories bring storm surges of up to 5 and 8 feet respectively. This "surge is the biggest killer," according to an American Meteorological Society *Statement of Concern.* "Ninety percent of those who lose their lives in a hurricane are killed by the storm surge. Wind and inland freshwater flooding claim the remainder. Thousands are injured. More than 6 million people are currently exposed to the storm surge hazard."

"Major" hurricanes start with Category 3 on the Saffir/Simpson Scale. These have winds up to 130 miles an hour and a 9- to 12-foot high storm surge. In this century such a one has struck the Gulf or Atlantic coast on an average of every other year. They wreak this kind of havoc, according to a terse National Hurricane Center manual:

> Foliage torn from trees, large trees blown down. Practically all poorly constructed signs blown down. Some damage to roofing materials of buildings; some window and door damage. Some structural damage to small buildings. Mobile homes destroyed. . . . Serious flooding at coast and many smaller structures near coast destroyed; larger structures near coast damaged by battering waves and floating debris. *Low-lying escape routes inland cut by rising water 3 to 5 hours before hurricane center arrives. Flat terrain 5 feet or less above sea level flooded inland 8 miles or more.* (Italics added.)

Given the numbers of people who flock to coastal areas today, one of the greatest potential problems is leaving. Cape May County, N.J. (population 60,000), may have a summer-weekend populace of 1 million. The Outer Banks, which has one two-lane road for much of its length and only two bridges that eventually reach the mainland, has 150,000 visitors on a busy summer weekend. The people who reach high ground ahead of a hurricane will be those who leave the barrier islands first. Keep in mind that flooding occurs hours before the storm arrives and can cut off escape routes, if traffic through a bottleneck hasn't already done the job. Because of the topography along most of the Atlantic coast—low marshland crossed by a few long roads—this scenario applies almost everywhere south of Boston.

Alarmed by the inadequacy of evacuation plans for summer communities especially, the Meteorological Society warns "If we do not initiate ways of informing our coastal communities of the hurricane problem, Mother Nature will impose her own education program, which is swift and severe." How swift? Hurricanes frequently travel 30 miles an hour, and sometimes over the legal highway speed limit of 55. How severe? A Class 5 hurricane brings winds above 155 miles an hour and storm surges higher than 18 feet. Such a one is not likely to strike the Atlantic coast; indeed the last Category 5 hurricane here occurred in 1960 and the last Category 4 bludgeoned the Carolinas in 1954. But hear this from the AMS *Bulletin:*

> The Georgia coast has not been struck by a major hurricane this century. Many Georgians feel immune from hurricanes. A survey by a Savannah newspaper showed that most of the people on Savannah Beach do not plan to evacuate if threatened by a major hurricane. The same is true at beautiful Hilton Head Island, S.C. Yet in 1893, a storm surge of 15–20 feet inundated many of the islands along the Georgia and South Carolina coasts and killed over 2,000 people.

This may sound like doomsday stuff, but the rarity of hurricanes in recent years has encouraged beach development and made people complacent. And the long lapse just means we're due.

One final hazard on the beach: the occasional threat of lightning. The dimensions of these electrical extravaganzas stagger comprehension: Sometimes 5 miles long but rarely thicker than a pencil, a single bolt lasting less than one second can carry 100 million volts and reach a temperature of 70,000° F., or five times as hot as the sun itself.

By all means get out of the water at the first hint of a thunderstorm. Probably the safest place to be on the beach is crouching down behind a dune—and keeping well below its crest. Since lightning often strikes the tallest local objects, don't hide under an isolated tree, bush or metal watchtower, which may just draw the next bolt like a magnet. (Seeking shelter in a forest is okay.) A source citing National Oceanic and Atmospheric Administration instructions says if "you feel your hair stand on end—indicating that lightning is about to strike—drop on your knees and bend forward, putting your hands on your knees. Do not lie flat on the ground."

Remember that a little rain must fall everywhere—even at the beach. Resign yourself to a good rinsing and enjoy the spectacle.

Driftwords:

What's in a Name?

Having reached the shore and put down roots (perhaps as temporary as a tomato's but roots nonetheless) most summer people perform a certain rite: They christen the beach house. It may be a one-room hutch called "Shan-Grila" with trashcans on the torn-screen porch or the Newport mansion Vanderbilt built and plainly dubbed "The Breakers." But plywood or palace, it gets a name. Some are simple, some inscrutable.

In the last century my grandfather built a summer home large enough to later become a boarding school on seven spacious acres. (A residence again, it's now surrounded by split-levels and ramblers like an Arab steed among asses.) A civil engineer with a mathematical bent, he named it "Azimuth," a term astronomers and surveyors use to describe the apparent elevation of a star. His heirs never knew why. By the same token, a passing stranger hasn't a clue to the cottage signs in a squalid hamlet near the pristine expanses of Plum Island Wildlife Refuge: "Dartmouth," and "Gemini." A few years back Johnny Cash sang a song about "A Boy Named Sue." On the North Shore I've seen a house called "George."

Most modern dwellings have self-explanatory names, like the remote and tidy fishing shacks along Nauset Beach: "Out of Reach" and "Tax Shelter." A colleague recalls a house on one narrow island called "Chateau Frontenback." At Sandbridge, Virginia long-legged boxes on stilts are called "Seaduce" and "Mermaison." In one Fire Island town the locals call single folks who share their digs "groupers," a term only a little less graphic than the names of the houses they lease. These places are modest in everything but rental prices (upwards of $10,000 a season) and titles: "Six Sex" (or "Sex Six" depending on how one reads the logo), "The Sensuous Bear," "Inn the Bushes," and "R. U. Naked." These names would hardly be permitted in nearby communities so proper that nonfamilies cannot be admitted. But then "groupers" might not be able to relax in a "Wee Kirk o' the Heath."

From one end of the coast to the other there must be a hundred "Driftwood" motels (each with a mandatory stump on the porch) and a like number of "Sea Shanty" restaurants, most of them overgrown huts charging mansion prices. There are more "Sandpiper" gift shops than shore-bird species; more "Sea Breeze" cottages than directions the wind can blow. Yet the most unlikely cliché of a name applies not to a structure but a stripper. On a beach highway north of Boston a neon sign announced the appearance of an entertainer called "Sandy Shore." Apropos of names, it's high time someone examined America's athletic totems. By that I mean the Chicago Bears, Baltimore Orioles, Princeton Tigers and the like. How the current menagerie evolved is a mystery.

The University of Maryland fields team after team of able competitors called Terrapins after an indigenous reptile. The animal itself is rather sluggish and lackluster. Not possessed of any particularly valorous trait, it's best known as the main ingredient of an epicurean soup. Does Louisiana State University go rah-rah for its Gumbo eleven? Of course not. Lions are ubiquitous sports symbols—not native pumas but the imported kind à la Phineas T. Barnum and M-G-M. Bears also show up on sports pages everywhere. Yet in the American west, where the Ursidae are most common, the ubiquitous black bear appears most frequently as a garbage thief, a pest—hardly Hall of Fame material. My alma mater identified with the bulldog, a member of the genus *Canis* that was bred by British gentry (if memory serves) for pit fighting in an age when blood sports were considered amusing. Harvard might as well have sponsored the Cambridge Gamecocks but muddled through without a totem.

All this seems so biologically inept. I am not suggesting that every bestiosthenic icon needs to be replaced. Dolphins are swift, intelligent and agressive so the Miami team seems well named despite the animal's reputation for playfulness, a trait that has no place on the football field. The Los Angeles Rams is another well totemed organization, given the amount of head-to-head contact that occurs on an NFL line of scrimmage. If *Ovis canadensis* does most of its butting when in rut, the football players don't seem to mind the association.

So let well enough alone where teams have traditional identities. But all the professional athletic leagues seem to be expanding and I submit that each new team has a golden opportunity to employ a degree of zoological sensitivity. Let them chose symbols with a brighter eye to accuracy and select animals noted for some trait that's useful in the particular game. Consider these characteristics and candidates:

For tenacity (useful in any sport) *Balanus* or *Crepidula*. Thus the Beaufort Barnacles and Savannah Slipper Shells. Yes, the latter do change their gender as they grow older, but most athletes retire before menopause. Nobody's perfect.

A capable foot is the prerequisite for skillful soccer so a Pacific Northwest owner might hire Pele to sparkplug the Walla Walla Lightning Whelks. (The impression of speed is always desirable.)

Group coordination wins highest respect on the basketball court where aerial acrobatics—so far as man can achieve them—are important. I nominate candidates from the Charadriiformes: the Pensacola Peeps. But if the owner has a fondness for fishing perhaps he'd prefer to call his team the Miami Menhaden.

Football is such an intrinsically territorial game it seems a shame not to recognize the proprietary determination of some *Sternidae*. Thus, the Salt Lake City Sea Swallows or Terra Haute Terns.

Speed and defensive acumen are valuable in hockey so if that game spreads far enough south, Dixie might root for the Chattanooga Chimney Swifts or Lauderdale Lobsters.

As everyone knows, the ability to throw an object with deadly accuracy is the sine qua non for baseball players at every position. In the natural world this talent is best exhibited by an Egyptian bird that preys on ostrich eggs which are notoriously hard-shelled. *Neophron percnopterus* throws rocks to break them. Thus, when our national game expands with a franchise in southern Illinois, what could be more fitting than the Cairo Vultures.

Before the beach feast.

Chapter Ten

Delicacies de la Mer

There are few secrets to eating well at the shore—unless a newcomer thinks that fish and shellfish come from a frozen-food case tasting like their cardboard wrappers. The sea is where seafood lives. So catch it, net it, dig it, trap it. If all else fails, buy it from the local grocer or a skipper on the dock and tote it home. If there's no place to buy fresh seafood, you must be in Ohio. Pack up and drive east. Another thing about catching and cooking your own: When the sea serves up dinner it doesn't order the diner to "enjoy your meal," a remark about as conducive to good appetite as "eat those brussels sprouts."

Unless you are spectacularly sedentary, it's most rewarding to gather seafood yourself, whether from the surf with rod and reel, from the marsh with a baited string, or from a clam flat with your toes and muddy fingers. No license is necessary to catch fish from the sea. In many National Seashores you can take reasonable amounts of shellfish "for personal use" without anyone's by-your-leave. However, the most heavily visited Seashores discourage this. In Massachusetts towns non-residents need a permit, but the fees are reasonable enough. The best rule for strangers anywhere is to check first about local caveats with local authorities, whether wardens, rangers, troopers, the grocer or post-master. Certain likely-looking clam beds may be closed. Sometimes the reason for a ban is public health; nothing is quite as certain to make a person very low with a leveler like hepatitis than bivalves fresh from a polluted bay. (Since these animals are filter feeders which strain water continually to extract their own microscopic food, they retain and con-centrate a number of toxic substances from a tainted environment.) Or the dread red tide may have passed that way—an inexplicable popula-tion explosion of certain plankton that can render fin and shellfish fatally poisonous for brief periods. In other cases clam beds are closed for a season to let depleted mollusks recover their numbers in peace.

Assuming it's open season, here's where you find dinner: Quahogs and cherrystone clams live in mud or sand. Hunt for them at low tide on sandbars, particularly in the protected waters of bays and tide-fed pools. On soft bottoms east of the Hudson, the traditional way to stalk a hardshell clam is with bare feet: Scuff slowly through the shallows, burrowing your toes into the sand. You'll soon learn to feel the differ-ence between a clam and a rock. Take along a sack or basket floating in an inflated innertube to tote them back; if you're in the right place, you'll soon have far too many to hold in one hand while picking them up with the other. (If you're in the wrong place, you'll find none at all and can go rafting in the basket.) Savvy Virginians wait for low tide to leave a mud flat bare, then walk the mire, looking for the southern quahog's telltale sign of an almost T-shaped hole, shaped like a kind of antique key slot. North or south, you'll be surprised how many kinds of similar holes are made by dissimilar animals, including worms that only a bottom-feeding fish finds edible.

In New England particularly, softshell clams live in everything from the densest mud to rocky bottoms. Armed with 12-inch siphons, they may be too deep to feel with your toes, which are useless on a stony flat anyway and vulnerable in bays near towns where broken glass abounds. The proven approach to these animals is made with a clam rake. Walk around when low tide has drained what a local savant says is an unpolluted clam flat. Look for jets of water shooting from the gravel or mud 10 yards ahead, then study the shape of the hole before destroying it. Since a softshell doesn't squirt continuously—but most visibly when first frightened by human footsteps—many holes without a fountain contain a sweet clam. With the rake's long, flat tines, dig around the hole to pry away a large chunk of mud, then finger through it. The critters may be hard to see because their shells are stained the color of the mud. Dig gently several inches from the most likely hole or you'll smash the quarry. (This does more aesthetic than actual harm; though broken clams don't keep well and should be eaten soon.) Find one clam and there's likely to be half a dozen within the radius of a foot. Harvest the large ones but leave those less than about 2 inches long for next year. Lightly cover them with mud so the gulls don't get them.

Depending on the kind of grounds they come from, softshell clams need anywhere from an hour to a couple of days in clean water to rid themselves of internal sand. I've heard of people grinding fresh pepper into the water to speed up the process, but can't vouch for it. Clams from soft mud will flush out their grit fast in a dishpan of fresh water. Friends in Maine dig a few clams daily and keep them tied to the dock in a lobster car—a floating wooden crate with slits wide enough to let water in but not wide enough to let animals slip out. This assures a constant supply of sandless steamers.

Blue mussels live in active wave-washed places, clinging to rocks and pilings with their byssal threads. Gather them there—again at low tide, of course. Better yet, at a low spring tide—the best time for any shellfishing on foot—since the water falls an extra distance to lay bare rocks and flats that have been covered for a fortnight, a month or half a year.

Low tide is also the time to find lobsters on the right kind of coast. Near Plymouth, Massachusetts a boy told me he hunted them on mud flats, seeking out their burrows, plugging the escape tunnel and digging them out! I didn't believe him—I had lobstered only in Maine, where the animals are taken in sunken traps. Mea culpa. John Hughes, director of the Lobster Hatchery in Vineyard Haven, confirms that lobsters will burrow in a muddy bottom to seek the same kind of shelter by day that their kin find in rocky caves and crannies off other coasts.

Hunting mollusks may be the easiest part of the prefatory process. Opening them is harder. Start with cherrystones if you've never done this before. All it takes to secure a small quahog is a dull knife designed for the purpose and a firm grip: Hold the clam with the hinge cradled in your left palm; with the right hand lay the knife edge in the slight straight groove between the outer lips of the shell and squeeze with the left fingers. The knife enters—insinuates itself between the valves. Pivot it inside, snip the adductor muscles and presto! The clam opens with a twist of the right wrist. Toss one shell away and serve on the other.

Oysters are much more difficult. An oyster has an irregular shape. The valves are rough and their lips hard to find. Crooked and wrinkled, the hairline crack between the valves can't be widened with the blade of a knife; the point must enter first. Furthermore, a big Chincoteague doesn't fit the left hand. One must hold the animal slanting against the edge of the kitchen sink and poke around, seeking the slot by touch as much as by sight. It takes painful practice. When the knifepoint finds a purchase, push carefully and quickly before the oyster realizes what's afoot and gets a firmer grip on itself. Push in the wrong place—it's easy to mistake a growth line for the groove—and the knife takes a life of its own. It can skid and open up your hand. This delicate work requires patient agility to find the groove, push the knife in, then slit the muscle and open the critter without losing too much juice. (Restaurants serve oysters on their flat shell. It's better to throw that one away and lay the delicacies on a bed of crushed ice in the roundest half-shell which holds its delicious liquor. Sprinkle each one with lemon juice—a healthy oyster will wriggle the slightest bit at this to prove it's alive—lift the dishlike shell to the lips, and drink the oyster down. It's a delicious, addicting experience.)

(A word about culinary/molluskan terminology. Most oysters marketed in America are *Crassostrea virginicas,* though they'll be called a multitude of names: Chincoteagues, Wellfleets, Blue Points, etc. These names simply indicate where the beasts came from. Differences in appearance result largely from the kind of bed that nurtured them. Crowded beds produce rather contorted oysters that tend to be oblong as the animal grew into whatever space it found. Open, well-culled beds produce more nearly round bivalves. To my taste the best are informally called "salt oysters" and the best of these are Chincoteagues. These come from beds in nearly undiluted ocean water, rather than from the uppermost reaches of long, protected bays.)

Periwinkles can be found at almost any tide in their varied habitats and boiled. Live whelks wash up on beaches after storms, or you can dive for them in sheltered seas, like in the lee of Nantucket's Great Point. They make an interesting chowder. Horseshoe crabs can be taken after they've come ashore and mated along a quiet sandy coast near the mouths of bays. Steam them like blue crabs, in a laundry tub. Of course, a compelling appetite or unusual culinary curiosity is a prerequisite for these entrees.

For people who prefer more cunning shellfish prey, the blue crab's the thing. "Hardshell" crabs can be caught in a variety of manufactured or homemade traps. This is the easy southern way practiced in Maryland and Virginia where the traps are 2- or 3-foot cubes of metal fabric like chicken wire (but sterner stuff to survive salt water). Each trap has an entrance to a large compartment, a straight-sided funnel, then another chamber. There's also a wire cylinder to hold bait of fish heads and the like. Attracted by the bait, the crab pokes around the contraption until it finds the entrance and enters the large chamber. To reach the bait, the animal enters the wide end of the funnel and follows it into the next chamber, where he's trapped, unable to escape again through the narrow end of the funnel. Ideally, you bait such a trap after breakfast, drop it in a bay and empty it for dinner.

For slightly more active crabbers, there's a wire cube or pyramid with sides that open when the attached lines are slack. Tie the bait inside it and drop it to the bottom from a dock, slackening the line so the sides fall open. Wait a few minutes, then close the sides with a jerk on the lines and pull the thing to the surface with a few crabs inside. Empty the trap carefully; blue crabs bite. Repeat. (This method also works for rock crabs much farther north.)

Crabbers with a sense of sport go armed with a ball of string, a mess of chicken necks and a long-handled net. Tie a neck to a string, toss it in the water and stay very still for a few minutes. Holding the string between thumb and forefinger, tug it very gently to feel if anything tugs back; or the string may move when a crab starts walking away with the bait across the bottom. However you tell crab's nibbling, pull the string in very slowly until the crab is close to the surface within netting distance. Then snatch with the net fast! Aim well below the bait, since the crab will flee as soon as it sees you move. This is a diverting pastime; moments of motionless waiting, then the quick stab for the wary prey.

Softshell crabs are taken by net alone from their hiding places in marsh grass. Just walk along the shallow fringes of a bay looking for quarry that's just cast its shell (or is about to) and scoop it off the bottom with a net. Of course its easier said than done until you practice.

As for acquiring fin fish, my own experience is slim. I've caught a few and had them in a pan when the flesh was still cool from the sea. There's nothing like such recently live food. But it would be presumptuous of me to recommend methods of fishing, an avocation many people devote their lives to. Some go at high tide, some at low. The most serious fish only at night, and all night long at that, for species like striped bass. Ichthyological authorities Bigelow and Schroeder note: "The best advice we can give the surfcaster . . . is to go fishing whatever time of day he is free to do so." Amen.

Once you've acquired a finned fish, clean it as soon as possible—before the viscera—digestive juices in particular—taint the meat. On a wild beach, simply gut it on the spot (being careful not to perforate stomach or intestines) and toss the innards to the gulls. In the case of shark, which can be delicious when simply fried in butter, bleed your catch as soon as it's dead or the urea-laden blood will make it barely fit to eat—even after marinating in lemon juice. But whatever you catch, finned or shelled, don't take any more than you'll eat. If you fish for sport, put everything back that isn't bound for the table.

The best fish in the world is caught fresh and then baked, broiled, sautéed or (sometimes) poached without much fuss. Lemon or lime juice, herbs like thyme, rosemary or dill, a garlic clove and perhaps a little white wine are the only secondary ingredients needed. (Some finicky friends of mine who live off the littoral when visiting Nova Scotia pack seasonings along since no herbs fresh enough for their palates can be bought at that latitude. Most folks can find what they need in local groceries or gas station/general stores that serve even the smallest coastal hamlets. However, bring your own wine to strange territory. Some seaside emporia only offer choices between Thunderbird and two flavors of Ripple.)

Generally speaking, as far as shore fare is concerned, follow Thoreau's maxim: "Simplify, simplify" as written. (If he meant it absolutely, he would simply have said "Simplify" and left it at that.) Utter simplicity is eating cherrystones as you pluck them from their bed without bothering to wade ashore. They're delicious that way, but I wouldn't want a crab uncooked, and my fondness for raw fish is limited to the confines of a good Japanese restaurant. So if some of the following recipes have a few twists of the *cordon bleu,* it's because even simplicity has its limits. But almost all of them can be followed in a simple kitchen—the kind found in a rented beach cottage. Most can be fixed on a camp stove. They were compiled with a couple of criteria in mind: They depend on fresh seafood that's found easily along the coast; they're easy to prepare; they're part of the fabric of living along a beach.

You can do two things wrong to fresh seafood: overcook or deep-fry. The only reason to do the latter is to fix a dish worth smothering in catsup for anyone who likes catsup. Any fish is better underdone than overdone; no fish is harmed by being put back on the fire if it comes out rare the first time. One rule of thumb is to cook a fish about 15 minutes per inch of thickness, then test with a fork. This applies to any kind of fish and any method: frying, baking in a preheated 450° oven, or poaching. (Start timing when the water returns to simmer after a cold fish is put in.) A fish is still underdone if it looks gooey-wet between the muscle segments. It's ready when the flesh flakes at the poke of a fork. Cook it past that point, and you might as well eat warmed-over packages. If a fish is big enough to handle a meat thermometer, serve it when the internal temperature is 140°; at 150° it's ready for a crematorium urn instead of a platter.

Fresh fish is more tender than frozen, juicier and each species more distinctive in flavor. The different fish and shellfish available at surf or dockside are so varied, even when cooked simply, that meat is easily forgotten as an inland oddity. For the uninitiated, some technical hints:

To clean a fish: First, sharpen a knife. Then slit the belly from vent (the anal orifice) to throat and throw out all the innards. (There is one notable exception to the gut-first rule: fresh-caught northern puffers, a.k.a. blowfish or store-bought "sea squab." The flesh of this odd fish is said to be delicious and healthy, but the viscera—particularly roe, gonads and liver—are poisonous, as is the skin. If you catch a northern puffer *(Sphoeroides maculatus)* don't gut it at all. Just skin it, slice fillets from the back and throw the rest away. Fishing and food fish authority A. J. McClane suggests staying away from puffers entirely noting that "the flesh of the southern puffer is frequently toxic." *Sphoeroides nephelus,* which looks very much like its northern cousin, generally doesn't appear north of Florida.)

After gutting a fish, scale it—if it has scales. Hold the fish firmly by the tail against a cutting board and use the back of a knife to scrape all the scales off with a brisk back-and-forth motion. To remove the fins with their little bones down the roots, cut deep into the flesh around (or along) the appendage, then pull the fin toward the head with a quick jerk. Don't bother to skin a fish—unless it's a thick-skinned species or a puffer. For any cooking method except sautéeing fillets, leave the head and tail on if your pan's large enough to hold it all; they'll keep more juices in.

To cut fillets: The object is to remove all the meat from one side of the fish in a single piece, cutting close to the backbone and wasting as little as possible. First find a slender knife that's longer than the height of the fish—i.e., the distance from the belly to back. Lay the fish on a hard flat surface, preferably a plank or cutting board. Hold it by the tail and work toward the head. Slice down into the fish just in front of the tail fin, then smoothly slant the knife parallel to the board and cut along the backbone all the way to the gills. In the smaller, softer-fleshed species, this can easily be done in a single slow stroke. With some bigger or tougher fish, a sawing motion works best. I know a veterinary surgeon who holds the knife steady and pulls the fish by the tail, wiggling it back and forth. Use any method that works comfortably; anyone who isn't all thumbs can master filleting in a week's vacation.

To fry fillets: Melt some butter in a pan over moderate heat (stir in some minced garlic if you like). When the butter bubbles, lay the fish gently in it, skin (or outer side) up. Add lemon juice to taste, any chosen herbs and perhaps a little white wine. Having estimated the total cooking time —15 minutes per inch—leave the fish alone until two-thirds of the time has elapsed. Then turn it over for the remainder and test with a fork.

To bake or broil: Preheat the oven. Grease the pan or rack well and dot the top of the fish with butter. Sprinkle with lemon juice and any seasonings. Cook the total time without turning (except in the case of thick steaks if they threaten to burn).

Charcoal methods: Wrap the whole fish, dotted with butter and seasoned, in an aluminum foil cocoon. Place it as close to the coals as possible and cook 20 minutes to the inch of thickness, since the foil reflects some heat.

If you have any large leafy herbs or rockweed handy, try this variation: Soak the herbs in fresh water (or rockweed in sea water) and lay them wet on the coals so that they smoke and steam. Put a piece of foil slightly larger than the fish on the grill with the edges curled up to catch the juices; place the fish on that. Then blanket the whole grill and fish with foil to hold in the smoke. Some will escape; don't worry about it. Make sure the coals are at their glowing peak when you begin and open the damper to allow a draft or it'll all smother. Allow a little extra time.

Clambake Supreme

This meal deserves a mob, a family reunion, a wedding on the beach or no excuse beyond a gathering of good friends organized by an energetic host and hostess with willing helpers. The preparations are complex and some odd hardware's needed, but complexity is part of the fun here. Special events take special work. This method is nearly foolproof, given enough firewood. (The hot-rocks-in-the-sunken-pit method can fail miserably and never be set right, because the rocks cooled off before anything got cooked.) The best place for such a feast is an island, of course. Second best is a piece of Maine riverfront with cold tidal water to coddle the shellfish and chill the drinks. Third best is wherever you can build a roaring fire without setting a roof ablaze and spread out without tumbling the neighbor's carport. Here's the rite as it occurs on Chanterelle Island, Me.

Two days before the feast hard- and softshell clams are gathered around the island to fill the lobster car floating off the dock. Then they're left undisturbed while they contentedly siphon out their sand. Supplies are laid in with each boat: beer, white wine, net cooking bags, paper plates and cardboard bowls. Kids gather heaps of driftwood and deadfalls. One day before the feast, another car is floated with the 1 1/2- to 2-pound lobsters (one per person at least, kids included). There are two schools of thought about lobsters. Some folks like "shedders," which have recently molted and whose shells are still somewhat pliable. These devotees say that because the beast wears his shell loosely he'll be juicy, soft and tender. I prefer animals with the hardest shells that are ready to molt again. These may be a better buy since they have more meat. But they're firmer too, though some people call them tough. (And they're hard to find in summer.)

The morning of the event, all the accessory dishes are prepared in a kitchen: cakes baked, salads tossed, bread bought, and everything ferried to the island along with a watermelon that's tethered off the dock. Two hours before dinnertime the real work begins. A fire is lit in the antique stone fireplace by the old boathouse. Folks arrive to watch and work their share. The tide starts going out to make room for more on the pocket beach. The host says in vowels rarely heard west of the New Hampshire line, "Get it hot as the hinges of Hades and gradually increase the heat." When the fire roars, pile on more wood and make it bellow. The iron sheet across the hearth starts to take the heat, plus the weight of a huge kettle two-thirds full of sea water.

The last boat from the mainland brings the last guests and new potatoes. The latter were rolled in salted oil (1 teaspoon of salt per half-cup oil), then partly roasted in a 400° oven for half an hour and oiled again. Sweet corn arrives now. It was picked minutes earlier since its sugar starts turning to starch as soon as it leaves the stalk.

An armload of rockweed from the shore is spread on the hot steel plate and starts to steam. Nestle the potatoes in it, cover with another layer of seaweed and an inverted pot which later becomes what they still call "scultch bucket" here. The term, a variant of "culch" was more common in seventeenth-century England where it meant the broken pottery, shells and other rubbish used to make an oyster bed. Now it means the remains of a sea feast, shells and other rubbish included. A pot of butter (1/2 stick per person, please) is placed where it'll melt without burning. The net bags are filled with clams.

Keep feeding the fire. Have a beer; this is hot work. Check the potatoes—heavy canvas or asbestos gloves are a must—and turn them as they brown. When the water is rolling like Vesuvius ready to surprise Pompeii, toss in the bagged clams and cover. Feed the fire; the water mustn't stop boiling volcanically. Wait 3 minutes and pull out the bags of clams which should have just opened. Feed the fire.

Empty the bags, serve the clams, feed the fire, crack a beer, check the potatoes and fill the bags with lobsters. Feed the fire, down a couple of clams and toss the lobsters in. Cover and let boil, dividing the time between feeding clams to yourself and wood to the fire. About 20 minutes does it. Test a representative lobster by picking it up by an antenna and jerking. If it pulls out, he's done. Serve the lobsters (with melted butter of course). Serve the potatoes, breaking each one open with a gloved hand and lacing it with butter and salt. Bag the corn and toss it in for barely 5 minutes—or long enough to switch to wine and crack a claw. Let the fire die and feed yourself till dark, or dawn.

Blue and Brew

Blue crabs make something more than a meal. Properly done, they become a delicious, difficult and messy ritual. I learned about it all in Baltimore from a native who was doing time in the Navy while I apprenticed at the local paper. When my college pal came home on leave, I'd wangle an evening away from the police beat and we'd go to one of the local crab houses. These were the only restaurants where two young men (on a cub reporter's pay and a lieutenant j.g.'s respectively) could hire a table for several hours of food and talk without being either fawned over by supercilious French waiters or hurried by sullen American ones. Sit down in one of these establishments and they didn't want you to leave until closing time—so long as there was another crab and another beer on the paper-covered table.

The best way to enjoy crabs at home is à la Frederick Road with beer in the can, a length of 2-inch dowel, a dull paring knife and a fresh roll of paper towels. Here's how:

First haul or lay in some crabs. Catch them if possible; buy them if necessary. Next get some beer, a tin of prepared seafood seasoning—Old Bay is the only kind I know—and a large covered pot. A proper steamer is nice, a sort of huge double-boiler affair, but any big kettle with a lid does fine. Just put something solid in the bottom like a few old saucers or clean rocks to keep the crabs out of the liquid. These critters should be cooked by the rising steam, not boiled.

Open a beer, pour it in the pot to the depth of about an inch, and drink the rest. Set the stove on high. When the beer comes to an active boil, toss in a third of the crabs alive and kicking. Do this carefully; given the chance, they are as willing to bite you as you are them. (Chuck out any dead ones). Sprinkle seafood seasoning on them as they pile up in the pot according to taste and/or directions on the label. By the time you've finished another beer the crabs will be bright red. But cook them for at least a total of 20 minutes. Spread Sunday's paper—all of it—on a table and tong the crabs onto it in a pile. Then sit everybody down and get to work because work is what it takes.

Callinectes sapidus is a miracle of packaging. If you've never eaten one before, don't be discouraged. You'll learn how with time and practice. Pry off the apron—the pointed plate covering the rear of the bottom shell. With this gone, the top shell will flip off to reveal the gills. These feathery gray things should be scraped away with the dull paring knife. Eat everything else that tastes good—namely all the meat you can find, the yellow tomalley (spelled "Tom Alley" in one restaurant) and the whitish fat in the body cavity. Then go for the meat. This is easier said than done because each morsel is diabolically encased in ectoderm and partitions. A crab surrenders its meat one nibble at a time.

Using both hands, break the remaining crab in half along the seam that runs front to back. Crush each half slightly. Break off one leg at a time, doing your damnedest to keep a segment of muscle attached. This is a little tricky; practice is the only teacher. With thumb and forefinger, grasp both the inner joint of the leg and the body segment to which it's attached, squeeze, and twist the leg off gently. Start with the hind legs; it's easiest with them and, when done properly, results in a legitimately bite-sized piece of "back fin" meat jutting from the end of the leg. After dispatching that morsel, nibble at each pliable leg joint; sort of squeegee them between upper and lower incisors to get the meat out.

To get inside the claws, tear off the entire appendage from the body and lay it on the table. Hold the blade of the dull paring knife across the claw and smack it gently with the dowel, broomstick, or whatever's handy. (You could always tell if a crab house had pretensions; it provided little mallets for this job.) Repeat with each segment. The notion is to cut about halfway through the claw, then snap it apart with your hands and nibble at the exposed meat. As you proceed, pick out elusive bits of meat with the knifepoint. Go back over your first crab, making sure you haven't missed anything. Morsels hide in all sorts of nooks, crannies, and cubbyholes. You'll soon know the animal's anatomy better than it did.

Needless to say, the entire procedure creates a good deal of scultch and beer cans. That's why you spread the table with so much newspaper. When things get out of hand, roll it all up in a few layers of classified ads, chuck the bundle and start fresh on the sports section. This cannot be a tidy meal, nor a delicate one, nor a fast one. A hungry man can eat a dozen jumbos—if he has the patience and a couple of hours. (One never gets sated on crabs; one gets tired first). When the party is on the way to finishing the first batch of crabs, put another on to steam and fetch another six-pack from the fridge. The ratio of crabs to cans is sometimes on the order of 1 to 1; peppery seasoning warms a thirst. Outlanders sometimes accompany crabs with french fries and/ or coleslaw. Some people even drink good wine with this meal, though fingering a wineglass with crabby hands seems gauche, at least, and all that pepper dulls the palate. Beer goes best.

Discussing the corruption of the mother tongue, H. L. Mencken rather proudly observed that "in Maryland *crabfeast* has never yielded to *crabfest.*" (He probably knew more about Maryland food ways and the American idiom than anyone of this century, and wrote about both at greater length.) A crabfeast traditionally includes she-crab soup, crab imperial, crab cakes, and sautéed soft crabs. Some Baltimore restaurants —the places that had moved from dowels to mallets and from newspapers to brown wrapping paper to gingham tablecloths—featured fried hardshells too: hard crabs covered with butter and cooked in deep fat. This practice is slightly more obtuse than gilding lilies.

Simple Shrimp

Euphemisms have their place no doubt. With no intention of taking a bath we ask to use a host's "bathroom." People talk about someone's having "passed away" to ignore the brutal fact of death. The commercial world has long since elevated such high-sounding prevarication to an art form on the order of playing Strauss on a color-coded electric organ with the rhythm set to Waltz Time.

Food mongers of all sorts perpetrate the euphemistic lie with the "fresh frozen" label. Certainly frozen vegetables taste better than canned and Minute Maid brought the magic of OJ within the reach of everyone regardless of season or latitude. But regarding seafood in particular the operative word in that obnoxious phrase is "frozen." Even if it was alive 24 hours ago, when a fish is frozen it suffers hypothermic crystalization. It may be better than canned or none at all, but it's tougher, more rubbery and not nearly as tasty as fresh fresh.

When fresh shrimp can be had, have it. What size? Medium for reasons of economy and common sense. Huge shrimps are magnificently expensive while small ones come in such numbers per pound that shelling becomes slave labor. Buy two pounds of fresh shrimp and shell them. First, with a thumbnail pinch the tail shell hard crosswise (so the tail segments will come out intact), then handle the headless animals like so many pea pods: split them lengthwise, save the contents and throw the husks away. Sauté the shrimp with three crushed garlic cloves in two-thirds of a stick of butter. When the shrimp turn pink, add a 12-ounce can of Italian tomatoes (which taste better than the fresh supermarket kind), two bay leaves, a teaspoon of dried oregano, a half-cup of dry white wine and the juice of a lemon. Simmer for ten minutes, sprinkle with chopped parsley and serve with rice.

Rebecca's Surefire Clams

Clams of any genus get tough as hawk's feet when cooked too long. Here's a way of knowing when to turn off the steam.

Put an inch of fresh water in a pot with a lid that fits loosely and fill the pot with clams (steamers or littlenecks—i.e., *Mya* sp.; cherrystones or quahogs—i.e., *Mercenaria* sp.). Cover and set on a high flame. When the water boils, the clams start lending their juice to make broth; then the pot boils over, literally flipping its lid in the process. Put the lid back on. When it pops off again the clams are done. Pour off the broth and serve the clams.

A Maine native who swears by this method adds one word of warning: Make sure all the clams are alive. One bad one in the pot, like a rotten apple in a barrel, can spoil the lot. (Nothing tastes worse than a dead bivalve.) It's easy to tell a healthy clam. Touch a softshell's siphon and it flinches slightly, withdrawing into its shell. A quahog closes tight when handled.

Serve softshells with a cup of broth and a cup of melted butter on the side. To eat: Grasp the whole clam in the left hand (right for southpaws), peel the black membrane off the "neck" (siphon) like a sock and discard. Pull the whole animal from the shell, swirl in the broth, dip in butter, devour. Serve hardshells with butter or nothing. Pluck them from the shell and pop them down.

Eyeballed Clam Chowder

There are no eyes in this stew; they're what you measure with. Clams in the shell, plucked from a low-tide flat, are not labeled as to weight, volume or unit price. Yet the best chowder depends on the proper ratio of solid ingredients. Eyeballing (or using a measuring cup if you want to get fancy) is the answer.

Acquire some hardshell clams, a.k.a. quahogs of the northern or southern persuasion, and a few razor clams, if possible. Let them wash themselves out in cold water. If one isn't firmly closed, chuck it out; it's dead and hazardous to your palate, if not to your health. Put them in a good-sized pot over a high flame with an inch of water in the bottom and cover. Peek at them soon; remove them with tongs as they open. Remove the clams from the shells and toss out the latter (unless you're short of tippy ashtrays). Strain the broth to remove sand and return the broth to the pot.

While you were resting you should have chopped some onions and sautéed them until translucent in a little butter and salt pork or bacon fat. You should also have diced some potatoes (without peeling them) and parboiled them until almost soft. Now, with a sharp knife, mince the clams into small pieces. Eyeball the amount of clams (or count handfuls) and put them back in the pot with the broth. Now add the cooked onion. How much? About one-third the amount of chopped clams. Pour in the pan drippings as well. Add potatoes—about two-thirds the amount of chopped clams, or twice the amount of onions. Stir. Then double the whole mixture by adding an equal amount of milk or, preferably, light cream, or both. Add salt to taste—careful, it may not need any. Heat to the simmering point and dish it all out in bowls, being sure to ladle up a fair share of solids—half of which should be clams. Twist a pepper grinder once over each serving, add a pat of butter and serve.

Coquina Broth

This is a real beach treat, and a dish you simply can't get inland. I've never seen it sold anywhere. It is the simplest and purest fish soup in the world, a delightfully evocative first course or thermos drink. All it takes is the discovery of some coquina clams at the beach and a container to carry them in. If you're going back to a beach where you've seen coquinas the day before, pack a colander or a sieve along. Coquinas are the small triangular and sometimes varicolored clams that live in the swash zone, moving up and down the beach with the tides, always staying in the shallowest active water. You'll see them on the surface of the sand when a wave washes up the slope; as it recedes they'll start burrowing out of sight. Though they may be less than half an inch long, they're not hard to spot; when they're around there are literally millions of them. Since they're so small, the best way to take them is by the double handful, sand and all. That's what the colander or sieve is for. Fill it up with coquinas and sand, step a few feet to seaward and wash the sand out in the ocean like a forty-niner panning gold. Take them home in a bucket of sea water.

Now comes the easy part. Measure out a cup of fresh water for each serving into a saucepan; add a generous handful of clams for each serving. (Some people gussy it up with various extras; onions, potatoes, spices—things this soup needs like a cello needs chrome.) Boil gently for about 10 minutes. That's all there is to it. Strain into cups and serve a steaming marine nectar.

Deep-Fried Fish

Eschew it. Like rubber. Fish and seafood that come in naturally small pieces or thin slabs—fillets, picked crabmeat, shrimps, scallops—may be sautéed in butter, perhaps with a crushed clove of garlic, a teaspoon of basil, rosemary or thyme and/or a little white wine. Thick fillets or steaks can be baked, broiled or roasted over charcoal. Most fin fish are delicious steamed, baked or roasted whole, dotted with butter, laced with spices if you're feeling fancy, and stuffed with a bread, mushroom, or crab stuffing if you're looking for a way to pass the time before dinner. But nothing good ever came from taking a self-respecting marine creature from the sea and drowning it in a boiling surf of deep fat. French-frying a fresh fish is close to sacrilege. This is as certain as the promise that the tide will rise again.

Mary's Miracle
(or Breakfast in Paradise)

First, way ahead of time, learn to make a French omelet, the light, fluffy kind that is nothing but eggs, butter and dexterity. Practice a few

Sundays running before a beach weekend in a month with an "R" in it.

Saturday afternoon, beg, buy, borrow, or poach a dozen fat salt oysters—six apiece, this breakfast for only two. (If you're uncertain about opening them yourself, buy them on the halfshell; covered with a cellophane wrap, they'll stay moist and firm in a refrigerator overnight. Avoid pre-shucked and packaged oysters; they've been washed in fresh water until nearly flavorless.)

Sunday morning brew a pot of real coffee, squeeze some fresh orange juice and invite your best friend, lover or spouse to the table. When all's ready, whip up the eggs and start making an ordinarily exquisite omelet while, in another pan, sautéeing the oysters with butter, a splash of white wine and freshly ground black pepper. Do it briefly—don't cook them to death (literally) but just until the edges start to curl. You will have timed this to happen just as the omelet is ready to fold—it takes a little planning and luck at first. When the eggs are still wet on top (but have that delectable golden-brown on the bottom) slide the warm buttery oysters onto the omelet, fold the sides over gently, count to ten in any language, and serve on the flip side. The results are extraordinary.

Correction: Don't bother with the coffee. Open a bottle of champagne instead. You won't be going out this morning anyway—it's too glorious inside.

Indoor Lobsters

Robert Lautman, the Escoffier of architecture photographers, cooks seafood on the side—for the love of it. After building a new kitchen at home, he christened it by having ten for dinner and serving us a lobster. One lobster. Weighing in at 20-some-odd pounds, it looked a yard long and proved that the big fellows don't have to be tough. In fact, when you can get (and afford) a jumbo, it's likely to be sweeter than a runt since these are the ones that grow slowest in the coldest deep offshore waters.

I've stopped eating chicken lobsters—one man's poor protest against our genocidal greed. The point is simple: A lobster in the 1 1/4-pound class is probably a juvenile and never had the chance to mate. Because of shortsighted regulations—and the inability of the Atlantic states to take a momentarily unpopular stand—people are eating the breeding stock of *Homarus americanus.* This kind of simple conservation, as traditional as tossing back little fish, is mandatory if our grandchildren are to eat lobsters and the lobstermen's grandchildren to catch them. Otherwise there may be none left to speak of in another human generation.

The reason big lobsters have a bad reputation—one that's perpetuated by seafood stores and some culinary authorities—is that people overcook them. If a small lobster needs boiling for 20 minutes, they assume a 5-pounder wants 100 minutes. Nonsense. That might be the case if the critter were a perfect sphere, but he's not. He's built more like an eclair than a baked alaska, and cooking heat penetrates through the narrower dimensions. Hence, Lautman uses a sliding time scale. Boil a 1 1/2-pound lobster 20 minutes or steam it 25 to 30 if you prefer. Boil a 10-pound lobster 35 minutes, or steam it 40 to 45. A monster in the 40-pound range should be boiled no more than an hour, Lautman says, or steamed 90 minutes. For lobsters in between these benchmark sizes, extrapolate the cooking time. When you open the lobster up before serving—indeed the jumbos need to be carved like turkeys—check the light greenish tomalley in the body cavity. If it looks runny, as it may one time in ten, toss the animal back. This isn't a cheese soufflé; nothing is lost in returning it to the pot.

How big a lobster should you buy? The biggest you can get, then divide its live poundage by two and invite that number of hungry friends to share.

Double–Bedded Mussels

Whether ribbed or blue, mussels needn't be overlooked. They're fine as hors d'ouevres, as an entrée or part of a seaside smorgasbord—a pastiche of whatever low tide offered for the taking.

First scrub each animal with a stiff brush and pull out the "beard"—the clump of byssus threads. Then steam the mussels briefly, till they open. In a separate pot melt a stick of butter, stir in 2 small cloves of crushed garlic and 1/4 cup of chopped parsley. Now the trick: Remove half the mussels from their shells, which seem too big to begin with. Put each animal in a half shell with another one. Double them up, as it were, like Ishmael and Queequeg in the Spouter Inn. Arrange the double-occupancy half shells on a cookie sheet, pour a little of the butter mixture into each, and bake briefly in a hot oven until the butter bubbles.

Stuffed Fish

Dressing up a dish comes easier than putting on shoes after a week at the beach. There are many popular stuffings, each as overwhelmingly filling as it is expensive. Here's a hearty one made from simple ingredients.

Peel and chop one medium onion. Clean and slice a pound of mushrooms. Dice 5 or 6 new potatoes. Rough-chop 4 celery stalks. Sauté all the above for 15 minutes with a half-stick of butter, 2 tablespoons of dry sage, salt and freshly ground pepper. Clean a fresh bluefish or striped bass and stuff the body cavity with the mixture. Lay 2 or 3 strips of bacon across the fish, bake in a 425° oven for about 40 minutes (depending on thickness), and garnish with lemon slices for instant class. Serve with a chilled white burgundy.

Driftwords:

Night Swims

Call me chicken? I don't swim at night when the moon rises behind the beach because from beyond the breakers I cannot see the edge of land, the place where home begins. Facing the shore, the shining light turns sea, shallows and wet sand into a twinkling blur. Twenty years ago I swam out in that kind of moonlight, turned, and was lost suddenly in black and silver water that had no visible scale, no reference point. I turned, kicked and thrashed toward the unseeable shore so blindly my arms scraped bottom before I thought to wade. The beach still looked vague, far-off. The next time I learned that the right time comes when a full moon hangs over the sea itself. It was a night that lingers in memory, in the perpetual present.

Walking between Yankee villages late at night, our shadows fall inland up the the slanting shore. The moon shines on the backs of breaking waves and their landward faces stay concealed. But the surface of the water shimmers, the moon's reflections reach the world's slightly scalloped rim, and I'd swim beyond it if I could, knowing that the edge of land stays visible.

"Let's go in." Yes, she says. Even in midsummer the air chills a little as we strip on the empty beach, the water too at the very first. "Don't dawdle." Dive through the first breaker, into its black, curling, hidden face. Swim straight out; it seems warmer. Beyond the surf the sea grows gentle and supports, rocking in its swells. Seen from there each wave toward land brightens as it grows, curls and breaks against the sloping land, its swash a bright line against the matte sand.

She hangs back, porpoising between the waves, her streaming hair a plume, then surfaces and waves a shining arm. Waiting for my mermaid, treading water, I see the farthest breaker rise in a distant curl that hides the lower beach again; then a ribbon of sand, the fringing grass and salt-pruned trees beyond. Except for a bleached log and our bundled clothes, the beach lies empty as the Sea of Serenity itself high behind me. The grass along the dunes is gray and the sky a royal blue behind counterpointing stars. She reaches me, we hug and sink laughing, to come up all coughs and sputters, holding each other afloat. It's time to splash the moonlight, then drift and float dead-man style (a misnomer of the first magnitude).

We were never so alive—fingers touching, rising with every swell toward the warm deep sky and easing back again, staring stars in the face, glimpsing the moon from the corner of an eye, fingers touching, almost out of reach, connected, moving, closing with the sky itself, floating down and up again. But we can't stay there forever. A jellyfish stings her arm; it's getting cold. We stroke away from the moon again, at last touching bottom waist-deep inside the outer surf. We wade ashore and dry ourselves, shivering together. On this perfect empty beach, the moon turning dark water bright and not another soul in sight or mind, the world seems ours alone. We two—we are the human race.

It's a little frightening the first time, a swim like that; as unlike land as space must be, a place and time of mesmerizing quality. Don't swim alone at night—that's dangerous, they say. And to swim together risks sudden overwhelming love on land again.

Chanterelle Island, Maine.

Chapter Eleven

A Scattering of Islands

THE RACECOURSE

One island near the tip of Maine has a moral history. Those who've seen it say Great South Beach is mythically beautiful. Even a botanist's cold catalogue of its flora sounds lush and alive. The beach curves huge and smooth for more than a mile. The west end, close to an evergreen forest, hooks sharply and stops at the foot of a sheer rock bluff that rises 40 feet jutting into the sea. Along most of the long gentle crescent, which arcs through one-quarter of the compass, the sand is soft and white. At the east end the beach becomes gravel to reach a tall sloping crag that runs at a right angle for another mile to the granite head. This beach is growing year by year. Protected from storms, it rarely receives the big waves strong enough to rob its sand. Instead the sea wastes its strength on outer islands and on the complex headlands that guard both ends of this sheltered, sandy stretch that's exposed only to the gentle southeast. Waves that reach into the cove bring sand from some off-shore lode, break on the foreshore and having spent their energy, sink into the beach face itself. And so it grows.

Punctuated by clumps of sea rocket and beach pea, uneven rows of beach grass slowly advance seaward each year keeping pace with the sand. Behind the grass are raspberry briars, blueberries, mustard, orach, alder and yarrow. Indians shared this place and left the heaped shells of their camping feasts. That was before the Europeans settled, laying claim to "real estate" and enforcing notions of private ownership. Today the island is private—a pity in that more of us won't see it; a blessing since our heavy presence won't change it into something tamed and common.

The man who first described it to me—an aesthete and a runner—was awed by the place. That may be why another man who knows it well told him the story, which changes with each telling:

As I remember the tale, this was a littoral arena, a place of final judgment. When two Indians fell into a dispute that grew out of all proportion, when they couldn't or wouldn't settle it until the tribe knew no simple peace, they went to the island and this beach. Not just the antagonists—the whole nation traveled to witness a days-long contest. They went to the beach and the two men ran. Only one would leave it living. They ran back and forth along the shifting mile of soft white sloping sand until one was dead. No weapons, no furious combat. Just fatal settlement of a stupid quarrel that had gone too far. Whether the best man won, the fittest surely did—unless a weaker man strengthened by certain knowledge that he was right beat a titan who knew his cause was unjust. Either way, there was no room for further argument, no hope for a new decision, no complaint that the deal was rigged or the judges biased or the counselors drunk. No appeal. The test was hard, the verdict final.

Would the whole tribe gather for the start? Men, women, children gathered in a mass? Or were the young barred from seeing so serious a rite? One imagines some witnesses watching from start to finish, at least one silent, trusted elder from each side. Some solon calls the start. Setting an easy pace—but not too slow for the sake of pride—the enemies match strong, long strides over wet sand where the footing's firm above an outgoing tide. Back and forth uncounted times beneath a high summer sun. Then the dusty heats through softer sand after the tide returns to nudge the runners higher up the beach face. One tries the swash but the water sucks at his feet like the other's ally and he too must move up to the hot, uneven sand. Some children peek, until their patience lags, then go off hunting hares and raiding bird nests. Women gather shellfish and tend the cooking fires. Night falls; the runners find second wind with the ebbing tide and the cooler offshore air. A chant rises from those waiting in circles around the fires beneath the pines. The sachems bear constant witness, old men with small appetites, judges who'd impose a ritual death on anyone who stains the sacred contest with a foul. The runners match stride for weakening stride into the night, one of them daring a pace a little too fast to tire his enemy under the rising moon. . . .

Wouldn't that be a way to settle arguments between two troublesome peers: "Put an end to this feud, you two, or one dies running an endless marathon. The tribe insists." If the gripe goes on, they hit the beach they called "The Racecourse" until one runs the other into the sand. A tradition like that would encourage peaceful settlement before things went too far. It might also end an argument once and for all.

But it wasn't quite that way. A single epic race ran its course here, according to a white man's much later history of the island. Hunting Wolf, chief of the Abnachi Tribe, had a daughter and Forest Flower had two suitors. Her father proposed a race—one lap down the mile-long beach and back—to win the bride. In the written account, the rivals sprinted from the west corner of the beach along the crescent coast on hard wet sand by the loud surf "whose mighty intimations presaged either death or victory." Neither had an edge at the far end. They reached the towering rock beyond the pebble stretch together, pushed off and started back, at a dead run too. Halfway down the beach one pulled ahead by inches. The other willed more speed, gained a narrow lead but couldn't hold and faltered, then came abreast again for a few last strides. He stumbled in the sand and fell, bleeding from nose and mouth, dying not from too weak a heart but one too strong for its vessels. The other panted on, ran toward the waiting princess, crossed the line and tumbled at her feet—as dead as the one who dared to race him. The runners each won remembrance but not the prize they sought. Their names live on, if history doesn't lie.

I like the first version better—the one my friend heard—embellished in remembering, "improved" in telling me and which I in turn amended in remembering. But that says more about us than beaches, history or Indians. Perhaps they did have simpler ways to settle disagreements than us litigious moderns. But not quite as simple as we hopefully construe according to our own criteria with each retelling of the saga this perfect beach deserves. I said there was a moral. There are two. First, it seems that even in simpler times people sought out islands for occasions too important to suit the trackless mainland. Islands are special places, more defined, more contained, and hence better able to contain an event of special feeling and significance. We pour the finest port in small glasses. The other lesson is that we hunger both for heroes and for more simply honest ways as desperately as Running Chief and Eagle Wing sought a princess for a bride.

CHANTERELLE

Cradled in a cranny of the Maine coast stands an island called Chanterelle—though not on any map or chart. It has another legal name: one that suits it about as well as Frederick Austerlitz fits Fred Astaire and Frances Gumm means Judy Garland. (Called by any other name a rose would smell as sweet, but it would take a bloody while for another word to evoke the bud.) Only a few miles from open ocean, Chanterelle lies in what Maine calls a river—really a twisted arm of the sea. Storm surges don't overwhelm it but the tides range 8 feet up and down its shores each day making a brackish heaven for lobsters, oysters, crabs, clams and fish. The river winds around steep land; tendrils of the continent and countless islands all covered with evergreen and hardwoods clutching bedrock through shallow soil of their own making. Parts of Chanterelle's little shores are sheer at high tide while at the ebb, dark sands strewn with rocks and rockweed slope gently out into the clear cold water.

At the turn of the century these 16 acres were owned by two sisters from "away"; genteel Philadelphians who contrived to have several small buildings erected and formal gardens sown. Paths were cut wide enough for the Victorian sisters and their gentle friends to stroll two abreast without snagging a hem. They dressed formally for dinner in their briefly tamed wilderness and left each year before winter locked them in. No doubt they read Sir Walter Scott aloud, emulated Evangeline's fidelity, held musicales and voted for William Howard Taft. Day lilies remain in profusion around the shingled cabins. About the time Calvin Coolidge frowned his way to the White House, the sisters began buying their fowl from an ambitious mainland boy. A chicken farmer by the age of eight, he sold his birds for 25 cents a pound—head, feet, feathers and viscera included. (It was expensive in those days. When Herbert Hoover promised "a chicken in every pot" he evoked luxury.) The boy left Maine, sought his fortune close to Boston and returned to buy the island during the Truman years. Perhaps he had a sense of Dickensian achievement: the distant goal grasped at last. Perhaps he just meant to preserve something special: a place for friends and scattered daughters, and their friends and grandchildren to spend particles of summer that lend savor to the winters passed in cities.

A friend of mine is privy to the place which I reached after a frantic few-hundred-mile solo drive to join close friends who'd had time to settle in. The island is hidden from the landing at the end of a dirt road; the boat ride takes 10 minutes. But climbing ashore in this strange sylvan place I felt suddenly unsettled. What if there wasn't enough food on Chanterelle? (The kind that comes from stores, I mean.) What if my hostess blew an appendix or one of the children split a chin running on the rocks? What if the water rose too high that night and swept the boat away? *What would I do all evening?* There was not a street nearby to stroll down, not a telephone or cigarette machine in sight. And if I had the itch, I couldn't just pat the Cherokee on the transmission and be somewhere else by morning. Call it island fever.

The cookhouse was well stocked. A safari lamp did lose its charge but there was a spare battery, and besides it was time for bed. We ate raspberries and felt the wind.

Next day everyone went off sailing or shopping in the mainland village leaving me alone to work at a kitchen table in one cabin. For a moment I snuggled in the peace, then sat up with a start. It was not *quiet.* Not at all. A squirrel ran across the roof. Some raucous birds began a debate that threatened to last till noon. Fishes jumped with no discernible pattern. But what lured me from the typewriter was a high-pitched cheep, a pure note that swelled so briefly, then stopped. It was repeated a dozen times, then answered. The call came now and then from every side. I had to learn its source and walked down to the island's southern point. Ospreys were teaching their young to fly over the water and high above the next island to the west. Soaring, gliding, diving, chasing each other, disappearing behind the trees to swoop back again. Sometimes half a dozen were visible at once; sometimes silent, sometimes singing that piercing, delicate note. I walked around the island once listening to all the sounds before finally settling down to work.

After dinner that night the erstwhile chicken farmer's granddaughter was troubled by a sound: an engine close offshore. It wasn't right, she said, knowing the night noises better than the rest of us. It made her nervous, so she and her suburban girlfriend crept through the woods to have a look. A large boat with no lights and several men aboard moved about, then anchored in the channel. Returning to camp, the girls urged me back with them. They imagined the worse. But the men were not raiders, drug runners or pirates (and the girls not fated Sabines). They were fishermen netting herring in the tide.

Another afternoon toward sunset we circumnavigated the island in the dinghy. One osprey stood watch on the branch beside a treetop nest on the next island. Ten more came and went, not fishing, just taking their constitutionals as the sister ladies must have done. We saw great blue heron too and another wader—I've forgotten which because of what happened next. Passing the north end of the island, I rowed slowly east around the sunken rocks. We were 100 yards from the mainland shore opposite a lush stand of hardwoods. The tide was high, the sun low, directly behind us and about to hide below the mile-distant evergreens. It appeared that a spotlight shone into the trees ahead. Broad daylight still, a half-circle shimmered brighter in the trees. The sun seemed a perfect hole in the pale sky through atmospheric haze; its light bounced off the water like a skipping stone into the trees and bounced straight back at us. There was nothing rare standing in that light; no primal deer come down to drink or bald eagle peering from a branch poised for prey. There was just bright phenomenon highlighting a half-round portion, a Giotto halo in the trees. A simple spectacle, beauty to the eyes of the few beholders blessed to be there to see it.

LOOKOUT

Even fine weather batters the Outer Banks. While a hurricane too distant to notice whips the Caribbean, Indian summer warms the Great Lakes. Tomorrow is Halloween; tonight is windy on Ocracoke and the ten-minute task of pitching a tent becomes an hour-long struggle with the fly streaming out like a battle flag, pulling up stakes and tossing them about in the dark. Next morning one orange pennant flies from the Coast Guard flagstaff: Small craft stay in port. The ferry to Cedar Island cancels its three-hour run across Pamlico Sound. By noon a second orange flag whips the wind. Local radio stations interrupt their rock and gospel songs to announce the gale warning. That high-pressure system to the north is feeding air to the donut low beyond the Devil's Triangle. These islands lie in the middle, and winds rake in from the northeast rising to 40 knots, then gusting toward 50. The tide will crest soon after sundown. Fed by waters pushed abnormally high by this fair-weather frenzy, it may flood the islands.

By dusk the sea's gone mad off Hatteras Lighthouse at the eastern-most corner of the land. For several hundred yards the shallow water churns white. As often as not six lines of breakers stand up to be counted, like a troop of mounted cops in riot gear waiting for orders. The waves in front rise and roll forward; one gallops in, breaks and crumbles. Another overtakes its swash, marches erect for several seconds further, rides up the narrow beach and strikes the scarp. Breakers beat beneath the long-gone foundations of the first lighthouse, under-mining ledges of sand precariously held by tangled bayberry roots and beach grass. A half-foot slab of shore slides away with every twelfth wave. The next eleven splash straight up the scarps like geysers; some splash inland down a narrow road.

After dark the tide turns without major flooding, but the beach a few miles north becomes an eerie place. Approach it with care, as if one can walk carefully in wind like this. It slants across the island, driving and dragging the Atlantic to the base of man-made barrier dunes, cutting them back. Beneath an invisible sky the surf shows white as far as can be seen—a ghostly white that has no depth, no leading edge, no ending. The peculiar thing is that human eyes can see at all. There are no artificial lamps; the electric power lines behind the dunes have shorted out, and the sky is overcast. There seems to be no source of light. But the furious surf writhes visibly in the dark. I crouch in the lee of a broken dune trying to see some order in the frenzy, but the wind whips tears from my eyes, replacing them with sand.

Hard to see, it's impossible not to hear. Each breaker makes its own sound, yet there are so many that the noise seems out of synch. Watch one specter of a breaker and the loudest sound comes from somewhere else. Wind screams through the grass beside me and from everywhere offshore comes a long, low groan of noise like a final phase of Inquisition torture. The whole beach is white and moving, but the sea doesn't eat my dune; nor does the berm sand reappear as it should between the flood and ebb of waves. This beach is covered with dry foam; no one ever drowned in foam. I walk toward where water must be. The surf rises more clearly. A wave charges in and breaks. Another overtakes it; distance and speed are impossible to judge. I turn and trot back from the invading white. After an hour or more, a spitting rain begins in fits and starts. I leave the beach and drive to a nearly empty campground. Too tired to wrestle with wet nylon in the gusting wind, I sleep in the jeep which rocks gently in the gale, cozy as a cradle.

By morning the wind has slackened. The Coast Guard lowers one warning flag. The ferry runs across the sound again to Cedar Island, a sparkling ride. But in the little bayside towns of Davis and Atlantic the work boats that shuttle across to Core Banks stay bobbing beside their crooked docks. The steep, short waves that built up are too much for them. It's been months since I articulated Kopper's First Law of the Littoral which states that a beach's merit depends directly on its inaccessibility; the more remote, the wilder and more beautiful a place can be. If the law is sound, Core Banks, which constitutes most of Cape Lookout National Seashore, must be fine indeed. It's taken four days to reach the place thanks to distance and conspiring weather. At last we're chugging through the marshes behind this barrier island. Once ashore it appears my Law has been repealed.

This place is as remote as any miles-long stretch of Atlantic beach, but fishermen have flocked to it for decades. They brought dilapidated cars to ply its 23 miles of narrow sand and when the cars collapsed they left them where they lay. The whole island comprises less than 5 square miles—it's only 1,000 yards wide in places and rarely twice that. But 2,000 junked vehicles of every kind—cars, trucks, buggies, buses— disintegrate all over it. They're most dense around two seasonal slums: clusters of the most squalid shacks this side of the Mexican border towns. Resentfully I propose the Second Littoral Law: Sport fishermen

Cape Lookout, N.C.

are slobs, and southern subspecies excels in this trait to a degree that Northerners cannot hope to match. At Ocracoke I'd wondered at this. Southern fishermen work in gangs; where one parks a pickup and wets his hook at dawn, a dozen will soon gather. By noon the storm-washed shore was bright with beer and soda cans, tattered with bread bags and cardboard cartons that held frozen squid. Here on Core Banks they strew the beach with fish carcasses too. The gulls clean up most of the organic mess but can't do much with the head of a big blue. So these corpses, their bones laid bare like the remains of a cat's dinner in a Looney Tunes cartoon, litter the beach, empty eye sockets big as inkwells. There are sharks, rays, blues, flounders, sea robins, even a handsome 15-pound tuna—all carrion bird food. Here I'll never see a fisherman throw a fish back once it's landed; they throw a dozen up on the berm, then take only one or two back to a shack for supper.

But soon the eyesores fade. This island never suffered the construction of an artificial barrier dune line. Because prevailing winds don't cross it from the seaward side (but blow along its length) its dunes occur in clumps of mounds anchored by sea oats. The berm is 100 yards wide —twice that in some places. It slopes away from a barely noticeable crest. Where spring and storm tides reach across it, only a few grasses take root. There is an expanse of natural pavement across the center of the island: shells, shards and coarse sand that have compacted into a glazed surface.

Toward the bay the marshes begin. A couple of clumps of land rise barely five feet above mean high water. These hammocks boast live oaks and pines. Even here whole and broken shells lie on the surface because storm tides inundate the entire island from time to time. Because there is no line of barrier dunes, the active beach remains very wide, so storm tides waste their energy over a large area. When they wash inland they carry sand, shells and nutrients across the island. These materials nourish the marsh behind the island and stimulate new growth. All the plants resist salt spray to some degree and can survive occasional flooding. After a storm has robbed the outer beach of some sand, normal wave patterns bring it back in succeeding seasons. Burial stimulates pioneer grasses like sea oats and these plants collect new sand in young temporary dunes that withstand the gentler storms. When a major tempest occurs, they succumb after retarding the storm surge a while. The dunes "retreat," but the dynamic "unstabilized" island survives pretty much in place, edging slowly west. The habitat survives too for uncounted centuries.

The drive along Cape Hatteras had been as boring as a turnpike between a wall of American beach grass (which doesn't naturally occur this far south) and a barricade of bushes. Both ocean and bay are concealed. But on Cape Lookout, as on the islands of the Virginia Coast Preserve, the virgin views extend from shore to shore—a marvelous panorama of surf, foreshore, berm, dunes, grassland, occasional clumps of maritime forest, marsh and bay. It's a varied, vibrant place. Forty-two species of reptiles, amphibians and mammals live on this Seashore's several islands among 188 kinds of plants. The catalogue of resident and migrant birds reads like John James Audubon's life list.

Returning to the mainland, my boatman said, "You got away from the world there. That's why the fishermen come year by year. But now the National Park wants to take it away from us. They want it all for theirselves." A mixed blessing. The Park people are hauling cars away and burning the fishing shacks, most of them put up by squatters with no legal right to occupy the land even before it became public domain. Though plans are not final at this writing, odds are good that most of the island will be preserved in a wild state: no permanent camps, no roads, no more private vehicles of any kind, and possibly no public jitneys or park vehicles either. It's painfully obvious that cars can cause ecological confusion. Not only do they kill grass, they compact the sand, interfere with percolation, make ruts. But the ruts collect ribbons of rainwater and nurture native grasses. Are RVs good or bad or both? Certainly they allow hundreds to ride where only tens would walk, carrying everything on their backs. The fishermen will scream and I'll miss the convenience of a jeep, but this place would be better without beach vehicles.

Here is a National Park island that can be easily returned to an entirely natural state. It is a rare opportunity to restore such a place that will be open to gentle human use by anyone willing to forego the "improvements" found almost everywhere else. Call it Eden by the Sea.

SANDY SERENDIPITY (OR LITTORAL LITTER)

On a Yankee island just after World War II, three boys engaged in what an English writer calls "the gentle art of wrecking." That means to go see what the tide dragged in and tote it home for fun or profit. Farmers used to harvest rockweed fertilizer that way along with horseshoe crabs for chicken or hog feed and sea-soaked firewood. People with metal detectors do it now in search of Spanish gold but settle for loose change and lost car keys. Traditionally one hopes for random flotsam (wrecked ships or cargo) and jetsam (stuff thrown overboard to lighten a foundering vessel).

Looking for anything the Gulf Stream might deliver, my friends and I found a large waterlogged crate on the empty beach. Its stenciled letters indicated war materiel—treasure of the highest price for kids whose generation barely knew peace and yearned to be fighting men when we grew up. We worked cautiously with pocketknives and driftwood levers—in case the crate contained explosives or hand grenades for the French Resistance. But we worked with zeal. It might hold bayonets or bullion for some fifth column.

The job took hours. We had to move the leaden thing twice from the returning tide. When the lid came off at last, our treasure was this: about one thousand gross cartons of matchbooks. They'd been destined for troops closer to the rear than the front because the covers had cartoons of hussies leaning against lampposts and the caption: "G.I. Joe Knows V.D. Can Be Prevented." We knew wet matches wouldn't light our grape-leaf cigarettes. Soon inquiring what V.D. was, we decided that military careers mightn't be as glamorous as they'd first appeared.

One beachcomber became a craftsman, one an oceanographer and I went into the word game. But I never gave up assiduous wrecking. In the subsequent three decades I have found two nearly complete whale skeletons, a recently deceased porpoise with lovely pearly teeth, a Chevrolet, three loggerhead turtles, enough bleach bottles to launder the Sixth Fleet and assorted barrels to fill a delicatessen, one rusty tricycle, a perambulator, many gloves and boots (always filled with sand), an 18-foot sailboat with her back broken, an almost whole pilot whale that couldn't be approached downwind without a gas mask, one 16-foot runabout with an outboard motor, uncounted pieces of wooden hulls and decks, a barge large enough to carry six freight cars, a hundredweight of antique iron ships' nails in worm-eaten timbers, a yard of oyster-encrusted cable that looked like a sea snake, one half-full squeeze bottle of Spanish pomade, innumerable bottles (never with a note), several fishnet floats, a gill net with about 100 pounds of spoiled fish, jet-fuel tanks, one anchor and chain, miles of hawser, two willing girls, half a catamaran, and one loving couple. (What then? Embarrassed at intruding, I went snorkeling on a beach bounded for several miles by 150-foot bluffs; there was nowhere else to hide. After studying a school of killfishes and the habits of a rock crab in its element, I surfaced again to see that the lovers were now sitting. They'd opened a bottle of rosé by then and hospitably offered me a drink. *Noblesse oblige*.)

Most of the objects I've come across had to be left behind. Once I negotiated a telephone cable reel more than a mile to a friend's bayside back yard where it became a breakfast table—a herculean labor stretched over several days. I have never found another sealed crate nor anything closer to a piece-of-eight than a sand dollar. Now I kick those echinoderms aside and keep on looking for rarer things to carry home: a loggerhead shell, the rib of a wrecked whaler. Many folks are content with starfish, devil's pocketbooks, sand dollars. I envy such simple acquisitive tastes and have long since stopped trying to explain the 2-foot whale vertebra beside my fireplace. But guests understand the bowl of seashells on the coffee table and finger them like worry beads. That heap evokes the ineffable mysteries of the ocean and its infinite designs.

Shells may be the most sensible things in the world to collect. Easily handled and carried, they're light, little trouble to preserve, more varied than a herd of Pet Rocks, and free. Dead shells need little cleaning; live ones can be buried in a back yard for a few weeks to emerge odorless. They have nice names too: little white trivia, fighting conch, greedy dove, strawberry cockle, sunray Venus, Humphrey's wentletrap, false angel's wing. People gathering dead shells have an easy task: Walk, look and pick—with R. Tucker Abbott's field guide in pocket or The American Museum of Natural History's *Guide to Shells* in a backpack. (It's a somewhat bigger book with more detailed text. The authors went to considerable trouble to compile translations of Latinate names.) Abbott includes instructions for people who want to get serious about collecting shells. Other useful information can be had by writing to the American Malacological Union, Box 394, Wrightsville Beach, N.C. 28480.

The rules of beachcombing are easy enough: Anything washed up is fair game for anyone who wants to take the trouble to lug it away. That stated, there are exceptions. The broken runabout I found had been "claimed" by someone who left a note to that effect in the belief that it was common salvage. Local police didn't honor the claim, however, since the boat had been beached by a couple of drunks. They planned to fetch it after drying out in the local lockup.

Some National Seashores set limits on collectors. You can take as many seashells as you can lug on foot, for example, not as many as you can carry in a pickup truck. This is to discourage commercial collectors from picking a beach clean. As for living plants, leave them alone; the beach needs them far more than your arboretum. Anything that man made and lost in the sea which then washed up on the shore is a beachcomber's for the taking—but the taking can involve considerable effort.

BACK TO BASICS

The beach moves different people in the same ways.

I knew a man whose life involved arguments, legalisms, and institutions. A cautious policy-maker in public life and a bachelor, he kept company with a distinguished career woman of esoteric tastes. They were both intelligent and urbane—he rather stuffy, she a little slim— the kind of couple welcomed at dinner parties where his polysyllabic conversation through a deviated septum was reliable as Muzak. In the city I never saw him unshaved, unbuttoned, or untied around the throat with rep silk and convention—except in the sauna of a humorless club. She was a member too but, more important, for part of every summer she visited an island that's long on simplicity but short on amenities like plumbing. She told me about it during a buffet.

Knowing my interest in natural places, the lady invited me to stop by if I was in that latitude. There'd be no way to phone and the mail's haphazard since days pass without anyone reaching the mainland to pick it up. "Come visit anytime," she said after the almond tart. It was the kind of vague invitation people offer in the happy belief it will be accepted but never acted on; the kind you accept with a certain postprandial enthusiasm because you'll certainly never be in the neighborhood. What's "nearby" an island, after all? But months later it happened that I was in sight of that island and had time on my hands. It was closer than any other place I had to visit. It had the undeniable attraction of being a bastion that doesn't admit strangers without invitations. In a mainland harbor I found a boat that could head that way, and I hitched a ride to this limpet of bleak and rustic land.

Some colonists, as ubiquitous as George Washington, had slept here, so it has a place in the pages of history—if only a footnote, progress has passed it by. There are a dozen dwellings, some foundations dating back to the seventeenth century; some mansions that suffered the heavy hand of Victorian renovators. One house has running water and another electric lights powered by a home generator. The others don't. On this private island, people walk to their own rhythms. It offers no public facilities, but then the public wouldn't like it; there's nothing very public to do. You can visit the graveyard where a family is planted under white marble stones—except for one black slate set apart and bearing the same surname. You can draw water from the common well, visit where a founding father prayed by a rock big as a Winnebago, hunt coon oysters, listen to the poison ivy grow, chase wild rabbits, and count the gulls.

These three wild species—rabbits, gulls, and poison ivy—dominate this place of absurd ecological equilibrium that has no predators except hunters in the fall. The cottontails are so sure of themselves that they'll hop down a path (between poison ivy banks) 15 feet behind a person toting water. The gulls are eerie. They own one end of the island more certainly than the old families own the other and fill the air with constant, monotonous screaming. To cross the island at their end is startlingly strange. Herring gulls and great black-backs are everywhere, the countless living, lame and dead. They nest on the beach, under bushes, and in an ancient fallow orchard. The cripples of each year's brood, which elsewhere would die before they fledged, hide among the brush and briars to scrape a living off the carrion of their kin. This is the only place I've seen gulls roost in trees—perhaps because there's nowhere else to rest. It was also the only place I've been afraid of birds that weren't defending nests or young. In this chaos there was no apparent pecking order—except lethally, one on one. It was so crowded that the normal rules of avian behavior seemed to have been abandoned. Inland beneath a flying flock so thick I saw two birds collide, the flightless ones ran into blind corners of bramble, then rushed past me almost rabidly in arm's reach. A one-eyed bird picked at a carcass undisturbed. It seemed an evil acre, as if that corner of the natural world had gone berserk. It is a place that all the islanders visit from time to time, to keep in touch with something.

Elsewhere there are mud flats full of clams, bays full of fish, sand beaches full of solitude, sheds full of firewood, and scattered houses bright at night with kerosene lamps. This island has the compelling attraction of the wild, the exotic, the remote—even of those birds themselves so obviously untouched by any man. But back to my host and hostess.

They would occupy "The Boathouse," she'd said. I took the term for one of those euphemisms in exclusive summer places where butlers in white jackets light the charcoal grills and lapsed debutantes pick wildflowers in picture hats. I expected a dock recently abandoned by Astor's yacht and was not surprised to see a house commanding a well-trimmed yard big enough for Scarlett O'Hara's garden party. Certainly "The Boathouse" would be a renovated storehouse built to serve blockade runners in 1862 or a bootlegger's cache. Not so. A single room with a bottled-gas fridge and stove at one end, it was smaller than a slaver's cabin. The policy-maker answered my knock in a five-day beard and cut-offs. She was reading Tolstoy barefoot. They greeted me with equal measures of warmth and surprise. After all, I was a man they saw at city dinners.

My host seemed as settled as a barnacle on a low rock at high tide —and equally aware of the rhythmic need to eat. He'd never soiled so much as a fingernail in a mud flat before first seeing this island a few summers before. But the tide was falling and he planned to dig clams at dead low, three hours hence, he said, with a glance not at a clock but at the water. If he missed the tide there wouldn't be much dinner. One thing he hadn't lost: his manners. Would I care to come along? He'd seen a new and likely spot for steamers and meant to try out a Yankee tool he'd bought by mail. In winter this man doesn't wield anything much more physical than a Dictaphone, I thought, but he hefted the clam rake deftly and called a halt when the bucket was two-thirds full. Leave some for tomorrow, for next year. Reading by hurricane lamp, bathing out of a bucket beside the privy (if at all), digging clams, bearding the mussels, catching fish, sharing the cooking and KP with his lady, he still talked through his nose. But the ideas were different. "I find I spend half my time gathering, preparing and eating food. I never give those things much thought at home. But out here they're important and I enjoy them."

There were moments over supper—a seafood smorgasbord with a bit of beef split three ways as an excuse to open a bottle of Bordeaux—that they were comfortably mute. We listened to the wind shift, and when the tide returned, went down to see tiny shrimp swarming near the surface of the bay.

THE OYSTER AND THE MARATHON

Variously and simultaneously a beach can be seductive, disciplinary, evocative and unforgiving. One spring I decided to join a 10-mile foot race as an intentional also-ran, one of several hundred unofficial participants. For some serious competitors this race was a preamble to the Boston Marathon; for many more it was a sweaty, panting test. For the friend who egged me on, and for me, it offered a simple challenge: to finish a "marathon" after forty. I'd been running a few miles several times a week and thought I'd try this race. To ice the cake of a short training stint, I went down to Assateague, where the Wildlife Refuge had always maintained mileposts along the dunes. If I could run a fast 5 miles on sand with a 10-pound pack on Friday, I could certainly double the distance over asphalt on Sunday morning.

Out on the beach I began to run, feeling good, feeling like the Athenian messenger himself ready to shout "Victory" when I saw the first milepost ahead. Then my spirits slumped: *1 km* it said. Assateague had gone metric over the winter. Remembering that a kilometer is 5/8 of a mile, I began computing and plowed on along the beach, past the dunes and the large-letter signs that mark dikes through the carefully managed marsh. My second wind arrived near the old pony fence, now a meaningless line of posts without wire stretching clear across the narrow island. I was still strong down the long slow cove where the beach broadens to a quarter-mile of dry white sand before the dunes. Feeling good! I made the eighth kilometer at something close to a plodding sprint and stretched for a tape as impalpable as the laurels I meant to win. Time: 42 minutes, which was good enough. Ambling back, I did a few wind sprints just to show off to the sandpipers. I was fit and ready. The 10 miles on pavement around the Tidal Basin and along the Potomac would be a snap.

My first oystercatchers of the year appeared, ostentatious as Easter Paraders with their beaks bright red for breeding season. I drank juice from my pack by the old fence that looked so desolate now, without wires, its outermost posts leaning bent and rusty in the low-tide swash. When it was intact, with four cables strung post to post from ocean to bay it had served a purpose: to keep a herd of healthy Chincoteague ponies safely apart from some quarantined horses suffering an infectious disease. Back then, a few years earlier, there had been an encounter:

I'd wandered up that beach mile after mile, fleeing something in the world of cities. Leaving lifeguards and children behind first, I passed surfcasters and a few scattered sunseekers, then finally found unpeopled solitude. There were only the skittering ghost crabs, ceaseless shore birds and the sea bothering the shore. Warmth and stillness filled the early summer afternoon. I swam in the cold, gentle surf, then floated, looking up at an incomparably clean sky, arms outstretched, rocked by the easy waves until I thought I could fly. Instead I walked from the surf onto a beach that had no footprints but my own, momentarily feeling like Robinson Crusoe. I wandered back toward the dunes. The wooden deck of a wrecked boat lay on the flats which are washed only by spring tides and storm surges. It had moved a hundred yards or so from behind the little hummock that hid it the year before—unless the hummock had moved. There was an enormous barkless tree trunk, its roots shiny in the sun, and a battered aluminum fuel tank jettisoned by some jet fighter-bomber on an unknown errand. It had come ashore during the winter; I *knew* this stretch of beach. Then, behind a barrier dune, there stood a little chestnut foal and her dam.

They eyed me with gentle curiosity, for though these stunted now "wild" horses come from domestic stock somewhere along the line, tradition has it the first horses here survived the wreck of a Spanish galleon. The more pedestrian historical truth is that Virginia farmers kept surplus stock on these barrier islands until this century. Also, the Chincoteague Volunteer Fire Department, which owns the present herd, culls sick animals (and secretly sells them to slaughterhouses, so it's said), then it brings in new horses from surplus herds of mustangs in the West. But none of that mattered just then; I was remembering my own summers in the Rocky Mountains.

I walked slowly toward the mare and her foal as I'd walked toward countless ranch mounts on a sagebrush rangeland with a halter hidden in one hand. The trick was to coax oneself within arm's reach, grab a fistful of mane, and slip the halter over the horse's head in the cold dawn, because morning was breaking and it was time to round up the night-scattered herd for the day's work. The halter rope served as a single rein; riding back to the corral without a bridle, a teen-age wrangler controlled the horse by legs and will, since halters have no bits. Walking up to horses became routine in my youth. Then riding back one morning I saw a spotted fawn beside a Colorado trail, a little thing that watched timidly and nibbled an aspen sapling while I dismounted a dozen paces away. I thought I would touch that fawn and nearly did, but I may have walked too slowly. Five steps away she finished the sapling, lifted her head, and seeing nothing else to eat nearby, walked off into the woods with one backward glance. I was seventeen that summer and a Shelleyesque Romantic.

So I walked toward this equine madonna—the pair of Chincoteague ponies—with nothing certain in mind but the sense of a distant memory, and without so much as a string of whelk eggs in hand for a halter. The air was hot that far from the surf, the horses quiet and standing almost easy, flicking flies. The mare didn't move; the foal wandered toward me a little. It seemed to be twenty years or more before, the commonalities clearer than the differences, as I mounted the edge of a steep hummock, carefully skirting the dune grass that held it in place.

Then from out of the pages of history or mystery came the thundering hoofbeats of a runt horse rampant. Daddy! The dusty stallion, minding a harem that ranged among the dunes, was running my way, head down, ears back, teeth bared. My reverie fled at a gallop but I stopped in my tracks. He was 30 yards away, 20. I might have stood taller than he eyeball to eyeball, but under the circumstances I was no match for those brown incisors and splayed unshod hooves. I didn't even have a Stetson to spook him. I leapt down the face of the dune, breaking a dozen rhizomes, no doubt, putting a fragile physical barrier of sand between us. Out of sight out of mind? The alert stallion didn't follow and I pursued my ramble a little chastened, somehow very conscious of the fact that I was stark naked. Farther along the flat I found a beautiful oddity, a talisman of sorts. It was a single perfect mushroom, big around as a tennis ball, pure white across the crown and fringed in silver-gray. It grew atop a dry pile of horse dung.

But all that was a year or so earlier. Thinking about the race two days away, I walked back to a crossing through a marsh where I'd once found the skull of a sika deer, an exotic species imported from the Orient decades ago by Junior Conservationists. I saw sikas alive that day, whitetails too, and slept well at the hospitable Refuge Motel on nearby Chincoteague, the settled tourist-loving island that lent its name to a tame children's story and then to those sometimes-wild horses.

Next morning, feeling up to running another beach from end to end, I fed on pancakes on the theory that lots of carbohydrates the day before a race sate muscles with stored energy. The beach and the amenities of its nearby town were standing me in good stead for my rite of passage, the mini-marathon. If only I could have ignored the coast's seductions. But no, before driving back to Washington I bought half a bushel of Chincoteague oysters on-the-hoof for about the price of a dozen on the halfshell in a French restaurant. Mary was having several special friends to dinner and these would be extraordinary openers.

John Benson would be there: calligrapher, stonecutter (viz. inscriber of the Kennedy graves at Arlington), windsurfer, fiddler, earthy aes-thete and epicure. In town to carve some words on I. M. Pei's wing of the National Gallery, he'd appreciate Chincoteagues. He'd also help open them, being as deft with an oyster knife as a stone chisel. Arnost Lustig was also invited with his wife: professor, writer, Auschwitz survivor, catalyst of *The Shop on Main Street* and author of several novels about the Holocaust as seen from within the Nazi flames. Knowing life's fragility so intimately, he takes more kinds of joy in living than most men can enumerate. He might not know Chincoteagues by name, as Benson would, but he'd relish them. I bought champagne and arrived in time to start opening the tenacious oysters.

As the remoteness of a beach relates directly to its beauty, the difficulty in securing a bivalve from its shell is an index of its excellence. A steamed softshell clam opens easier than a softboiled egg. But oysters? *Crassostrea virginicas?* They're harder. Hardest to open and best to eat. Especially Chincoteagues. I only ventured to buy such a big basket of them because I knew I'd have capable help.

Benson arrived first and joined me in making a midden. We couldn't help it: For every two or three we put on ice, we ate one. When the other guests arrived, the party grew in the kitchen. We finally got far enough ahead so that a silver tray covered with shining ice was filled edge to edge with opened oysters and quartered lemons. We all adjourned to the living room and champagne. We laughed, we drank the dry bubbling wine that set off the slippery shellfish like diamonds against blue velvet. It was a noisy party almost, without many articulated paragraphs just then—only declaratives and sounds of delight. In the middle of it the Professor had something to enunciate, an inspiration.

"You know how oysters taste?" he said in his thick accent—and everybody else shut up. When he speaks the words are worth hearing, imbued with contagious feeling. But caught up in the moment he'd started to talk without thinking. How do oysters taste? Who can say? Now we wanted to hear the pregnant simile. He was stuck, hoist by his own palate, his effusive mind trapped by an Eastern European tongue.

"Oysters taste like . . . Oysters taste like . . . the universe!" It made no more sense—and none less—than our appetite and glee.

I don't remember what happened to the entrée or dessert. I do know we ate oysters until I couldn't pry any more. Then Benson, whose forearms are like hawsers from carving stone for two decades, opened another trayful. We saved only a dozen or so, for breakfast perhaps. We stayed up too late, sated and strong, energized by Chincoteagues, euphoric with good company. (The conversation picked up once the mollusks were gone.)

Next morning I woke up alert and in plenty of time to run the race. A thousand people gathered near the Lincoln Memorial: curious spectators, slightly nervous unofficial runners, and the long-limbed racers who sat on the dewy ground bending heads to knees, stretching tendons, breathing, meditating. It was an inspiring crowd, and as the racers shed their sweatsuits they looked like heroes ready for an Olympiad and limber heroines of sagas yet unsung. But warming up, I felt sacks of wet sand hanging from my knees. My feet felt like clamshells, my legs like kelp, my stomach like the crest of a breaking wave.

The challenge of Friday's beach run had led to the easy seduction by delicacies from nearby waters. I'd celebrated too soon. The oysters had wanted champagne—only there were so many oysters they'd demanded too much sparkle, and I hadn't had the will to resist. The beach had been there, 30 miles of it or so. I'd needed only five of them. I'd met the challenge of that day, rested the next and forgotten about tomorrow, today, Sunday and the marathon. I couldn't have jogged 10 miles to see a whooping crane hatch out triplets, or the fabled phoenix nesting atop the Washington Monument.

So instead I ran the mini-mini-marathon, the race for ladies, kids, and some handicapped folks who hopped and hobbled 2 miles with the fighting, glorious will of that Athenian messenger. Two friends ran it too, and eight-year-old Andrew finished ahead of me.

Next year, older and wiser, I'll run without oysters.

Driftwords:

Flashes

Two days ago a northeast gale carried seas 100 yards beyond the berm along Core Banks and left the beach crest clean. Tonight at dusk I stopped between two steep round dunes, the closest to the shore. Only one set of tires had marked the sand since ebb tide; the fishermen left a dogfish dead and a cow-nosed stingray, nothing more. The surf is always visible from where I sit. It looks higher than the nearly level sand, though of course it cannot be. It seems threatening to swamp my little plain and carry everything away to sea, except the inevitable sand. I know the tide will peak at 8:02 far below the beach crest—but I wait to make camp until it has. At home I'd been reading randomly before this trip; some notions come to mind:

* E. M. Forster: "Under cosmopolitanism, if it comes, we shall receive no help from earth. Trees and meadows and mountains [and waves and dunes] will only be spectacle, and the binding force that they once exercised on character must be entrusted to Love alone. May Love be equal to the task."

* George Steiner: "The widening gap that separates most of us in the antiseptic West from a normal, active religiosity not only cuts us off from grasping the life forces still primary to much of the Third World but divorces us from much that is elemental to our own past. . . . The seasonal pulse and segmentation of the year, the articulations of the day . . . and feasts both fixed and movable derive their meaning from precise religious occasions." The essayist's elliptical elegance boils down to this corollary: Mankind evolved knowing God(s) and acted accordingly. In past ages we measured our lives by cycles seen as manifest divinity. But that's all passé.

* The antique *Book of Common Prayer* speaks of "the peace of God which passeth understanding. . . ."

A soft wind rattles the sea oats on either side. I can see only one human light, the beacon 156 feet above Cape Lookout 15 miles away blinking shyly four precise times a minute at anyone wanting to know its whereabouts. The quarter-moon set soon after the sun, but I've known far darker nights. No clouds hide the November sky. So many stars appear that the constellations seem pale among them; my star map is a puny thing, like a connect-the-dots rendering of a Winslow Homer seascape. These stars are beyond counting, yet astronomers have presumed to identify them with anonymous numbers. Every few minutes —after a dozen waves or so—a truly unnamed gleam appears: a meteor dying as it brightens. The night is cold, the surf alive. It is as quiet as it ever gets here, but nothing close to silent. The sea oats rattle; the waves growl; the wind murmurs.

The tide rises with rhythmic waves, then at last retreats, and I relax again, hungry from the vigil for a sea that never rose unaccountably. After supper I see that all tracks have been erased, the shark and stingray gone with them. The sand is smooth except where I have walked. The surf washes shoreward despite the tide's retreat. Polaris hasn't budged.

I wonder about Forster's "cosmopolitanism" and regret it. I think of "feasts both fixed and movable," the benchmarks of our years. Didn't every famous ancient culture observe the solstices, the promise of spring, the threat of winter death, the ebb and flow of life on land? Our word for equinox comes from a dead language. Then I get the joke I've played on me: This trip—the last before my deadline—began the day

Osprey.

the clocks were turned back to repay the hour stolen in the spring. What a way to mark a season! The Druids would call it blasphemy, and they might be right.

A dying meteor flares and fades high above the west horizon somewhere beyond the continent over another ocean. Something suddenly comes clear on this wild and utterly empty beach where I am the only man: The act of dying may be full of private pain, but death itself holds no fear for me—nor should for humankind until we cut all natural ties. Like those shooting stars, vanished to remain invisible and changed, we are a part.

Acknowledgments

In more lyrical times than these, every writer worth the sand to blot his ink began by invoking the Muse. Now it is more fashionable to finish the work, then list the people who provided help or inspiration, then wedge thanks up front between the dedication and the table of contents.

This tradition, once sincere and gracious, has fallen on hard times. Some academic writers acknowledge a benefactor and slap him in the next breath: "My esteemed colleague, Dr. Jekyl, read Chapter X . . . but the views expressed therein are the author's alone." It seems to say "Jekyl's advice was lousy. But if that chapter draws any flak he's the jerk who let me say something stupid and he should share the blame." Other writers go to such lengths to share credit that they finally take responsibility only for whatever gaffes got into print. Then there are those authors whose grateful thanks read like a starlet's Academy Award address. They mention absolutely everyone's contribution in painful detail until the reader wonders who was mostly highly regarded: The all-suffering wife? The dogged dictationist who typed all nine revisions of the entire book? Or the brilliant grad student who quantified the stool of 4,000 laboratory animals for seven summers? In hopes of finding a better way, I wish to make some things uncommonly clear: I freely acknowledge sole authorship of any errors. Nay, I claim each skewed speculation and dubious datum—not that anyone else wants them. I happen to have done most of the typing too. These admissions out of the way, let's turn to more important matters. First, the organizations that helped:

Having complained for years about taxes, I was repaid in part during 1978 through the good offices of the National Park Service and the Library of the Department of the Interior. The Smithsonian Institution also provided bibliographic and human resources, even unique physical opportunities, whether to handle a black skimmer's bill or to borrow a goosefish's corpse.

Turning to individuals, a number of authorities gave advice, some then offered thoughtful criticism on sections of text. The scientists named below also offered something beyond information, namely insight, encouragement to a nonscientist, or infectious enthusiasm for their specialties. Two companions in the world of letters read the entire text in its nearly final and most cacographic form. One stranger provided a motor vehicle for a summer. Several faithful friends gave moral support. Others provided stimulating ideas when my view became too narrow, others a well aimed toe when my problem was lethargy or hubris. Were these contributions more or less important than a private tutorial or a guided tour? Is a pomegranate as red as rare porterhouse? I'll beg such issues and try to obviate any ranking of my benefactors— as soon as I specify the roles three people played.

Behind every writer who doesn't go nuts (and some who do) stands a singular sustainer, a person who performs what Wordsworth called "little nameless, unremembered acts of kindness and of love." Mine listened to complaints, dared to offer unwelcome advice, shared a few travels but settled for tales of many more. She was there when I needed relief from writing and out of sight when I had to work alone. A part-time miracle worker, once she produced fresh raspberries on an island where none grew; another day she found the First Aid Kit just in time. The very versatility of her support makes a summing up next to impossible. This book is dedicated to her with love and gratitude.

I cannot thank another person personally for her crucial role. Two years ago Marion Clark, legendary editor of *The Washington Post's* magazine *Potomac,* accepted my proposal for a natural science survey of nearby summer beaches. The project she commissioned and published became the springboard for this book. An airplane accident took her life too soon, and Washington journalism is the lesser for that.

Neither can I contain my incredulity at hearing of one Anne E. Lacy's work at the Smithsonian a year ago. She was then in the process of drawing the genitalia of every North American water beetle known to science, which is on taxonomic terms with some 1,500 species. It sounded peculiar but the reason turned out to be simple. These insects' bodies look so much alike that the best way to distinguish all the species is by microscopic examination of their miniscule private parts which differ remarkably. And the only way to record the results for a definitive taxonomic catalogue is with exact line drawings. Hence, her odd preoccupation. Anne calls herself an illustrator. Her work, which illuminates this book, speaks for itself. But it cannot reveal the perseverance and joyful presence that this gifted artist of science brought to our collaboration.

The people named below know how they contributed. The reader need only know that their gifts of time, knowledge and caring enriched these pages. I have the happy honor to thank them publicly now for early help, for sustained support, for scientific counsel. These were my tutors, mentors and Muses:

Donna Ari; Richard D. Baker, Assateague National Seashore; Maxwell Boverman, M. D.; Anne Buchwald; Daniel H. Crowley, Esq.; Robert F. Dolan, University of Virginia; Molly Friedrich; Paul J. Godfrey, University of Massachusetts; Mary Hallett; Mary Anne Harrell, National Geographic Society; Jill Johnson and Maryanne Gerbackis, Fire Island National Seashore; Col. Robert J. T. Joy, M.D., Uniformed Services University of the Health Sciences; Stephen P. Leatherman, National Park Service; author Charles R. Larson, American University; Irene E. Magyar and Raymond B. Manning, Smithsonian Institution; John R. Pichurski, American Motors Corporation; J. W. Pierce, Smithsonian; Aaron Priest; Theron Raines; Joseph Rosewater, Smithsonian; Carl N. Shuster, Jr., Federal Energy Regulating Commission; George E. Watson, Smithsonian; Charles L. Wheeler, National Marine Fisheries Service; Austin Williams, U.S. Fish and Wildlife Service; Richard Zusi, Smithsonian.

Washington, D. C.
February 14, 1979

Index